HOCKEY, PQ

Canada's Game in Quebec's Popular Culture

A wide-ranging study that examines everything from the blockbuster movie franchise *Les Boys* to the sovereigntist hip hop group Loco Locass, *Hockey, PQ* explores how Canada's national sport has been used to signify a specific Québécois identity. Amy J. Ransom analyses how Québécois writers, filmmakers, and musicians have appropriated symbols like the Montreal Forum, Maurice Richard, or the 1972 Summit Series to construct or critique images of the Québécois male.

Close readings of hockey-themed narratives consider the soap opera *Lance et compte* ("He shoots, he scores"), the music of former pro player Bob Bisonnette, folk band Mes Aïeux, rock group Les Dales Hawerchuk, and the fiction of François Barcelo. Through these examinations of the role hockey plays in contemporary francophone popular culture, Ransom shows how Quebec's popular culture uses hockey to distinguish French-Canadians from the French and to rally them against their English-speaking counterparts. In the end, however, this study illuminates how the sport of hockey unites the two solitudes.

AMY J. RANSOM is an associate professor of French at Central Michigan University.

Hockey, PQ

Canada's Game in Quebec's Popular Culture

AMY J. RANSOM

UNIVERSITY OF TORONTO PRESS
Toronto Buffalo London

Toronto Buffalo London
utorontopress.com

ISBN 978-1-4426-4813-5 (cloth)
ISBN 978-1-4426-1619-6 (paper)

Library and Archives Canada Cataloguing in Publication

Ransom, Amy J., 1964–, author
Hockey, PQ : Canada's game in Quebec's popular culture / Amy J. Ransom.

Includes bibliographical references and index.
ISBN 978-1-4426-4813-5 (bound) ISBN 978-1-4426-1619-6 (pbk.)

1. Hockey – Social aspects – Québec (Province). 2. Sports in popular culture – Québec (Province). 3. Nationalism and sports – Québec (Province). I. Title.

GV848.4.C3R35 2014 796.96209714 C2014-900766-3

University of Toronto Press acknowledges the financialassistanceto its publishing program of the Canada Council for the Arts and the Ontario Arts Council, an agency of the Government of Ontario.

Canada Council for the Arts Conseil des Arts du Canada

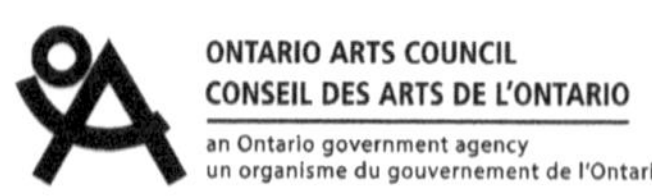

This book has been published with the help of a grant from the Canadian Federation for the Humanities and Social Sciences, through the Awards to Scholarly Publications Program, using funds provided by the Social Sciences and Humanities Research Council of Canada.

University of Toronto Press acknowledges the financial support of the Government of Canada through the Canada Book Fund for its publishing activities.

Contents

Acknowledgments

Working on this project has been one of the most fun and fulfilling academic ventures I have undertaken, and although writing an academic study is not as much of a team endeavour as the game of hockey, I could not have completed this project without assists from a number of individuals. I would like to acknowledge here the feedback and support I have received from colleagues in Quebec and hockey studies, from my home institution, Central Michigan University, and from my family. I would especially like to thank Andrew Holman and Jason Blake, along with other hockey experts in attendance at the 2009 Sports Literature Association Conference in London, Ontario, where I let fly the first ideas that eventually became this book. Had they not shared their knowledge and expertise, I'm not sure I would have known how to start talking about sport in any other way than as a fan. Luc Bellemare and Christi Brookes shared their musical knowledge, for which I am grateful. I also wish to mention Sophie Beaulé, my friend and native informant, whose invaluable e-mails bearing tidbits from *Le Devoir* always kept me up to date on breaking news from Quebec. And I would like to thank Siobhan McMenemy and Frances Mundy at University of Toronto Press, as well as the independent readers who evaluated the manuscript; their knowledge, insight, and careful reading were invaluable in the final stages of this book's process. UTP's copy editor Matthew Kudelka earns a star for his insights into clarity of style and the game of hockey itself.

In addition, I would like to recognize the support for my research in this and other areas that I have found at Central Michigan University, from my colleagues in the Department of Foreign Languages, Literatures, and Cultures, and from Dean Pamela Gates of the College of

Humanities, Social and Behavioral Sciences, as well as from CMU's Office of Research and Sponsored Programs, all of which have provided funding for travel and research related to this project. Similarly, the staff at CMU's Park Library, especially at the Documents on Demand service, deserve my thanks. Above all, I want to express my love and thanks to my son, Richard, who now refuses to wear the jersey of our home team, the Detroit Red Wings, and has become a staunch supporter of the Montreal Canadiens. He is my most valuable player for his amazing patience and understanding when I needed to read, to write, or to travel and could not spend time with him. I love you, buddy!

Permissions

Passages from the following sources have been used here with the following permissions:

François Barcelo, *Ville-Dieu* (© François Barcelo, 1999), reprinted with the permission of François Barcelo.
François Barcelo, *I Hate Hockey*, translated by Peter McCambridge, reprinted with the permission of Baraka Books.
Bob Bissonnette, lyrics from "L'Affamée," "Les Barbes de séries," "Chris Chelios," "Enweye donc," "Hockey dans rue," "Les Hommes zébrés," "J'accroche mes patins," "J'haïs Montréal," "La Machine à Scorer," and "Y sont toutes folles," reprinted with the permission of Bob Bissonnette.
Les Dales Hawerchuk, lyrics from "Dale Hawerchuk," reprinted with the permission of C4 Records.
Denis Côté, author of the original novel *Hockeyeurs cybernétiques*, reprinted with the permission of the author.
Denise Duguay, for Gilles Tremblay's original novel *Les Nordiques sont disparus*, reprinted with the permission of the author's estate.
Loco Locass, lyrics from "Le But," and "Hymne à Québec," reprinted with the permission of Loco Locass and Avenue Editorial.
Loco Locass and Samian, lyrics from "La Paix des Braves," reprinted with the permission of Loco Locass, Avenue Editorial, and Septième Ciel Records.
Mes Aïeux, lyrics from "Le Fantôme du Forum," reprinted with the permission of Mes Aïeux and Les Disques Victoire.
Amy J. Ransom, "*Lieux de mémoire* or *lieux du dollar*?: Montreal's Forum, the Canadiens and Popular Culture." *Quebec Studies* 51 (Spring/Summer 2011): 21–39, reprinted with the permission of Jane Moss, Editor, *Quebec Studies*.

HOCKEY, PQ
Canada's Game in Quebec's Popular Culture

Hockey as Nationalist Marker in Quebec Film, but Which Nationalism?

Hockey holds a privileged space in the Canadian imagination, producing a distinctive form of national celebrity: the professional hockey player. As a potent signifier of class, nationalism, masculinity, and race, the Canadian hockey star is a locus for contestation between popular and highbrow articulations of what constitutes the acceptable range of Canadian identities.

Bart Beaty[1]

Hockey in Québec is a significant site for popular expression.

Anouk Bélanger[2]

One of Quebec's biggest box office hits in the last decade,[3] Érik Canuel's action comedy *Bon Cop, Bad Cop* (2006) pits two mismatched investigators, one Anglo-Ontarian, the other a Franco-Quebecer, against a serial killer who chooses his victims among various "members of the hockey community" (1:03:05). Nicknamed the "tattoo killer" after the clues he leaves imprinted on his victims, the murderer views himself as a righteous avenger, targeting individuals involved in the pending sale of a fictional Quebec major league franchise to the United States. Perhaps unfortunately, the two very different yet complementary detectives manage to thwart the killer's final escapade targeting the head of the entire league, Harry Buttman, a figure clearly meant to parody the NHL's commissioner since 1993, Gary Bettman. Both provinces' love of hockey creates a context for the humorous representation of the two solitudes – and an ultimately federalist message that "we can get along despite our differences" – in the form of the film's two heroes, the wild, non-conformist Québécois, David Bouchard (Patrick Huard) and the straight-laced, by-the-book Torontonian, Martin Ward (Colm Feore).

As Canada's national sport, like the film *Bon Cop, Bad Cop*, hockey bridges the gap between the two solitudes, uniting Quebec and the Rest of Canada through the parallel broadcast of CBC's *Hockey Night in Canada* and Société Radio-Canada's *La Soirée du hockey* (now replaced by RDS's *Le Hockey du samedi soir*) every Saturday night from October to May. Leaving aside the occasional grousing about provincial representation when Canadian national teams are chosen, Franco-Quebecers support Team Canada during the Winter Olympics. They recall landmark international events like the historic 1972 Summit Series / *Série du siècle*, endowing these with the same significance as their English-speaking counterparts in the Rest of Canada.[4] This book examines how popular hockey narratives (film, television, popular literatures, and even pop songs) in Quebec participate in discourses about national identity and sovereignty, but also how they work in dialogue with contemporary images of gender roles and sexuality, as well as discourses about the sport of hockey itself. The common thread between national(ist) images and images of masculinity and femininity is, of course, the relationship of gender to identity; these hockey texts project images of "who we are" both as men and women, and as Québécois and Québécoises. In addition to having an impact on individual conceptions of national and gendered identity, the sport allows for the creation of a collective "we" (hockey players, hockey fans). But the adversarial nature of sport and hockey's relationship to hegemonic forms of masculinity also involve negative aspects of identity formation, based more on "who we aren't" and on the creation or identification of Others for the sport's fans. As critics have repeatedly asserted, hockey has only recently begun to include women and minorities as rightful participants in its unique liturgy.[5]

Because of US hegemony in the National Hockey League, which is the image of hockey most present and accessible to media viewers, particularly for those of us south of the border (and I don't mean Mexico here),[6] it is not necessarily self-evident that the "National" in NHL refers to Canada. We are a long way from the ironic comment in the classic American hockey film *Slap Shot* (1977) that the Chiefs' star player Ned Braden (Michael Ontkean, himself a former University of New Hampshire hockey player) is "a college graduate and an American citizen." Over the past three decades, but more so since the mid-1990s, intense debates about the meaning of hockey for Canadians and as a symbol of

Canadian culture have been undertaken in English by sports journalists and fiction writers (John Macfarlane, Roy MacGregor), by former players (Ken Dryden), by sport sociologists, economists, and historians (Richard Gruneau and David Whitson, Bruce Kidd, Jean Harvey and Alan Law, Michael Robidoux, and Andrew C. Holman), and lately by literary critics (Jamie Dopp, Jason Blake). Hockey has been posited as perhaps the *only* originally and uniquely Canadian cultural form, and the sport has been depicted as a unifying and assimilationist force in a nation of immigrants. Counter-discourses began questioning this image in the 1990s, pointing to the sport's exclusionary aspects (white, masculine, and increasingly middle-class) as well as its appropriation by big capital. Nonetheless, as Bart Beaty asserts, "hockey holds a privileged space in the Canadian imagination [... as] a potent signifier of class, nationalism, masculinity, and race."[7] For example, there seems to be no question that for Anglo-Canadians, Paul Henderson's winning goal in the Summit Series of exhibition matches between Team Canada and a Soviet all-star team represents a defining moment in national history. For Daniel Francis, "The Goal" provides Canadians with "our 'where were you when?' question."[8] Brian Kennedy would later argue that "the events of September 1972 helped to create the Canada of today through giving a generation of people a touchstone moment with which to mark their participation in a shared culture."[9]

For better or for worse, hockey represents *a*, if not *the*, dominant cultural marker of "the Canadian." Yet as a *Québéciste* (someone specializing in Quebec studies), I always seem to perceive – except on rare occasions – that when English-language scholars talk about "Canada," they really mean English Canada. I find this both revelatory and ironic, given the great national debate about Quebec sovereignty and the fears it might come to pass. While it rarely supports a "separatist" agenda, English-language scholarship on the "nation" of Canada often elides *le fait français* (the French fact), seeming already to imply Quebec's status as separate, addressing the notion of Canada-without-Quebec *avant la lettre*. Such Anglo-exclusive imaginings of the community of the nation speak volumes about the reality of the "solitudes" metaphor,[10] notwithstanding those rare voices like Charles Taylor, Will Kymlicka, and John Ralston Saul, whose proposed conception of Canada–Quebec as Siamese twins never quite took off.[11]

In many English-language popular culture and literary texts, French Canadians continue to appear just as marginalized and stereotyped as they did thirty-five years ago in *Slap Shot*, in which the only other

French Canadian besides the nearly silent Jean-Guy Drouin (Yvan Ponton) is the outspoken, "crazy" goalie Denis Lemieux (Yvon Barrette). Such token appearances similarly occur in "Canadian" – that is, English-language Canadian – discourses about and representations of hockey. From the foundational hockey film, *Face-Off* (1971), and from novels like Frank Orr's *Puck Is a Four Letter Word* (1983), to much more recent and sophisticated works like Bill Gaston's *The Good Body* (2000), the stereotype of the crazy French goalie lingers. For example, while eight French Canadian players appeared on the Team Canada roster for the now epic 1972 Summit Series,[12] T.W. Peacocke's CBC television docudrama *Canada Russia '72* (2006) includes only Yvan Cournoyer (Louis-Philippe Dandenault), Serge Savard (Marc Savard), and J.-P. Parisé (Jason Thibodeau) in the credited cast list. Yet, while their "air time" in the film is largely limited in favour of more colourful anglophone players like the narcissistic Phil Esposito (David Berni), the goon Wayne Cashman (Gerry Dee), and the paranoid Frank Mahovlich (Jeff Roop), it is the Montreal Canadiens' star, Cournoyer, who utters these significant lines in French: "C'est pas comme un rêve qui devient une réalité; c'est plus comme une nation qui devient une réalité" (It's not like a dream that's become a reality; it's more like a nation that's become a reality).[13]

Although French Canadians appear on the margins of Anglo-Canadian media depictions of "Canada's Game," and sociologists and former players have even argued that French-speakers face a systematized culture of discrimination in the recruiting and draft system of the NHL and in the Canadian minor leagues that serve as its farm system,[14] hockey remains central to Quebecers' depiction of themselves and to their specific *French* Canadian culture. From its earliest days, argues Michael Robidoux, the developing game of hockey appealed to a notion of French Canadian masculinity,[15] a connection Anouk Bélanger links to the appropriation of a certain image of Maurice Richard for later nationalist debates.[16] Such notions of French Canadian masculinity and national identity were often constructed against those of anglophone or Metropolitan French Others, and again, hockey offered a site of rivalry and occasionally of dominance to a people who at one time had considered themselves conquered, as historian Steve Lasorsa observes.[17] Jean Harvey further examines the changing meaning of hockey for Franco-Québécois and the relationship of sport to various forms of nationality, both ethnic and civic.[18] The number of book-length studies of hockey, both popular and scholarly, published in Quebec has been rising since the turn of the millennium. Quebecers like Simon Richard have written their own homage accounts of the Summit Series, while Steve Lasorsa and Jean-François Chabot eulogize the short-lived but intense rivalry between the Quebec Nordiques and the Montreal Canadiens.[19] Academics Normand Baillargeon and Christian Boissinot have devoted an essay collection to the links between philosophy and hockey; Olivier Bauer and Jean-Marc Barreau have edited a volume on religion and the Montreal Canadiens.[20] Benoît Melançon has written the cultural history of a single player, Maurice Richard.[21] The latter was quickly translated into English, and plans are in the works to translate yet another edited volume on the Canadiens, this one by Audrey Laurin-Lamothe and Nicolas Moreau.[22] Yet, apart from essays published in English by Jean Harvey and Anouk Bélanger, much of what Quebecers have to say about hockey and its significance to them remains inaccessible to anglophones. One of this book's aims is to make that discourse available to an English-speaking audience. More importantly, though, it seeks to interpret for that audience a vast array of French-language popular culture texts which reveal that, in spite of its recent problematization, hockey remains significant, even central, to conceptions not just of Canadian but of a specifically *Québécois* culture and identity.

Indeed, hockey appears almost omnipresent in Quebec's popular literatures, visual media, and music, and it is often explicitly or implicitly linked to issues of masculinity and national identity. For instance, in Sébastien Rose's comedy-drama *La Vie avec mon père* (Life with My Father, 2005), two sons (David La Haye and Paul Ahmarani) reconnect with their dying father (Raymond Bouchard) by bringing him to an outdoor rink to watch them play hockey from his wheelchair. The sport rejuvenates the family ties that have been stretched to the limit, allowing a momentary return to the joyful bonding of father and sons. Even *Dans une galaxie près de chez vous* (1999–2001), a cult science fiction television series parody, manages to pepper Quebec's future with references to hockey. As I discuss at length in chapter 5, the biopic of the late lead singer of the iconic 1990s rock group Les Colocs, *Through the Mist* (2009), depicts André Fortin (Sébastien Ricard) playing hockey in its opening scenes, mobilizing the sport as a motif for his fiercely nationalist Québécois identity. Indeed, as that chapter reveals, the link between hockey and francophone popular music is particularly strong. As in Anglo-Canada until quite recently,[23] hockey in Quebec appears to suffer somewhat from the stigma of being a lowbrow form of culture, so that relatively few of the province's major "literary" writers reveal their affinity for the sport.[24] Nonetheless, at least two significant icons in the province's literary establishment invoke hockey in their work: Jacques Poulin in *Le Cœur de la baleine bleue* (1979), and Roch Carrier in *Il est par là le soleil* (1988) and the well-known story "The Hockey Sweater" (1979), discussed briefly in chapter 1. Here, however, I focus on popular literary genres like science fiction and juvenile fiction.

As an interdisciplinary study that examines a range of popular culture forms, including film, television, music, and literature, this book necessarily draws from a number of disciplines to support its claims, including history, sport sociology, film and media studies, and literary theory. As a work of cultural analysis, its goal is to situate its objects of study (songs, films, short stories, and television shows with prominent hockey thematics) in the context of their sociocultural production (contemporary Quebec) and then to interpret their meaning(s). It takes as a given the basic tenet of cultural studies that cultural products both reflect the culture that produces them and in turn offer up images of themselves to members of that culture. As an academic specifically invested in the study of *popular* cultural forms, I propose that, because of the sheer numbers of individuals they reach, products of mass culture like television and music may reveal far more about a particular culture than do elite forms of art and literature. In Quebec, I believe, the personal and creative investment, as well as the sense of participating in a collective endeavour, is all the greater for the province's writers, musicians, actors, and filmmakers because the commercial stakes are much lower, often nearly non-existent. The production of culture in the tiny market of Quebec is for many a labour of love and often a means of political engagement. Iconic filmmaker Jean-Pierre Lefebvre describes a national cinema for Quebec in a manner that we may apply to the other six arts as well:

> Hors de tout doute, le concept de création nationale, et de cinéma national, est d'une importance tout à fait capital parce que relié à la notion d'*appartenance*, laquelle est reliée à l'*instinct de survie*, dont la *création* – je l'ai souvent répété – est l'une des manifestations les plus spontanées, directes, nécessaires, dynamiques.[25]

> Without a doubt, the concept of national creativity and of national cinema is of completely vital importance because it is linked to the notion of *belonging*, which is linked to the *survival instinct*, of which *creativity* – I have often repeated it – is one of the most spontaneous, direct, necessary, and dynamic manifestations.

The films, television shows, songs, books, and stories examined here all represent expressions of their producers' sense of belonging and their will for a vibrant and dynamic contemporary French-language culture to survive in North America. Lefebvre further reiterates the very notion that subtends all of cultural studies, the interdisciplinary field to which this book belongs, a notion that we apply to the texts examined in the pages to come, namely, that there occurs *"une osmose exemplaire entre de nouvelles formes de représentation de l'imaginaire québécois, et le milieu ambiant québécois d'où il était issu"* (an exemplary osmosis between new forms of representation of the Quebec imaginary and the Quebec environment from which it comes).[26] The following section, then, offers a brief introductory sample of the work to be found here, engaging the questions of hockey, national identity, and masculinity in the film referred to in our opening paragraphs, *Bon Cop, Bad Cop*.

Hockey, National Identity, and Masculinity in *Bon Cop, Bad Cop*[27]

Typical of the thriller genre, Érik Canuel's *Bon Cop, Bad Cop* opens with the first in what will prove to be a series of murders; also a comedy, it lovingly parodies its precursors, paying homage to the cult franchise *Friday the 13th* (1980) films, in which serial killer Jason Voorhees hides his identity from his victims by wearing a hockey mask. In those American films, the reference to hockey was purely gratuitous; in this Quebec film, it is highly significant, as its serial killer specifically targets key figures in the hockey industry. Not only does his accomplice prove to be a disgruntled sidelined ex-pro hockey player, but he also uses various articles of hockey gear as murder weapons, whacking his first victim over the head with a hockey stick, planting the blade of a skate in the skull of another, and so on. Yet he is still a loyal fan: after completing his gruesome first murder, he turns up the volume on a muted television in order to watch the match. Eventually, his motives will be unravelled by the two intrepid detectives assigned to the case: on the eve of the sale of yet another Canadian hockey franchise to the United States, the tattoo killer (Patrice Bélanger) seeks revenge for the earlier sale of the Quebec "Fleur de Lys" and hopes to blackmail the league into stopping the departure of the Montreal "Patriotes."

The villain's most striking feature is that he speaks both of Canada's official languages with an accent; thus he cannot be aligned politically with either charter nation. Of much greater interest are the film's unlikely and mismatched heroes and the circumstances that bring them together: the discovery of the first victim. The body's location – dropped from the sky, it straddles a road sign marking the border between the provinces of Ontario and Quebec – establishes the pretext for their cooperation through the jurisdictional problems it creates. By forcing Bouchard and Ward to collaborate, the murder sets up the film's ultimate message: that the provinces need to work together to defeat a common adversary, namely, American expansion into the sacred territory of hockey. Of course, the first instinct for each detective is to attempt to foist the investigation onto the other, and the humour of this particular sequence underscores the irrational and petty nature of gut-reaction tribal antipathies.

The two groups – anglophone and francophone – approach the same problem from completely opposite viewpoints. This is reflected in Ward's and Bouchard's opposite approaches to solving the problem of jurisdiction, which they support with metaphors from the sporting world, in keeping with the film's hockey theme. As each prepares to leave the case in the other's hands, the battle of words begins:

> WARD: What do you mean our case? It's very clearly your case.
> BOUCHARD: How do you figure that? His feet are on your side.
> WARD: Exactly. And his head is on your side. What's your point?
> BOUCHARD: You play football or tennis or whatever, you step over the line ... you're out [...]
> WARD: May I remind you that in the 100-yard dash, it's the head and chest that break the tape. In horse racing, it's by a nose. [...] As you can see, the subject is a true Quebecer. His heart is in Quebec.
> BOUCHARD: Et en Ontario il a le cul aussi. [laughter from Québécois cops] I just said, 'his ass belongs to you.'
> MARTIN: Okay, we'll take it from here. (12:05–13:20)

The gauntlet having been thrown down, the consequences of failing to cooperate immediately become clear. As the two detectives examine the body precariously perched atop the road sign, they somehow manage to kick away the ladder supporting them; Ward and Bouchard hang suspended above the ground, one on each side of the border, their weight supported by the victim's corpse, until, like the metaphoric body of the nation, it is ripped in two because of their rivalry.

The manipulability of individuals weakened by irrational differences at this point becomes evident; both detectives now do an about-face, each claiming the case as his own. But eventually, the two individuals, each representing his respective province, are compelled to work together by forces higher up. Bouchard's superior officer, richly played by character actor Pierre Lebeau (Méo of *Les Boys*, of whom more in chapter 4), accompanied by his Ontario counterpart (Ron Lea), informs the two detectives that in the spirit of interprovincial cooperation, they will work together to solve the crime, "to show the RCMP that they can't have the whole pie. [...] And that if we can cooperate, it would be very good for our image and next year's budgets" (16:45–47). The two rivals are thus forced into a reluctant partnership.

As might be anticipated, this Quebec film offers a deliciously stereotyped image of the uptight, cultivated, polite Anglo-Canadian. During the Quebec-situated aspects of the investigation, actor Colm Feore plays his character as a fish out of water; his tall elegance and velvety voice become objects of derision as he enters a biker bar wearing a turtleneck and suit jacket. Similarly, his Parisian French gets him almost nowhere with roughnecks in la Belle Province. Ward's deejay teenage son and post-punk sister accentuate his nerdiness, as does their admiration of the hip Quebecer, Bouchard, who charms them both. Ward's domesticity (he first appears ironing his trousers), inept parenting skills, and apparent passivity (he agrees to work with Bouchard in part because he is promised the desk job to which he has long aspired in exchange) further emasculate the urbane cosmopolitan. Through contact with his crazy French partner, however, he will recover his zest for life, his sex appeal, and his hegemonic masculinity.

As a product of Quebec's culture industries, the film's portrayal of David Bouchard, while exaggerated and stereotyped for comic effect, nonetheless depicts a certain fantasy image of a desirable form of Québécois masculinity. Fit and active, Bouchard can chase down his man on foot or in his vintage 1975 Chevrolet Chevelle Malibu,[28] which he drives like a madman, over the sidewalk and against oncoming traffic, heedlessly parking in spots reserved for the handicapped. Not afraid to shoot, refusing to wait for back-up, iffy on the Canadian equivalent of the Miranda warning required by the Charter of Rights and Freedoms, and unfettered by the need to obtain a search warrant, Bouchard does everything necessary to get his man. Unfortunately, because of his independence, non-conformity, and refusal to grow up, he remains fixed in an adolescent stage of rebellion against the very authority he represents, and while Bouchard always gets his man, he has lost his woman. As trendy, modern Québécois, however, the divorced couple live together platonically in order to ensure that their teenage daughter is raised in a two-parent home! Nonetheless, Bouchard does everything with flair, although not with perfection; for example, as he cruises up to the crime scene, exits the car, and flicks away his cigarette in slow motion, the car mirror clatters off, revealing the wreck under the hip demeanour. His style remains decidedly populist: strictly jeans-and-T-shirt, drinking beer and swearing with the best of them. Indeed, one of the key cultural exchanges between Bouchard and his new partner involves a lesson in "how to swear in Québécois."[29]

Actor Patrick Huard's quirky sex appeal adds charisma to the over-the-top maverick antics of the role. If we accept Richard Dyer's theorization of the "star," which asserts that viewers bring to their interpretation of an actor's role in a given film their knowledge of both his previous on-screen casting and his off-screen private life image,[30] a quick look at Huard's career illuminates the efficacy of this casting choice. As we will see in chapter 4, Huard – who is also credited as a writer on the film – has a history with hockey-themed films, having played Ti-Guy, one of the garage league players featured in the highly popular *Les Boys* (1997) and two of its three sequels. While the physically clean-cut but boyishly attractive Ti-Guy's masculinity and heterosexuality were explicitly questioned by his own mother in *Les Boys III*, Huard had established a different persona for himself by the time of his casting in *Bon Cop, Bad Cop*. In *Comment ma mère accoucha de moi durant sa ménopause* (2003), breaking away from the boyish innocence of the asexual (rather than homosexual) Ti-Guy, Huard played a sexy, intelligent-but-working-class boy toy for an oversexed mother-and-daughter team. Huard's image is that of an idealized, hip, thirty-something, independent, individualistic, contemporary Québécois male.

Replaying the reversal premise deployed in the *Lethal Weapon* franchise (1987, 1989, 1992, 1998), in which the minority actor plays the straight man (Danny Glover's Mertaugh) to the crazy white near-pariah figure (Mel Gibson's Riggs), *Bon Cop, Bad Cop* allows its minority figure to embrace the stereotype. And while it builds its comedy around exploiting and exaggerating stereotypes of francophone and anglophone Canadians, the film also deconstructs those stereotypes. After prolonged and intense exposure to each other, these figures arrive at a state of recognition that allows each to see through and benefit from the other's traits. Indeed, their talents are revealed as complementary: each detective brings to the table a different skill set, and this allows allows them to solve the crime, but only once they begin to work together.

We already see the blurring of the borders – a trope quickly established in the film with the corpse's border-crossing location – in the film's marketing package. The theatrical release poster, also used for the DVD cover, plays on the anglo–franco binary even while rendering impossible a complete separation and distinction of the two. Huard takes star precedence in the Quebec production, with his image on the left and slightly to the fore, yet in the English-market versions, his name appears on the right, above the image of Colm Feore.[31] The actors themselves appear side by side, both wearing stern, determined expressions. Bouchard's T-shirt and leather jacket appear to distinguish him from Ward's suit-and-tie approach; however, both men are in jeans with visible belt buckles, and wear their police badges stylishly at the waist rather than pinned to a uniform breast pocket like a beat cop. At their knees appears the title lettering, which makes brilliant use of the Canadian and Quebec national logos. Obviously, the film's very title blends French and English; while the words "Bon cop" appear on the left under the image of David Bouchard, a half-red Maple Leaf lies under "cop"; conversely, half of a royal blue fleur-de-lys – partly merged although not quite in alignment with the Maple Leaf – lies under "bad." While the initial images of the two detectives suggest that Bouchard is the bad cop because he fails to respect police procedures or suspects' rights – indeed, he shoves an arrestee into the trunk of his car in order to watch his daughter's dance recital – and that the by-the-book Ward is the good cop, this identification is reversed on the film's publicity image. With the Maple Leaf and the "bon" under Bouchard's image and the fleur-de-lis and the "bad" under Ward's, national icons and expected images are completely blurred. As the intrigue develops and the partnership becomes a friendship, the two cops take on some of each other's characteristics, forming a complementary whole.

In its marketing strategy, but also through visual cues that punctuate the narrative, the film draws not only on national iconography but also on hockey motifs. Radio commentary running off-screen over establishing shots of both Toronto and Montreal, the home cities of the two protagonists, informs the viewer of the hockey rivalry between the fictional franchises of the Loyalists of Toronto and *les Patriotes de Montréal*. The real-life Maple Leafs/Canadiens rivalry, besides the now defunct rivalry between the Canadiens and the Quebec Nordiques, appears in the images of the red Maple Leaf and the royal blue fleur-de-lys featured in the film's title logo. Ironically, the NHL Maple Leafs' colour is royal blue – a hue close to that of the provincial Quebec flag. The fleur-de-lys on that banner recalls the province's former relationship to the French monarchy. At the same time, the Canadian flag adopted in 1965 sports a bright red maple leaf, and the colour red and the name "Canadiens" are associated with the historically francophone Montreal NHL franchise. Furthermore, the name of the fictional "Loyalists" obviously refers to those loyal to the British monarchy who fled the new American Republic at the end of the eighteenth century. Ironically, fans of this team would be horrified if the film's "Canadian Hockey League" sold them south to the United States, yet the team's namesakes were originally Americans who fled in the opposite direction. We may also, though, read this symbol against the grain, as referring to the monarchical attitudes – including a rejection of French Republicanism and an acceptance of the British Crown – promulgated by the Catholic clergy in pre-1960s Quebec. The "Patriotes" are a reference, of course, to the 1837–8 Patriots' Rebellion, which eventually called for the independence of Lower Canada from the British Crown. Although this was hailed as an early bid for French Canadian sovereignty, it is often forgotten that republican anglophones helped lead that uprising.[32] With all of these cross-references, it becomes impossible to identify one colour, name, or icon with one of the two solitudes; this in turn forces a semiotic confusion suggesting the ultimately federalist message that Canada and Quebec simply cannot be separated.

What unites the two detectives is, of course, their quest for a murderer who is attacking their shared national sport – a murderer whose rage focuses, in turn, on a common foe that is threatening the authenticity of hockey, that foe being the United States, personified by Buttman. Mainstream hockey narratives typically link the sport to religion; by contrast, *Bon Cop, Bad Cop* holds nothing sacred, parodying even the names of the murder victims, who are prominent members of its fictional major league hockey world. For example, the name of the lawyer Fred Grossbut (Gilles Renaud) offers a cheap laugh with a bilingual pun referring both to the French *gros but*, "great goal," but also to the English "gross butt." It also jeers at the one-time president of the Quebec Nordiques, Marcel Aubut. When Bouchard and Ward find their chief suspect's lair, complete with tattoo equipment and walls covered with news clippings (46:55), the latter are not news items about his own or other murders, although they are related to his killings. Rather, the walls are covered with hockey clippings and paraphernalia; in this way, the film pokes fun at the extreme hockey fanatic by linking him to the media's stereotypical image of the serial killer. These articles reveal that their prime suspect, Luc Therrien (Sylvain Marcel), was a former player whose career ended with a drug bust, and that Grossbut was involved in the sale of a former Quebec team, the Fleur de Lys, to Colorado (47:43) – an obvious reference to the Nordiques, who are now the Colorado Avalanche. Ward points out, "The next year they won the Cup, right?" To which Bouchard can only snidely mumble in response. While Ward photographs evidence, Bouchard plays with a display of bobble-head dolls. The sound of Ward's camera – invoking the flash used by Clarice Starling (Jodi Foster) to navigate the killer's home in *The Silence of the Lambs* (1991) – coupled with eerie background music as the detectives explore this dimly lit room full of hockey memorabilia, beautifully denaturalizes the nation's and the province's love of the sport. At the same time, the film invokes that love through its repeated *roman-à-clef* insider references to the sport's history, teams, and personalities.

The tattoo of Colorado found by Ward on the dead Buttman's forehead (50:38) leads the detectives to the next victim. Once again, radio voice-overs provide additional context for the murders, which have now moved to Ontario, as the anglophone host of a call-in show complains about the pending move of "a major Canadian team" south: "What's the point of hating Montreal if they're in Houston!" (59:08–25). The third victim is found outside her suburban Toronto home with a skate blade firmly planted in her scalp (59:30); she is Martina Flapcheeks, the first female agent in the league. Ten years ago she refused to let her client, a first-round draft pick, play in Quebec, instead signing him to Toronto and then to a team in the States. Once again, Canuel lampoons real-life hockey politics with this obvious reference to the Eric Lindros affair,[33] as Ward sarcastically remarks, "Of course she deserves to die." Here and elsewhere, he expresses impatience with Québécois attitudes and their insistence on harbouring old grudges. Earlier, he had told Bouchard: "You Québécois are all the same. You've got some lunatic going nuts over a hockey team that doesn't exist anymore. […] 'Je me souviens.' You're living in the past. You've got to get over it" (58:10–13). Canuel uses the voice of the stereotypical anglophone to lampoon his own compatriots who take both their history and their hockey far too seriously, as Ward now scorns, "I suppose some people still aren't over the Plains of Abraham" (1:01:01–02), referring to Montcalm's 1759 defeat by Wolfe outside the walls of Quebec City. This victim's tattoo says "I Love Philadelphia" (1:01:40), with the letters L and A missing; our genius detectives figure out that this is a clue to the next murder. Ward assumes that the new target may be "the best player in the world […] the Great One" (1:02:25–28), an obvious reference to Wayne Gretzky, while Bouchard realizes instead it is "the one who sold him" (1:02:30–33). Again, the film invokes yet another hockey betrayal that would be highly familiar to its Canadian audience: Gretzky's move from Edmonton to Los Angeles in 1988.

Hockey becomes more completely the focus and setting of the film at this halfway point. A sequence opens with an establishing shot of Toronto at night and a title informing us that we are looking at "Centre Loyalists." Then what appears to be an opening television credit – a montage of hockey images with the letters "CSN" (Canadian Sports Network) – underscores the media's role in building the hype that leads to fandom, fanaticism, and ... murder. Ward and Bouchard are on the set of a sports TV talk show. Its obnoxious host (Rick Mercer—a well-known Canadian television personality in his own right) is upset because his guest, one Pickleton (a jab at Peter Pocklington, the Edmonton Oilers owner who traded Gretzky), described in the film as the man who sold the world's greatest hockey player to the United States, has not shown up because of the murders targeting "members of the hockey community" (1:03:05). Although physically much younger, with his name "Tom Berry," his self-admitted inability to pronounce a French name (1:05:20), and his pro–hockey violence rhetoric, the host resembles CBC hockey commentator and former Boston Bruins coach Don Cherry. Ward and Bouchard are commandeered to appear on the show as fill-ins for the missing Pickleton. By demanding to know, "What about the cowards who want to abolish fighting in hockey and make the game of hockey look like golf?" (1:03:15–20), Berry manages to incite the killer to call in. Their identity revealed to the killer, they themselves have now become targets. The exchanges between Bouchard and Berry allow for some gratuitous frog-baiting by the latter – yes, he actually calls Bouchard a "frog." Now labelled as such by Berry, the Tattoo Killer gets the last word: "You are trying to stop me in my heroic effort to save our national sport" (1:07:40–43).

The next tattoo points towards New York, a Big Apple with the dollar sign etched on it, but a showdown occurs as the killer kidnaps Bouchard's daughter and wants to trade her for his final target, the league commissioner, Buttman. Buttman becomes the butt of the joke: playing him is an extremely short actor (Richard Howland); Ward and Bouchard plan to kidnap him at a press conference that will be held at the Montreal Patriotes' arena. There, photo ops for fans include the Patriote mascot, an enormous beaver (Canada's national animal), who is wearing a Patriote jersey, which is modelled on the Canadiens jersey but with a P replacing the iconic CH. Behind the scenes, Buttman receives a video conference call from the Patriotes' buyer in Texas, Mr Arbusto – Spanish for "bush," a thinly veiled reference to the former US president and onetime owner of Major League Baseball's Texas Rangers – who claims he will "make hockey as Texas as a big fat American steak; none of that poisoned Canadian shit" (1:30:33–38), referencing the then contemporary mad cow disease scare in Canada. Ward and Bouchard arrive and order the diminutive Buttman to get into a hockey bag, which they use to carry him out for the exchange.

This collaboration as "bad cops" marks the true beginning of the partnership between Ward and Bouchard; indeed, Ward takes credit for devising the plan of trading Buttman for Gabrielle Bouchard. He enjoys putting Buttman in the trunk of a car, claiming that it is "a Quebec tradition," since he learned to treat suspects this way from Bouchard. Later, he demonstrates that he has also learned to swear in Québécois, marking his initiation as an honorary member of the tribe. The killer holds Bouchard's daughter in a ship docked at the Montreal port, the hold of which is rigged to look like a hockey rink complete with cardboard cutouts of players, along with creepy half-dismembered mannequins that mark the clichéd serial killer's lair. There is apparently one thing more sacred even than hockey for all Canadians: family. With Bouchard's daughter's life on the line, it is even more imperative than ever that Ward and Bouchard function as a team.

Bon Cop, Bad Cop, then, offers a federalist message about working together against a common threat (serial killer; US hegemony in Canada's game); at the same time, it also sends the message that sport represents a unifying force at a time when the nation, both as a concept and as a geopolitical entity, appears increasingly in question. As we shall see, however, hockey has been appropriated by popular film, literature, television, and music in Quebec for a range of ends. Like the analysis above, the rest of this book teases out those sometimes contradictory but always fascinating meanings, interpreting the role of Canada's game in Quebec's popular culture.

So ... What's in the Rest of the Book?

Each of the chapters that follow focuses on a specific corpus of popular texts, examining them through a range of critical and historical perspectives. At the same time, the chapters follow a roughly chronological pattern as I situate these various hockey narratives within the socio-historical context of their production. In order to address texts of a similar genre or corpus together, though, I do make certain temporal leaps. Chapter 1 goes back furthest in time, drawing upon Pierre Nora's concept of the *lieu de mémoire*, the site of memory, to outline the historical and contemporary significance of the Montreal Canadiens NHL franchise and its former home, the Forum.

It draws in particular upon the insightful analyses of scholars like Anouk Bélanger, Jean Harvey, and Benoît Melançon to tease out the meaning of the man known as the Rocket. To illustrate how one Canadiens star, Maurice Richard, galvanized the province to become a national hero, I call upon Roch Carrier's beloved classic story "The Hockey Sweater" (1979) and its film adaptation. I then discuss in greater detail the recent biopic *The Rocket: The Legend of Maurice Richard* (2005), directed by Charles Biname, which tells the story of the Montreal Canadiens great right winger, who wore the number 9. It adopts a discourse that has been constructed around Richard, depicting him as a defender of French Canadian rights and dignity, a national hero who prefigured the modern sovereignist movement, and a model for the construction of French Canadian masculinity.

In chapter 2, we turn from the visual arts to the world of popular literature, specifically examining hockey's representation in the genres of science fiction (SF), fantasy, and *noir*, a spin-off of the detective genre. Various texts dating from the immediate post-1980 Referendum era reveal how hockey can be both exploited and critiqued in fantasies of empowerment and disappearance. In particular, the novel *Les Nordiques sont disparus* (1983) introduces the significant role of nationalism in the development of fans' loyalty to the Quebec Nordiques and in the meaning of their rivalry with the Montreal Canadiens. Besides offering political allegories, texts like François Barcelo's *Ville-Dieu* (1982) and Denis Côté's *Shooting for the Stars* (1983) explore the issue of the hockey player as male body and exploited worker. A similar text from the early 1990s – another period of conflict, this time over the breakdown of the Meech Lake constitutional negotiations – Guy Bouchard's "Au jeu" (1992) also engages the issue of hockey player as labourer, albeit it targets instead the inflated salaries of elite athletes and the Eric Lindros affair. The chapter concludes with a discussion of how a very recent novel, François Barcelo's *I Hate Hockey* (2011), appropriates and reverses the tropes of the hockey novel, transposing them onto the *noir* genre by exploiting recent coach–player sexual abuse scandals.

Chapter 3 takes on the first hockey-themed franchise in Quebec's visual media, the long-running prime-time soap opera *Lance et compte*

(1986–91, 2002–12), which was meant to compete with such popular US offerings as *Dallas* and *Dynasty*. It examines how this television series, first produced in the 1980s as a *pure laine* (dyed-in-the-wool) Québécois show, reflected the concerns of its day and how those concerns changed (or did not) when the series was reprised in the first decade of the new millennium. The analysis demonstrates to a certain degree that *plus ça change, plus c'est la même chose* (the more things change, the more they stay the same),[34] and that in spite of official governmental efforts towards accommodation and inclusiveness, as well as a massive feminist movement in the 1970s, neither the industry of hockey nor Quebec society itself has changed that much in the past three decades – at least if you believe the images of that society found in this television program. Unlike many of the other popular texts analysed in previous and subsequent chapters, which contest the dominant ideology even while celebrating the positive aspects of "la game," *Lance et compte* offers a largely ideological vision of the world – that is, a vision that works to reinforce the dominant social, economic, and political system.

Lance et compte fictionalized the elite lifestyle of an NHL team modelled on the Quebec Nordiques; another hockey-themed media franchise – *Les Boys* (1997–2005, 1997–2012) – stormed the late 1990s with the lowbrow antics of a *ligue de garage* team. *Les Boys* is the topic of chapter 4. The massive popularity of the four *Les Boys* films, which were followed by five seasons of a spin-off television series, certainly reveals their resonance for the people of Quebec. This chapter examines in particular how *Les Boys* constructs both national and masculine identities, and how – like many popular texts – although these films cannot be said to offer an extended social critique, they nonetheless participate in contemporary social debates about those identities. *Les Boys* and its sequels largely reinscribe a conservative image of Quebec as comprised of Franco-Québécois *de souche* (of old stock); nonetheless, they attempt to come to grips with changing aspects of society, from fostering a tolerant attitude towards homosexuality to attempting to deal with the presence of visible minorities, and even tackling the quite recent advent of elite women's hockey (in the third instalment, *les* Boys play the Canadian Olympic women's team).

In chapter 5 we look at how artists within Quebec's vibrant contemporary popular music industry have appropriated hockey as a marker of Quebec identity. In their 2008 song "Le But (à la gloire de nos glorieux)," an homage to the Montreal Canadiens, nationalist rappers Loco Locass celebrate the sport's ability to unite the province's increasingly diverse population. The neotraditionalist group Mes Aïeux use their blend of folk sounds with alternative contemporary rock to honour the sport's past heroes and explore its legends and superstitions, but they also offer a more critical view of its increasing commercialism in "Le Fantôme du Forum" (2008). While a growing number of groups are happy to exploit references to hockey to signify their authenticity as Québécois, Les Dales Hawerchuk and Bob Bissonnette integrate the sport much more fully into their music. The former named themselves after a Winnipeg Jets hero of the 1980s, and their breakout hit and its accompanying music video draw upon many of the images of hockey discussed throughout this book, including masculinity, history, and identity. The chapter concludes with a discussion of how Bissonnette, a self-proclaimed former pro hockey player, has based an entire career on a new musical subgenre; nearly every song on his two albums is about hockey.

Finally, the book's conclusion weaves together the threads of these analyses of diverse popular culture forms via observations about the varying meanings of the representations of hockey discussed at length in the previous chapters. It then returns to the problem of how French Canadians are represented in Anglo-Canadian and Anglo-American texts. Finally, it briefly examines how hockey has been offered to and adopted by cultural communities other than those of the "two charter nations."

Like hockey itself, this study aims to bridge the solitudes, offering for English-speaking hockey fans and scholars a view into the rich and complex manner in which Quebec's popular media have appropriated hockey as a marker for national identity, as well as a commodity that sells products and engages audiences. While I refer to French-language secondary scholarship as often as possible, I also use the large body of English-language hockey scholarship as a frame of reference. Conversely, I also wish to expose Quebec studies scholars to a broad corpus of popular culture texts that demonstrate the continued relevance and centrality of hockey to the Quebec imaginary. Because of this dual aim, my analyses will include background information on hockey that will appear well rehearsed to the hockey scholar; they will also include historical and cultural background that will seem basic to Quebec scholars. In the end, I hope that all readers will discover here a largely unexplored body of film, music, and popular literature texts that appeal not only to those who love hockey but also to a wider audience, and that this analysis ultimately will lead to a better understanding of how and why hockey is so omnipresent in contemporary Québécois popular culture.

Chapter One

From Canadiens to Québécois: Maurice Richard as National Hero

In a young country lacking in national symbols, hockey provided a common cultural reference point for Canadians from diverse regions and backgrounds. [...] The most obvious example is the powerful identification that formed between the Montreal Canadiens and the team's francophone fans.

David Whitson and Richard Gruneau[1]

[We] were five Maurice Richards taking it away from five other Maurice Richards [...]. On our backs, we all wore the famous number 9.

Roch Carrier[2]

Maurice Richard ...
C'est tout le Québec debout,
Qui fait peur et qui vit.

[It's all of Quebec on its feet,
Alive and scary.]

Félix Leclerc[3]

Sheldon Cohen's animated film adaptation of Roch Carrier's beloved story "The Hockey Sweater" literally transforms ten young boys in Ste-Justine, Quebec, into ten miniature copies of Maurice Richard (1921–2000), who in his day was the most revered French Canadian hockey player both inside and outside "La Belle Province" (and who still is today, in Quebec). Originally titled "Une abominable feuille d'érable sur la glace" (1979; an abominable maple leaf on the ice), the nostalgic text has been appropriated as an important nationalist parable. Its young protagonist – an avatar of Carrier himself as a boy – abhors the fact that for an entire winter he must wear a jersey sporting the logo of the despised Toronto Maple Leafs because Eaton's department store, a bastion of anglophone dominance, has botched his mother's mail order. What straightforward pro-francophone allegorical readings elide, however, is the boy's own accusation of reverse discrimination, since the priest–coach refuses to give him ice time while he wears the hideous sweater. Certainly, franco-nationalist discourse gets the last word with the priest's assertion that "just because you're wearing a new Toronto Maple Leafs sweater unlike the others, it doesn't mean you're going to make the laws around here."[4] The seed has nonetheless been planted that ethnic, nationalist, and linguistic prejudices can cut both ways.

Of more direct interest in this, the first chapter of a book on the meaning of hockey in Quebec, is the story's opening paragraph:

> The winters of my childhood were long, long seasons. We lived in three places – the school, the church and the skating rink – but our real life was on the skating-rink. Real strength appeared on the skating-rink. The real leaders showed themselves on the skating-rink.[5]

In rural and small-town Quebec during the 1940s (Carrier was born in 1937), hockey represented "real life." Furthermore, among this society's "real leaders," Maurice Richard, the famous Montreal Canadiens' right wing, for whom the NHL trophy for highest goal scorer is named today, stands head and shoulders above the rest. With this story, Carrier – a prominent literary figure in Quebec and at one time Canada's National Librarian and Archivist (1999–2004) – codifies the legend of Maurice Richard as a Québécois hero and that of the Montreal Canadiens as Quebec's "national" hockey team. This chapter begins to unpack such images, which link hockey to national identity in Canada's predominantly French-speaking province. First, we will examine how the *bleu, blanc, rouge* of the Montreal Canadiens has – somewhat problematically – been constructed as a *lieu de mémoire* in French historian Pierre Nora's sense. Then we will analyse how a recent, highly acclaimed biopic, *Maurice Richard* (2005; dir. Charles Binamé, writ. Ken Scott; *The Rocket: The Legend of Rocket Richard* in English), has reinscribed Richard as a national hero. The film draw upon the clichés established by Richard's earlier biographies – including one by Carrier himself – and also takes at face value the now commonplace assertion that Richard offered post–Second World War French Canadians a national hero around whom they could rally, thus planting the seeds for the Quiet Revolution of the 1960s and 1970s, a powerful campaign for political, social, economic, and linguistic reform in the province.

Hockey Night *Is* Canada, but It's *La Soirée du Hockey* in Quebec[6]

Richard Gruneau and David Whitson invoke CBC/Radio-Canada's weekly broadcast in their 1993 study of hockey and Canadian identity: "Perhaps the strongest of all our feelings of commonality came when we watched *Hockey Night in Canada* on Saturday nights. Even at an early age the TV program made us feel like part of a national community."[7] Similarly, one night a week, French Canadians sat around their radios, then their televisions after 1952, for the Saturday broadcast of *La Soirée du hockey,* as so poignantly demonstrated in the opening sequence of Cohen's film adaptation of Carrier's "The Hockey Sweater" (1980). André-A. Lafrance's memoir of the one night a week that he experienced a bond with his father links hockey to memory with nostalgia: "La communication du samedi soir. [...] Nous nous assoyions tous les deux devant l'écran de télévision pour regarder le match de hockey du Canadien" (Saturday night communication. [...] We would both sit down in front of the TV screen to watch the Canadiens hockey game).[8] Deeply connected to identity and memory, hockey represents a unifying force, as Tony Patoine clearly articulates, invoking the nation's very motto: "Deux nations: le Canada et le Québec. Un même sport national: le hockey. [...] Le hockey est le principal élément de culture unissant les Canadiens *a mari usque ad mare*" (Two nations: Canada and Quebec. One national sport: hockey. [...] Hockey is the principal cultural element uniting Canadians *from sea to sea*).[9] Gold medals for both the men's and women's national teams on home ice at the 2010 Vancouver Winter Olympics and again in 2014 at Sochi further cemented hockey's value as a marker of Canadian unity and identity.

Hockey appears here as a common ground where the two solitudes may meet, particularly through the Montreal Canadiens' rivalry with the Toronto Maple Leafs – the teams' very names reveal their connection to distinct national identities – while also allowing the symbolical acting out of their discords in the safe arena of the national sport: "The Canadiens' rivalries with the Montreal Maroons and, later, the Toronto Maple Leafs provided for the regular dramatization of the French and

English identities that were so much a part of the popular consciousness of the day. There was no other cultural form, no other popular practice, that brought the 'two solitudes' into regular engagement with each other in quite the same way."[10] Since Gruneau and Whitson's path-breaking interrogation of the "hockey as Canada" metaphor, a growing number of critics have questioned its applicability as an *inclusive* image of Canadian or Québécois identity. Michael Robidoux insists that his goal is precisely to "provide a counter-discourse" that acknowledges "the pervasive discrimination within professional hockey."[11] Robert Pitter and Cecil Harris point to the paucity of players of colour in the NHL,[12] and Nancy Theberge, Mary Louise Adams, and Julie Stevens examine the limited roles that hockey allows for women in "the context of a cultural practice that is intimately connected to notions of masculinity and national identity."[13] The very title of Whitson and Gruneau's second book, *Artificial Ice: Hockey, Culture, and Commerce* (2006), signals the constructed, rather than natural, status of hockey as a metaphor for Canadian identity.[14]

More recent essay collections from Quebec offer relatively unquestioning analyses of hockey's links to religion and philosophy;[15] even so, the equation "hockey = Quebec" has not gone unchallenged. Marc Lavoie conducted a statistical analysis of Canada's junior hockey leagues and the NHL and its farm system and found that francophone players face systemic discrimination in scouting and hiring practices; he titled his study *Désavantage numérique* (1998), "numerical disadvantage," troping on the French term for playing short-handed during an opponent's power play.[16] Jean Harvey's incisive essay "Whose Sweater Is This? The Changing Meanings of Hockey in Quebec" (2006) asserts that "hockey has historically served to represent and give voice to French-Canadian identities."[17] It concludes, however, that "today for Quebecers, hockey involves mixed and confused meanings," in particular in relation to the Canadiens of Montreal, a club that "has not been seen as 'French' for more than twenty years, and is perhaps now better understood as a brand name."[18] Yet significantly, even these critiques assert the longevity and omnipresence of hockey as metaphor for Canadian or Québécois national identity, implicitly supporting the description of the sport franchise as a *lieu de mémoire*. Moreover, as this book will demonstrate, the sheer proliferation of hockey-themed popular texts and of hockey references in non-hockey-themed texts, even since the publication of Harvey's essay just a few years ago, reveals that the sport continues to be significant for the people of Quebec.

The Montreal Canadiens as *Lieu de Mémoire*

Since the publication of *Les Lieux de mémoire* (1984–92; *Rethinking France: Les Lieux de Mémoire*, 1999–2009),[19] an epic, three-volume collection of essays on a wide range of places, monuments, works of literature, and other icons that have served to invent and reïnscribe the French nation, Pierre Nora's concept of the "site of memory" has taken on a life of its own. These "sites where a sense of historical continuity persists"[20] identified by Nora and his contributors include not only actual locations, such as the Arc de Triomphe in Paris, and the *Monuments aux Morts*, the war memorials found in every small French town, but also conceptual sites that have been invested with particular significance for the French people as symbolic of their nation and identity, such as the motto "Liberté, Égalité, Fraternité" and the *tricolore*, the blue, white, and red of the national flag. In this book, I will be referring to a number of no-brainer *lieux de mémoire* that have come to define a Franco-Québécois vision of the "nation of Quebec," such as the Plains of Abraham and Charles de Gaulle's "Vive le Québec libre!" speech during his 1967 visit. In this chapter, we look in particular at Quebec's own blue, white, and red, the iconic colours of the Montreal Canadiens, and how a man and a number, Maurice "Rocket" Richard, who wore number 9 for that storied team, have become sites of memory for French Canadians.

The scholarly and popular culture texts referred to in these pages, as well as the commercially motivated commemorative activities surrounding the hundredth anniversary of the Montreal Canadiens in 2009[21] – such as the installation of "La Place du Centenaire" with statues of its history's great players in the courtyard outside the team's home ice at the Bell Centre – all seek to preserve a cultural phenomenon that has begun to exceed the limits of lived memory. "Material, symbolic, and functional"[22] – the Canadiens and the Forum clearly fulfil the three functions that Nora associates with *le lieu de mémoire*, which is "simple and ambiguous, natural and artificial, at once immediately available in concrete sensual experience and susceptible to the most abstract elaboration."[23] What could be more natural than a founding date? Yet the year 1909 represents a reconstruction, a choice, for it predates the existence of both the NHL and *le Club de hockey canadien*, aka the Montreal Canadiens per se. Similarly, the popular culture texts analysed in this and subsequent chapters appropriate the material facts of the hockey team and exploit the functional nature of its home arena, drawing upon the symbolic valences of both, thus participating in "the endless recycling of their meaning."[24]

As Audrey Laurin-Lamothe and Nicolas Moreau assert, "le Canadien est le lieu d'une consolidation historique, identitaire, économique et culturelle" (the Canadiens are the site of a historical, identitary, economic, and cultural consolidation) in Quebec.[25] The very name of the franchise invokes history and signals its identity politics, not only through the obvious use of the French language in its official version – *le Club de hockey canadien* – but also through its original function. Founded with the specific goal of exploiting Anglo-French rivalry to boost attendance by Montreal's blasé hockey fans,[26] this supposed hallmark of an "authentic" French Canadian identity was inextricably linked with capitalist entrepreneurialism from its very beginnings. Yet "French-speaking east-end Montrealers [...] embraced the *bleu, blanc, rouge* as their own and nicknamed them *l'équipe des habitants* – team of the habitants," referencing the term for the original French settlers in the Saint Lawrence Valley.[27] English-speakers reinforced the team's identification with French Canadians, the original *Canadiens*, with nicknames like the "Flying Frenchmen" or just "the Frenchmen."[28] When "Habs" was appropriated by Anglo-Montrealers, French Canadian initiates began referring to the team as "nos Glorieux" (our glorious ones) or simply in the singular, *le Canadien*, a form I sometimes adopt here. As Jean Harvey explains, what began as a Montreal phenomenon developed into a province-wide passion through the combined influences of media dissemination and the NHL's efforts to monopolize professional play. "The most important factor in the national significance of *les Canadiens*, however, was the phenomenal success of their teams in the years from 1930 to 1980," Harvey writes. "The Canadiens' success in their glory years was built upon their virtual monopoly on good French-Canadian players."[29] Even in the team's earliest years, *le Canadien* was never *all* French;[30] nevertheless, they remained a source of fierce pride for francophones; until 1999 the Montreal Canadiens were the most successful franchise in all of major league sports, with twenty-four Stanley Cups. A sports dynasty rivalled only by that of the New York Yankees, the Canadiens owned the ice during the 1950s, 1960s, and 1970s, winning sixteen of their championships in those three decades. Hockey fans in the United States and Canada alike recognize the names of past Montreal stars, who include Howie Morenz, Jean Béliveau, Guy Lafleur, and Patrick Roy; the Vezina Trophy for the NHL's best goaltender is named after the pioneer Canadien *gardien de but*, Georges Vézina.[31]

Throughout this period, playing in an NHL always dominated by Anglo-Canadians and increasingly sold to the United States, the Canadiens' recruitment of the best French Canadian players allowed for their relatively authentic representation of a French Canadian national identity. Harvey argues, however, that hockey today "is no longer the national game that it once was" and that by the 1980s the Canadiens' "representative significance had been diminished, both by changes in the game and by larger changes in Quebec society,"[32] a point echoed by Lafrance.[33] In the 1950s, Maurice Richard's battles on the ice seemed to represent the only battles being won by French Canadians; but since the Quiet Revolution and the rise of the Parti Québécois, says Harvey, "Quebecers have found new avenues for their national confirmation through politics and the economy."[34] This point is well illustrated by Ken Dryden, former Canadiens goalie as well as a federal MP from 2004 to 2011, in his account of the night of 15 November 1976 in the Forum. On that night of the Parti Québécois's dramatic electoral victory, spectators watched the scoreboard anxiously, not because of the contest occurring on the ice before them, but for updates of election returns, which were being posted as "Lib" versus "PQ" scores.[35]

The link between Canadiens hockey and watershed events in Quebec's history provides the organizing structure for Toronto playwright Rick Salutin's *Les Canadiens* (1977), which Benoît Melançon interprets as depicting that night as marking the end of the myth of the Canadiens.[36] Yet the Canadiens' continued presence in popular culture appears to belie these assertions of their waning importance. Indeed, Michel Brunelle, a minority voice among Richard's eulogizers after the icon's death in 2000, argues that by the end of the millennium "les Québécois ont abandonné le combat, préférant la conquête de la coupe Stanley à celle de leur propre territoire" (Quebecers have abandoned the fight, preferring the conquest of the Stanley Cup to that of their own territory).[37] Jonathan Cha similarly argues that recent campaigns in a number of Canadian cities – but perhaps most extensively in Montreal – have led to hockey's increased hegemony as "une marque de l'identité culturelle évoluant au cœur et à l'échelle de la ville" (a marker of cultural identity moving at the heart of and on the scale of the city) – if not of the nation.[38]

Hockey and the Canadiens seem to be as ubiquitous as ever in Québécois popular culture, and their meanings can be exploited to a variety of ends, as we will see in subsequent chapters. Laurin-Lamothe and Moreau have observed that the Canadiens take up 85 per cent of all sports coverage in Quebec and that the coverage of just over three of the franchise's games equals that of an entire year of the province's news coverage of Africa.[39] Perhaps nothing so clearly illustrates the continued power of hockey to motivate Quebecers as the highly publicized reality show aired on TVA beginning on 24 January 2010: *La Série Montréal–Québec*, which pitted teams of amateurs (including two women each) coached by Guy Carbonneau and Michel Bergeron, former head coaches of the Canadiens and the Nordiques, respectively.[40] Each team also had its own anthem; Montreal's was sung by hard rock icon Éric Lapointe, Quebec City's by none other than ultranationalist rappers Loco Locass, whose hockey-related work is addressed in chapter 5. The program's popularity led to a second season in January 2011; however, there appear to be no plans for a third.

Blood, Sweat, and Tears: The Legend of Maurice Richard[41]

The most glorified player in the history of *les Glorieux* remains Maurice "the Rocket" Richard, described by his biographer Jean-Marie Pellerin as *L'Idole d'un peuple* (1976 [1998]; The Idol of a People). Although often hailed as a heroic figure in all of Canada, for many Richard symbolizes a more specifically French-Canadian pride and resistance to domination by Anglo-American elites.[42] Indeed, in his biographical memoir of Richard's omnipresence in the daily life of Quebecers, *The Rocket* (2000), Roch Carrier describes the player's presence on the ice in precisely such mythical terms: "Quand le Rocket traverse les défenseurs comme un passe-muraille, les Canadiens français voient un guerrier légendaire qui refait la bataille des plaines d'Abraham et reconquiert le territoire perdu" (When the Rocket magically passes through the opponents' defences, French Canadians see a legendary warrior who re-enacts the Battle of the Plains of Abraham and reconquers the lost territory).[43] So powerful is Richard's presence in Quebec that Benoît Melançon has dedicated an entire volume to the cultural history of Maurice Richard.[44] It reveals that Richard is, hands down, the Canadien most often invoked in popular culture texts, such as Carrier's "The Hockey Sweater." Richard's excellence on the ice provided a model, as did his frank observations about anti-francophone policies and prejudices in the NHL and elsewhere, expressed in the *Samedi-Dimanche* column "Le Tour du chapeau," ghostwritten by Paul St-Georges for Richard in the early 1950s.[45] Popular and scholarly texts link Richard with struggles to promote French-Canadian identity to the extent that he has been seen as a precursor-figure of the Quiet Revolution.[46] But as Fred A. Reed's translation of Melançon's study asserts, through product endorsements, the hockey star also became a commodity: "Maurice Richard is a brand name."[47]

In 2007, Charles Binamé's biopic of the hockey star, titled simply *Maurice Richard* in Quebec, won more Genie Awards – the Canadian equivalent of the Oscars – than Richard won Stanley Cup rings.[48] The film is in many ways a conventional sports biography. Writer Ken Scott included many of the well-known episodes in the hero's legend through 1955: his humble origins in working-class Montreal; his employment at a young age as a machinist (4:04–5:00), and thus his self-made status; his determination to improve his skills through hard work (39:50–40:00);[49] and the early comparisons made between him and former greats like Howie Morenz; but also injuries during his early career and concerns that he was too fragile for the NHL (22:04–25; 30:35). The film documents his struggles with the English language, which dominated the league (21:28; 1:06:35–1:07:18; 42:35–50), and his rise to success and popularity, as well as the later pressures he felt as such a star (1:14:44–1:15:23). Of course, it reveals the origin of his celebrated number 9, chosen because that was how many pounds his first daughter, Huguette, weighed at birth (43:45–44:00; 45:00–45:30). Above all, Scott's scenario features Richard's oft-recounted, near mythical feats on the ice, including his 28 December 1944 moving day exploits (he scored 5 goals 3 assists against the Detroit Red Wings for a 9–1 Canadiens victory after toting furniture all day down and then back up several flights of stairs) (1:01:25–1:05:10); his scoring a goal on 3 February 1945 while carrying renowned goon Earl Seibert on his back (51:27–53); and the 8 April 1952 goal he scored while dripping blood from a concussion-causing injury that had been stitched up earlier in the game (1:26:22–25).

Sequences like these mine the rhetoric of sports films: slow motion and close-ups of the athlete's determined visage establish exploits like these as extraordinary, heroic. In particular, Binamé bathes the Seibert sequence in a bright, almost heavenly light: the ice glows, but the spectators in the stands are occluded so that we can only see the opposing team's goalie ready to face Richard (Roy Dupuis) as he advances with an almost gigantic Seibert draped across his back. The sequence of 8 April 1952 portraying what the team president, Senator Donat Raymond, terms "le plus beau but que j'ai jamais vu" (1:27:50–55) appears almost as an incident of *déjà vu*, having been set up by an earlier sequence recounting the 17 December 1944 game in which Richard foiled the New York Rangers' head-hunting plans by beating up a former boxer, Bill "the Killer" Dill (54:43–1:01:06). In this case, the second round play-offs against the Bruins, Richard is not so lucky; he is struck from behind by an unidentified player and knocked unconscious.[50] A dramatically circling shot of him lying spread-eagled on the ice heightens the impact of the injury, as do reaction shots of Richard's wife Lucille (Julie LeBreton) and, indeed, the entire crowd in the stands (1:22:30–1:23:35).

Above all, Binamé employs more than once in his film the striking image of the hero's bright red blood, sometimes dripping, but here actually pooled on the stark blue-white ice (1:23:55). Another close-up of the prone hero being stitched up in the locker room further invokes the metaphor of the hockey rink as battlefield; the player's injury is vividly revealed, a deep gash above his blinking eye underscoring both the perils of his profession and his courage. Without flinching, he takes the stitches and returns to the bench (1:24:00–1:25:00). Bandaged, yet still dripping blood from the hastily repaired wound, Richard carries the puck down the ice and after a series of feints arrives at the opposing team's goal, bringing the crowd to its feet as he scores (1:26:22–25). Invoking the sports film cliché of the slow motion shot, with the player's breathing laid over the music soundtrack, Binamé cuts from close-ups of the player's determined visage to longer shots that situate him on the ice, allowing the viewer to experience the beauty of his drive forward; all the while, he intercalates these with reaction shots of the crowd and specifically of Lucille. To an ovation and chants of "Maurice! Maurice! Maurice!" he circles, seeking his wife's gaze; his sweat and blood, married with her tears of relief, seal the pact of the hero's effort for the nation and his long-suffering spouse's support and sacrifice that allow him to do so.

The media's presence seems essential to the creation of the historical moment. The transition from the ice into the locker room occurs via the device of black-and-white still photos coupled with the sound of flashbulbs (1:27:21–30). Lucille's are not the only tears shed that night; in the locker room afterward, still dripping with blood and sweat, the great hero breaks down into near hysterical sobs, a release of the great pressure and tension he now feels (1:28:00–50). It is precisely through these depictions of the blood, sweat, and tears of the athlete that Binamé constructs the image of the hero, human after all in spite of the almost superhuman deeds he has accomplished. But his greatest feat is yet to come: Richard's defiance of the anglophone-dominated league in the form of its president Clarence Campbell and the events leading up to what is commonly referred to as the Richard Riot of 17 March 1955.

Indeed, the biopic places its hero's struggles to succeed in the game of hockey in the context of pre–Quiet Revolution French-Canadian oppression and resistance. It does so in a number of ways that we will examine here, but most literally by framing its narrative trajectory with the Richard Riot, an event that has become a *lieu de mémoire* in the province's history. The film bookends its narrative with the Riot, an event interpreted by nationalist historians not as a mere outbreak of fan violence, but rather as a precursor to Quebec's intense period of modernization, secularization, and consolidation of political and economic power in French hands between 1960 and 1966, stretching according to some into the 1970s, a period now known as the Quiet Revolution.[51]

The film's opening sequence (0:00–4:04), which is intercut with black title cards containing the opening credits, underscores the media's role in creating the legend of the Rocket. A radio announcer's voice-over describes the scene of "destruction," while a title card informs us of the date and setting: Montreal 1955. A close-up of a clock radio pans out to reveal a concerned family huddled around a kitchen table; a transition shot returns to the white radio centred on the table.[52] Between more black title cards with the principal stars' names, a disorienting and relatively rapidly moving tracking shot brings us into the halls behind the scenes at the Montreal Forum. We follow a news reporter, camera in hand, arriving at a chaotic scene in which Canadiens' head coach Dick Irvin (Stephen McHattie) rails at the situation, explicitly articulating the stakes involved in the suspension of this game for the Canadiens: "There is no reason why we cannot finish this game. [...] We cannot afford to lose. This is Detroit. It's the end of the goddam season." But the fire marshal is emphatic that he is clearing the arena. The lack of explanation here reveals the extent to which a Quebec audience already knows the story about to be told. Another cut jumps to an office, where a businessman hands a sheet of paper to an individual who determinedly sets off down another hall, stopping at a door marked "PLAYERS ONLY";[53] the door is opened, the message is handed in, and jeers of disappointment emanate from the now closed door. The viewer realizes that the players have received the fateful verdict: the game has been suspended. Because most viewers are already familiar with the story he is telling, Binamé need only worry about *how* he tells it, and he does so stylishly and effectively, except that now, having begun with his ending, he returns to the beginning, with a general shot of an industrial setting and a title card reading "Montréal 1937 / – La Grande Noirceur – ." Although revisionist historians now question this appellation,[54] the film's reference to this period, translated as "The Great Blackness" and corresponding to the conservative – some say nearly fascist – leadership of provincial premier Maurice Duplessis, further contextualizes Richard's biography in a nationalist discourse of oppression and its overcoming.

By 1955, quite late in his career, Richard had already been publicly criticizing league president Clarence Campbell and generally accusing the NHL and its players of anti-French prejudice in a weekly newspaper column ghostwritten by Paul Saint-Georges since the summer of 1952. When a fight broke out during a game against the Boston Bruins on 13 March of that year, Richard punched an official and was suspended for the rest of the season, including the play-offs. The film depicts the sequence of events as yet another example of anti-French-Canadian bias on the part of the NHL and Richard's actions as largely justified acts of resistance. Not only were the Canadiens in contention for the play-offs, as asserted in Dick Irvin's speech quoted above, but Richard was also working towards his first highest-scorer trophy, which the film suggests he had heretofore failed to win because other teams cheated by giving unearned assists to their stars (1:18:45–1:18:50).

Richard's willingness to fight back, to shed his own blood and that of others, is a significant aspect of his hero status. Not only through his critical words expressed through the pen of Paul Saint-Georges, but also with his fists, Richard resisted the oppression of French-speaking Canadians, both in Quebec and in all of anglophone North America through his battles against the Maple Leafs, Black Hawks, Bruins, Red Wings, and Rangers. Again, the film establishes a context for Richard's violence, as when Irvin shows him the Boston papers on the train "so you really know just how much they hate you down there" (1:41:25–35). Increasingly a target for goons because of his skills and his scoring prowess, expressing his frustration over officials' looking the other way while French players are consistently punished for similar actions, the film portrays Richard as simply seeking justice after he takes an apparently unprovoked slash from behind from Hal Laycoe on 13 March 1955 (1:43:30). Once again, the hero's sweat and blood drip onto the ice, but this time he is quickly on his feet, having perceived the injustice – he espies the official who failed to see or pretended not to see the foul, noting his number 2 jersey (1:44:04). Up and at 'em, Richard skates quickly over to Laycoe and slashes him over the back in return (1:44:15-25), and a melée breaks out. As the film depicts the sequence of events, while Richard is being held by an official, Laycoe skates out of the melée to strike him squarely in the face at least twice, again shedding the hero's blood (1:45:10-20). The enraged Richard frees himself, and as the official tries to grab him again, he strikes back at the official (1:45:23). The situation is presented in such a way that one almost perceives that the official is holding the francophone hero *in order that* he can be struck by the anglophone Bruin, a player hailing from a team and from a city whose record of racism is renowned even today, as demonstrated by a series of racist Tweets occurring after the Washington Capitals' forward Joel Ward, who happens to be black, knocked the Boston team out of the Stanley Cup play-offs in April 2012.[55]

While it is outside the scope of this study to tease out the precise sequence of events that led to Richard's ejection and subsequent suspension, it remains nonetheless pertinent to note Scott's and Biname's portrayal of their unfolding in a manner that heightens both their dramatic effect and their weight among francophone nationalists. Indeed, historical accounts vary widely, ranging from that of D'Arcy Jenish, who does not mention Richard being punched while held and who sets Richard's suspension in the context of an earlier assault on an official.[56] We owe perhaps the most detailed account to biographer Jean-Marie Pellerin: enraged at the sight of his own blood after Laycoe had slashed him over the ear with his stick, Richard sought retaliation. Having dropped his own stick as he circled around to face Laycoe, the Rocket picked up another and hit Laycoe over the back. Restrained from behind by linesman Cliff Thompson, according to Pellerin, Richard warned him twice: "If you want to stop me, do it to my face, not from behind." As Richard sought to break loose, a struggle brought both men to the ice; having finally freed himself Richard then struck the linesman.[57] Like Jenish, Pellerin never mentions Laycoe striking Richard once the latter was restrained; we owe this element to Carrier. The filmmakers appear to have drawn heavily on the latter's account, which – like the dramatic film – uses rhetoric to heighten the reader's excitement and clearly accuses Laycoe of punching a restrained Richard.[58]

Furthermore, in the film Laycoe appears to receive no punishment for provoking the sequence of events, although actually he was given a five-minute major. Richard's suspension is thus depicted as a prejudicial and even vindictive action on the part of the commissioner, who has targeted Richard because of his prior criticisms. With Richard suspended and protesters already picketing outside, Campbell's attendance at the St Patrick's Day game in Montreal versus the Detroit Red Wings appears as not only arrogant but also clearly provocative. Fan disgruntlement makes itself felt inside the arena, and when a fan inside the Forum hurls a smoke bomb, the game is suspended. Rioting and demonstrations spill out onto the street, with looting and vandalism along Saint Catherine Street and elsewhere. Once again, the film underscores the media's role by focusing on television coverage – watched by Richard's children at home with Lucille – of the unfolding events, which the announcer frames as having "all the makings of a racial conflict" (1:51:00–1:51:20). It also depicts Richard's radio plea the following day for the violence to stop (1:57:10–1:58:15). The film then closes with a black-and-white montage of hockey sequences spanning his career, wearing both the number 15 and the famous 9, and then of him striding along, his head held high, with final title cards informing us that he played for five more years, during which the Canadiens won five consecutive Stanley Cups, and stopping on a close-up of his eyes, the Rocket's most celebrated feature, as highlighted in the French title of Melançon's cultural history, *Les Yeux de Maurice Richard* (The Eyes of Maurice Richard) (1:59:40–49).

Binamé and Scott thus faithfully rehearse the widely held image of Maurice Richard as a hero of franco-nationalism. In addition to using the Richard Riot to bookend their telling of his story, they frame his determination to succeed on the ice with depictions of English-speaking management's oppression of French-speaking workers' efforts to unionize in the machine shop where he laboured as a youth and his own punishment for refusing to betray the organizers (4:04–5:00; 5:28–6:41). Early in his career, Richard's barber implies that he hasn't been chosen for the All-Star Team because he's French-Canadian (48:48–50). Later, Canadiens star Émile "Butch" Bouchard (Patrice Robitaille) becomes the mouthpiece for the largely silent Richard in the locker room and on train trips when French-Canadian players including Richard, Bouchard, and Bob Filion (Sébastien Roberts) repeatedly share a compartment. Filion complains that "we have to be ten times better than them to be in the League. [...] I've got four brothers and all four of them are better than Frank and ..." (1:08:44–57). Bouchard responds by seeking to raise his teammates' consciousness and spurring them to act for change. He asks, "Why aren't we allowed to speak French on the bench? [...] Somebody has to stand up and stop pretending everything's all right" (1:09:20–50).[59] The film frames Richard's passion to win as arising from an inner rage against such injustices, a rage that must be expressed on the ice; and it portrays Irvin as exploiting that fire by pushing Richard's buttons. For example, during a losing game, Irvin directly addresses Richard in his locker room speech between periods, arguing that "you Frenchies are all alike. It is in your blood. You are nothing but a bunch of no spunk, no stiff upper lip, chicken droppings" (48:35–45).[60] Later, when Richard is angry that the English-language papers are making fun of his English, instead of praising him for tying Joe Malone's record forty-three goals in a season, Irvin goads him: "You know what they're trying to do to you, Maurice. Now what are you going to do about it?" (1:07:21–1:08:13).

Richard's growing awareness of his own responsibility appears to follow directly from Bouchard's challenge to stand up and do something. In an interview with Michel Normandin (Normand Chouinard), the great Canadiens radio announcer of the era, after he has beaten Malone's record, Richard begins humbly, attributing his success to luck, but then he asserts that "more importantly, I established a record that will be an honor to all French Canadians." A reaction shot reveals Butch Bouchard listening in his car and shouting, "Yeah!" in triumph; other shots show the reaction of Tony Bergeron (Rémy Girard), Richard's wise barber, and of a random fan seen in earlier shots, thus establishing the impact of the Rocket on French-Canadians around Montreal and throughout the province (1:14:00–10). When first approached by Paul Saint-Georges (Benoît Girard) to give his opinions of the injustices he sees, Richard declines; the film depicts his breakdown in the locker room during the 8 April 1952 play-off game against the Bruins as a turning point. The very next sequence, dated July 1952 with a title card, depicts Richard arriving at Saint-Georges's office to assert: "I want things to change." Asked what he wants to talk about, he begins with, "When they insult me" (1:30:00–30); he also accuses officials of *not* helping when other players hit and attack him and Bouchard "for the sole reason that we are French Canadians" (1:30:30–53). The film uses their collaboration to build up to and set the stage for the closing sequences about the Riot.

In contrast to the largely federalist message of different-but-complementary in the contemporary era – a message identified in our discussion of Canuel's *Bon Cop, Bad Cop*, released just a few months later – *Maurice Richard* remembers *past* injustices to celebrate a hero of French-Canadian resistance against English-speaking oppression. The film's message is summed up by Richard's barber, played by one of the province's best-loved actors, Rémy Girard, who also plays Stan in *Les Boys:*

> Ils t'ont enlevé le droit de t'exprimer. Il t'ont enlevé le droit de jouer au hockey. Mais ils t'ont pas enlevé le droit de te battre. [...] C'était tout croche hier soir, mais je pense que c'était nécessaire. [...] c'est que c'est important qu'un Canadian Français gagne, même si c'est juste dans le sport.
>
> They took away your right to express yourself. They took away your right to play hockey. But they haven't taken away your right to fight. [...] It was all messed up last night, but I think it was necessary. [...] It's important that a French Canadian wins, even if it's just in sports.

By displacing the stereotype of the "damned Canuck,"[61] the "nègre blanc d'Amérique,"[62] the French-Canadian loser, and replacing it with a discourse of the "winner," omnipresent in contemporary Quebec hockey films and television since *Lance et compte* (see chapter 3), Maurice Richard thus appears as a legendary figure in the province's battle to preserve its distinct French-language society in the face of the continent-wide anglophone majority.

Setting aside the frankly legendary depictions of hockey heroism described above, Binamé works for a paradoxical effect of both realism and nostalgia by inserting period exterior stills and even some apparent footage into which Dupuis's image has been digitally edited (12:45–13:00) to situate the action in a "real," historical time frame. And these mimetic images have been lab (or digitally) treated to obtain a blueish tint, thus lending them the distanced feel of a bygone era; similarly, the place and date titles appearing over these images add an effect of realism and accuracy to the purportedly factual aspects of Richard's life while explicitly signalling that they occurred in a now distant past. In the rink, slow motion and close-ups, as well as extreme lighting effects and a minimized colour palette (significantly, tones of blue, white, and red dominate), highlight the legendary aspects of the hockey star; by contrast, the scenes of Richard's domestic life offer the viewer a sense of his simplicity and humanity.

In addition to its nationalist dynamics, the film portrays the hockey star as a model of French Canadian masculinity, and depicts Richard specifically as an object of female desire.[63] From its initial sequences, *Maurice Richard* introduces a motivating figure as important to the hockey star as his coach, Dick Irvin: his future wife, Lucille Norchet.

She first appears as a young girl of thirteen (Amélie Richer), scorned by her seventeen-year-old brother, who plays with Richard (5:10–5:26). During the first hockey sequence, she cheers on the young Richard (François Langlois-Vallières), but also shows her own ambition and determination, staying behind on the ice to kiss the star who has scored the winning goal for his team (7:35–12:16). The filmmakers appear to compensate for Richard's early silence – a trait of his real-life model, who hated speaking publicly[64] – by making him a sexually attractive object of desire for the young woman, a choice reinforced by their casting of Roy Dupuis, Quebec's biggest heart-throb actor, in the role of the adult Maurice, who makes his first appearance in the following sequence, not as a hockey player, but as a suitor, arriving at Lucille's home to request her hand in marriage. Once again, his working-class origins appear clearly in contrast to her middle-class status: her father rejects his suit, in spite of his future mother-in-law's vouching for his promising career in the NHL (13:13–15:31). As a strong-willed and even spoiled young woman who gets what she wants, however, Lucille soon has her wedding nonetheless (15:50–16:10). She also gets her wedding night, but in the type of apartment a still aspiring hockey star can afford in the 1940s, with neighbours audibly fighting and windows that rattle in the cold; their relationship idealized, the couple manages to make the site appear romantic, turning on the radio, dimming the lights, and dancing together before embracing passionately (16:11–17:50).

Thus far, through its depiction of Monsieur Norchet (Michel Barrette) – who talks a lot, but to whom no one listens – and even of the relatively inarticulate Richard, the film appears to reinforce a cultural stereotype of the "absent" or ineffectual father in Quebec.[65] Indeed, Richard's own father, Onésime Richard, seems surprisingly absent from the film precisely *because* he was present in the Rocket's real life. This absence reinforces the viewer's sense of Richard as largely self-made, but also motivated by the woman in his life. Although his pride occasionally gets in the way of domestic bliss – in one instance, for example, he refuses to accept steaks from his butcher father-in-law (22:30–45) – the couple remain surprisingly solid throughout the ups and downs of his dramatic career. Richard is a desirable mate, a hero on the ice and not bad to look at; but above all he is a proud father, as demonstrated by his desire to wear number 9 in honour of his first child, a daughter's, birth weight. The film thus positions him not only as a model of French Canadian determination to rise up and fight against injustices faced on a daily basis, but also as overcoming this stereotype in order to offer a model of engaged fatherhood. As Anouk Bélanger articulates it: "Hockey heroes like Maurice Richard became the embodiment of (physical) strength, power, and pride that came to fill the 'insecurity gap' of many male Québécois."[66] The hockey star offers Quebec's men a model to emulate; it also offers Quebec's women, embodied in Lucille, an object of desire. Combining both skill *and* fight, Richard represents the ultimate French Canadian, well on his way to becoming a self-confident Québécois.

Finally, the film establishes Richard's role in revitalizing and popularizing the game of hockey itself, which is perhaps one reason why, despite its nationalist message, it had great appeal in English Canada as well. As Richard arrives at the Forum in his rookie season of 1942, a conversation between Dick Irvin (1892–1957), who coached the Montreal Canadiens out of obscurity and into the limelight with Richard's brilliant presence from 1940 to 1955, and then Canadiens general manager Tommy Gorman, reveals Irvin's desire to win. His initial speech to the team also reveals the crisis faced by the NHL, a crisis that began during the Great Depression of the 1930s and continued into the Second World War, when budgets were tight for fans and the perception (and reality) was that hockey's best players either were or should be overseas. Attendance at NHL games had dipped dramatically, and in addition, to put it simply, the Canadiens were playing poorly.[67] The film portrays Irvin and Richard as helping make hockey exciting again and as revivifying the game, not just in Quebec but throughout the league. Aware that the francophone audience would know the game and its history, Scott's script remains largely accurate, taking few liberties with chronology. Furthermore, to add some excitement to the hockey scenes, the film ices actual NHL players. For example, in the final game sequence at Boston Garden on 13 March 1955, Vincent Lecavalier (a first-round draft pick of the Tampa Bay Lightning in 1998, now a Philadelphia Flyer) plays as Jean Béliveau (he has no lines, but we recognize the Canadiens great's jersey number 4, worn by Lecavalier himself during league play).

Conclusion

Precisely by focusing on the blood, sweat, and tears of Maurice Richard, Binamé's film reinscribes the hockey player's status as a French Canadian *lieu de mémoire*. In a province long dominated by the Catholic Church, and repeatedly offered up the Passion of Christ – also a trial of physical endurance marked by violence – such imagery of the

Rocket in many ways employs him as a replacement figure, a redemptive, sacrificial hero for a modern, secularized Quebec-in-the-making. Indeed, in his biography/cultural memoir of *Le Rocket,* Roch Carrier describes Richard's fall during the Laycoe incident in precisely such terms, referring to "le Christ crucifié" and then, when Richard rises, to "Le Christ ressuscité!"[68] Hockey itself and the Canadiens in particular have reached almost the status of a religion in a contemporary Quebec searching for sites of communion and meaning. "Le plus grand hockeyeur des temps modernes" (the greatest hockey player in modern times)[69] has physically passed, and other heroes, like Guy Lafleur and Patrick Roy, have come and gone, but Richard lives on, not only in the fans' memory but also in the nation's. Richard is dead! Long live the Rocket!

Chapter Two

"The Nordiques Have Disappeared!" Hockey, Science Fiction, and Nationalist Fantasies in Quebec

Hockey, the national sport of the Quebec people, occupies a place of choice in the imagination of our science-fiction writers.

Simon Dupuis[1]

Anyone living in Quebec knows well – hockey occupies an important affective space on television here, possibly out of proportion – that Guy Lafleur was a fantastic hockey player.

Renald Bérubé[2]

In his well-known memoir *The Game* (1983), Ken Dryden, the former star goalie for the Montreal Canadiens and later a federal MP, recalls the tension in the Forum on provincial election night, 15 November 1976. For once, the crowd appeared distracted by a reality outside the hallowed arena, the Mecca of hockey; the scoreboard intermittently reflected their preoccupation, flashing election results as "Lib vs PQ." A few miles away in Montreal's heavily francophone east end, at the Paul Sauvé Arena – once home ice for a Quebec Major Junior Hockey League (QMJHL) team – the Parti Québécois prepared for a victory rally.[3] Led by the extremely popular René Lévesque, the PQ hoped to gain a majority in the Quebec National Assembly, a reflection of popular favour for their sovereignist agenda. Dryden describes the moment that victory was declared, a moment in which Habs fans, usually united in support of the *bleu, blanc, rouge* of the historic Club de Hockey Canadien, were divided in their reactions:

> In the middle of the third period, the message board flashed again – "Un Nouveau Gouvernement." No longer afraid to hope, thousands stood up

> and cheered, thousands of others who had always stood and cheered with them stayed seated and did not cheer. At that moment, people who had sat together for many years in the tight community of season-ticket holders learned something about each other that they had not known before. The last few minutes of the game were very difficult. The mood in the Forum changed.[4]

The Canadiens, no longer fully living up to their former nickname the Flying Frenchmen since less than half the team's players were French Canadians, defeated the St. Louis Blues 4–2, but they had been upstaged by a victory in the only other arena bigger than hockey in Quebec, that of politics.

The euphoria felt by nationalists that night lasted another three and a half years as René Lévesque made good on his promise to hold a provincial referendum on Quebec negotiating a new relationship with Canada that he called "sovereignty-association." Offered as a compromise term to gain wider support, sovereignty-association meant that, instead of being one province among ten equals in a federal system, Quebec would be a sovereign state on the same footing as Canada itself. Quebec would, however, maintain a close economic association, including a common dollar, with its neighbour on two sides (secession would literally divide Canada, for Quebec lies geographically between the Maritimes and the rest of the nation). Lévesque felt that if he could reassure anglophone economic interests and calm moderate francophones' fears about the financial impact of independence, he had a chance to win public approval to begin negotiations. The PQ victory in the November 1976 elections had seemed to signal that Quebecers were ready to say yes to sovereignty.

The previous May, the Habs had defeated the New York Rangers to win the 1979 Stanley Cup. But with the Canadiens already eliminated from the Stanley Cup play-offs in the quarter-finals, thoughts of hockey occupied only a few Quebecers on the evening of 20 May 1980. On that date, all of Canada's attention was again riveted on Quebec, this time as its voters went to the polls to voice their opinion on the following question: "Do you give the Government of Quebec the mandate to negotiate the proposed agreement [for sovereignty-association] between Quebec and Canada?" PQ supporters truly believed they had a chance for victory, for the 1970s had been a decade of nationalist upsurge. Most francophones had condemned the violent terrorist actions of the Front de Libération du Québec (FLQ) during the 1960s, which had included the kidnapping and murder of provincial minister Pierre Laporte in

1970. However, during what became known as the October Crisis, the invocation of the War Measures Act, which led to tanks in the streets of Montreal and to the arrest of most of the province's political left, had backfired on the federal government; its actions had radicalized public opinion and heightened perceptions of a threat to French-language culture in North America. Yet even though a highly vocal, media-friendly intelligentsia had spoken out in favour of sovereignty, the referendum results in 1980 revealed that nationalist sentiment does not necessarily translate into a vote for Quebec sovereignty.[5]

A majority, not necessarily a silent one, but one whose voice had perhaps not been heard by the province's political, cultural, and intellectual elites, voted against negotiating sovereignty-association.[6] For those 40 per cent who had voted Yes, this defeat was all the more devastating because they had embraced the dream so tightly. The vocal pro-sovereignty elements among the intelligentsia and the culture industries, referred to as *The Shouting Sign-Painters* (1972) by Malcolm Reid in his colourful account of their rise to prominence, had shouted so loud and so long that they had apparently lost touch with the majority of Quebecers. The period immediately following the No vote in the 1980 referendum appears in contemporary accounts as one of melancholy, mourning for a lost dream, even as a trauma for some, including public intellectual André Belleau. In a morning-after essay dramatically titled "On ne meurt pas de mourir" (Dying can't kill you), the late literary critic described the impact of the defeat on his sense of identity: "Je ne sais pas ce que je suis [...]. J'étais 'X' qui n'a pas réussi à devenir Québécois" (I don't know what I am ... I was 'X' who failed to become a Québécois).[7] This sense of a failed identity, of a loss of self, of mourning for a potential not realized, would pervade nationalist political discourse and literary and cultural productions in the early 1980s; it would be felt even in a popular genre that few immediately associate with Quebec: science fiction. At the same time, according to Steve Lasorsa, "devant l'inquiétude et l'insécurité des Québécois face à leur avenir collectif, nombreux sont ceux à se réfugier, comme dans le passé, dans une valeur culturelle 'sûre,' le hockey" (Faced with the anxiety and insecurity of their collective future, many Québécois looked for refuge, as they had in the past, in a "sure" cultural value, hockey).[8]

In this chapter I examine the unique conjunction of science fiction, hockey, and nationalist discourse in Quebec. In particular, I demonstrate how texts published in the aftermath of the failed 1980 referendum directly engaged the question of nationalism in a variety of ways, using science fiction and hockey as tools for social critique. Jean-Pierre April's short story "Le Fantôme du Forum" (1981), and novels by François Barcelo, *Ville-Dieu* (1982), and Gilles Tremblay, *Les Nordiques sont disparus* (1983), offer ambivalent fantasies of empowerment and fear of extinction to Quebecers allegorized as hockey fans and players. Denis Côté's young adult novel series that begins with *Hockeyeurs cybernétiques* (1983; *Shooting for the Stars*, 1990) promotes political and social action for change at a broader, global level in its depiction of a hockey star leading a popular uprising in a future dystopia. In addition to the nationalist question, these texts engage contemporary debates about hockey itself, commenting on the then recent international battle between Team Canada and the Soviet Union in the 1972 Summit Series, paying homage to a different sort of national hero, Guy Lafleur, and critiquing the hockey industry's commercialization and objectification of players as commodities rather than human beings.

We will also look briefly at a broader critique of elite sports' general role in society, which engages hockey in its allegorized depiction of the highly publicized contract disputes between Eric Lindros and the Nordiques after the 1991 NHL draft. Like the other texts of science fiction from Quebec (SFQ) discussed here, Guy Bouchard's "Au jeu" (1992) was published during yet another tense period in federal/provincial relations – namely, after the failure of the Meech Lake Accord in the summer of 1990. Finally, in a coda to the chapter, we will return to the work of François Barcelo, whose recent novel, *J'haïs le hockey* (*I Hate Hockey*; 2011), re-engages the sport and contemporary issues in the current "post-national" era. Although not an example of science fiction, this *roman noir* or thriller revisits the dark side of hockey seen in Barcelo's earlier novel, *Ville-Dieu*, and engages the recently publicized problem of coach sexual abuse of young players in the world of amateur hockey.

Science Fiction in Quebec (SFQ) and Nationalist Discourses

Like many professional sports, but perhaps more so than others, the world of hockey is laced with superstition.[9] In addition to the ritualistic repetition of game day activities, such as always donning equipment in the exact same order or tapping the goalie's mask a certain number of times before entering the arena, for the historic Canadiens, references to the "Fantômes du Forum" appear frequently in both fiction and non-fiction literature on the team.[10] The image of the "seventh man on the ice" – identified by the pop group Mes Aïeux (discussed in chapter 5) as the ghost of Howie Morenz, a supernatural power providing the great team with additional support – has intrigued commentators and fans alike. Elsewhere, I discuss at greater length Jean-Pierre April's (b. 1948) short story of the same title.[11] A pioneer critic and writer in Quebec's active science fiction milieu,[12] April appropriates the well-known trope of supernatural forces at work in the Forum and gives it a science-fictional spin. He attributes to a fan, the drunken Gaston Ratté – whose name refers to his status as both a loser (*raté*) and a rink rat (*rat d'aréna*) – the telekinetic ability to control action on the ice from the stands. April envisions the Canadiens of the future as composed entirely of Guy Lafleur clones who battle an opponent comprised of the "Robots Russes" on the night of the "dernier Samedi Soir de la Super Série du Siècle" (the last Saturday Night of the Super Series of the Century)[13] in a parodic re-enactment of the 1972 Summit Series, known in French as the *Série du siècle*. Invoking the Canadiens star's nickname, "le démon blond" (the blond demon), the author directly addresses the real-life superstar from the podium of his story:

> Guy Lafleur, tu étais la chaleur de notre hiver intérieur, c'était toi qui resserrais les liens invisibles de la collectivité, toi le rédempteur, mi-homme, mi-démon blond, portant le sens de notre combat national sur LA SCÈNE SPORTIVE.[14]
>
> Guy Lafleur, you were the warmth of our internal winter, you tightened the invisible ties that bind the collectivity, you, the redeemer, half-man, half-blond demon, carrying the significance of our national combat to the SPORTS STAGE.

April thus explicitly links the sports battle to the national battle for sovereignty, a notion we will develop further in this chapter. Just as in chapter 1 we saw the image of Maurice Richard used as that of a redemptive national hero battling for the rights of French Canadians, science fiction writers in Quebec take contemporary hockey heroes to extrapolate the hockey player of the future. While he is often portrayed as a hero, he may also appear as a victim of a dysfunctional social and economic system.

April later comments on his story in an essay titled "Sport-Fiction: le hockey et la science-fiction québécoise," in which he remarks on the somewhat unique conjunction of hockey and science fiction in Quebec in the period following the failure of the 1980 referendum. He notes that between 1981 and 1983 several authors developed this trope and that there are a number of similarities between their hockey SF texts.[15] April's observation that "le hockey et la science-fiction [est] une rencontre plutôt inusitée, qu'on ne voit guère qu'au Québec" (hockey and science fiction [are] a rather unusual pair, rarely seen except in Quebec) continues to hold true.[16] Confirming Michael Buma's assertion that "Canadian hockey novels [in English] are predominantly realist in mode," only a tiny sample of the vast body of English Canadian hockey fiction contains science-fictional or even fantastical elements.[17] In contrast, a good part of the relatively small amount of hockey-related fiction published in Quebec reveals ties to the science fiction and fantasy genres.[18]

As Renald Bérubé asserts in his analysis of April's story, Guy Lafleur's success in hockey offered Qubecers a compensatory fantasy, translated into the power to overcome an autonomy denied the province since the failure of the 1980 referendum.[19] The popular literary genres of science fiction and fantasy offer writers the power not only to logically extrapolate the hockey of the future, but also to explore contemporary fears and realize individual and collective fantasies of power. Furthermore, theorists of science fiction often point to the genre's critical function, asserting that it extrapolates current trends into the future, not only to spur the trajectory of progress but also and more often to send warning signs about the dangers of that trajectory. Narratives set in the future or on distant planets tell us much more, then, about human society here and now than about any actual future or interplanetary reality.

This is very clear in the final imagery of April's "Le Fantôme du Forum," when – evoking the Richard Riot of 1955, discussed in chapter 1 – a riot breaks out after officials suspend play towards the end of the match between the Guy Lafleur clones and the Robots Russes. Indeed, as Gaston Ratté's fantastical power surges out of control, the Forum actually implodes, an image April admits to having exploited as a means of expressing the failed hopes of the Québécois after the 1980 referendum:[20]

> *Avec l'effondrement du Forum, le cœur de la nation venait d'éclater, le tabernacle qui renfermait les liens essentiels de notre fusion. Et le bon peuple besogneux de la ruche québécoise tournait en rond comme s'il avait perdu sa reine. Les partisans restaient là, à contempler bêtement cette plaie rouge au sein du pays, ce trou temporel par où fuyait la vie et l'espoir. L'incertitude nationale se répandait et ne cesserait pas tant que les experts ne refermeraient la blessure en validant la victoire du Canadien.*[21]

> With the collapse of the Forum, the nation's heart had just exploded, the tabernacle that held the essential ties that bound us together. And the good people working in the hive of Quebec turned in circles as if they had lost their queen. The fans stayed in place, stupidly contemplating this red wound in the breast of the nation, this hole in time through which life and hope bled away. National uncertainty was spreading and would not stop until the experts had closed the wound by validating the Canadiens' victory.

April's fictional destruction of the Forum, a monument of sport architecture but also, as Robert Dennis argues, a true public forum for French Canadians on the way to becoming Québécois,[22] stands in metonymically for the whole of the nation, with the fans as its inhabitants.

As the fiction's narrative voice steps out of the diegetic future, returning directly to the present with these italicized exhortations, for which April even apologizes, labelling them as an "intrusion personnelle," the author expresses his own clearly pro-sovereignist opinions. Yet the fiction's imagery, which describes how Gaston Ratté's fantasy of power ultimately goes very wrong, reveals a more ambivalent attitude towards the fantasy of separation and its potential for destruction. At the same time, in its depiction of Ratté and the rioting masses,[23] "Le Fantôme du Forum" offers up a critical discourse about the "beer–hockey synergy" and the sports fan in general. The relationship between Montreal hockey and beer became transparent in 1996 with the move to a new arena, then named the Molson Centre, but it was present well before, and Jean Harvey and Alan Law outline the long-standing links between the Molson family, the Molson Corporation (now Molson Coors), and the Canadiens.[24] With the hyperbolic portrayal of the drunken fan in the buffoon Ratté, "cet alcoolique transfiguré" (this transfigured alcoholic),[25] April suggests the ridiculousness of fan identity; he also articulates how, by commercializing spectacle, the major leagues have corrupted the very notion of sports' transfigurative power. April satirizes the ultimate fan fantasy through Ratté's "téléclikétique" powers[26] (the man's pathetic status is indicated by his inability even to utter the correct term "telekinetic"), which ostensibly have been behind the Canadiens-of-the-future's success. By channelling the collective energy present in the arena – "il avait puisé directement à ce qui unissait la foule" (he pulled [energy] directly from that which united the crowd)[27] – Ratté immediately impacts the game with his thoughts and wishes.

April's critique offers a foretaste of later academic work like that of Richard Gruneau and David Whitson, who include in their analysis of hockey a significant discussion of fan identity. Remarking that "fandom also draws upon a sense of fantasy," citing in illustration the desire of all the boys of Ste–Justine, Quebec, to be transformed into Maurice Richard in Carrier's "The Hockey Sweater," Gruneau and Whitson express concern about the potential for big business to exploit this desire.[28] Fan identity seems even more problematic, in my view, when it begins to represent a substitute for a national identity – a possibility April suggests when he invokes the charged term of "la collectivité," but also evident in such expressions as "Nordiques Nation" and "Red Sox Nation." Boston's MLB franchise has successfully combined these notions for commercial gain through this concept, which draws on the reality of fan diaspora – there are Red Sox fans throughout the United States – even while building a false sense of a national community in order to sell licensed merchandise and tickets to a larger market than the team's home in New England. As April observes in "Sport-fiction," three of the post-referendum texts that unite hockey and science fiction depict just such a compensatory fantasy of the sports fan's power; along with his own tale of Gaston Ratté, he mentions François Barcelo's *Ville-Dieu* (1982) and Gilles Tremblay's *Les Nordiques sont disparus* (1983), to which we now turn.

Fantasies of Power and Realities of Powerlessness in François Barcelo's *Ville-Dieu* (1982)

Unlike April, François Barcelo (b. 1941) never significantly participated in Quebec's active science fiction milieu, but the genre's historians, among them Claude Janelle, Jean-Marc Gouanvic, and David Ketterer, quickly appropriated Barcelo's first novel, *Agénor, Agénor, Agénor et Agénor* (1981), for inclusion in the growing corpus of "SFQ,"[29] in part because its title character happens to be an extraterrestrial. The little green man, Agénor, finds himself stranded in a thinly veiled allegory of nineteenth-century Quebec, a land inhabited by the Vieux-Paysans (Old Peasants, a reference to French Canadians' agricultural heritage and nickname, *habitants*). Making the best of things, the alien finds love, and his offspring carry his name forward, allowing Barcelo to develop the allegory into the twentieth century. As Marie Vautier observes, his second novel, *La Tribu* (1981), invokes the techniques of magical realism in order "to destabilize the accepted workings of traditional myth" regarding Europeans' colonization of the New World, and of New France in particular.[30] Barcelo's third novel, *Ville-Dieu* (1982), part of the same cycle of postcolonial allegories of Quebec society, concerns us here because of its direct engagement with hockey.

Like science fiction, the term coined for the late-twentieth-century literary mode referred to as magical realism comprises an oxymoron, as Maggie Ann Bowers points out.[31] Following Vautier, I adopt this label as best reflecting the stylistic idiosyncracies of Barcelo's cycle of novels featuring the Vieux-Paysans as an allegory for Quebecers. Bowers identifies the mode's most striking characteristic as the "matter-of-fact, realist tone of its narrative when presenting magical happenings."[32] Perhaps better described as "speculative fiction" – the broader category often applied to Canadian SF as a whole[33] – apart from the device of the extraterrestrial Agénor, these novels bear only a distant relationship to science fiction per se. As we will see below, although the events they describe are not quite magical, they are nonetheless unrealistic, fantasy-like, albeit described with the matter-of-fact tone that is the hallmark of literary realism.

Ville-Dieu continues in the allegorical vein of its author's previous work, which in terms of its generic classification blurs the lines, borrowing from the magical realism of Gabriel García Marquez and the satirical *conte philosophique* of Voltaire. While its cover illustration – a photograph of the Montreal skyline at dawn viewed from the heights of Mont Royal – suggests realism, Barcelo playfully yet transparently transforms toponyms and nationalities to establish a certain critical distance. The novel's title, *Ville-Dieu* (God City), with Mont Dieu rising behind it, refers, of course, to Montreal, originally named Ville-Marie (after the mother of God, the Virgin Mary). The story takes place in the fictionalized province of *Hauturie*, itself contained by the nation of *Panurie*, which we might translate as "Highland" and "Panuria." The region of Hauturie, which stands in as an allegory of Quebec, combines the generic topographical suffix *–urie* (–uria), with a reference to the former labels of colonial-era British North America: Upper and Lower Canada (*Le Haut Canada* and *Le Bas Canada*). This reversal – recall that Lower Canada referred largely to present-day Quebec while Upper Canada referred to present-day Ontario – typifies Barcelo's fantasist style. With its Greek root *pan–* (all–), present in such contemporary terms as pan-Canadian and pan-African, *Panuria* represents, of course, the Canadian Confederation.

In addition to such language games, which distance the fictional world from the real, the novel's narrative structure and character development set *Ville-Dieu* apart from the standard realist or even science fiction novel. Its plot is episodic rather than linear, and its chapter titles refer to character names; most of the characters are ethnic Vieux-Paysans (literally, "Old Peasants") with stereotypically French Canadian monikers like Hervé Desbois, Irénée Dubreuil, Sylvane Laforest, and Archangèle Gélinas. These personages are involved in adventures of an exaggerated, sometimes picaresque and even magical/fantastic nature, as we will see in our discussion of the two hockey-related characters: Noël Lachard and Fernand Fournier.

Lachard, whose name is a bilingual pun on that of the English playwright, Noel Coward, is actually courageous, a hockey star playing for the Paysans de Ville-Dieu, an easily decoded reference to the Canadiens, nicknamed the Habs (short for *les habitants*) after the original peasant settlers of the Saint Lawrence Valley. In contrast, the novel's other hockey-related character represents a typical French Canadian loser; in his forties, unemployed and abandoned by his wife, Fernand Fournier spends most of his time in front of an "énorme appareil de télévision" (enormous TV set), watching sports, above all, hockey.[34] Barcelo expresses this character's nostalgia for bygone days, a lost childish innocence and purity found in both Franco- and Anglo-Canadian hockey discourse:[35] "il raffolait du hockey, sport qu'il avait pratiqué dans sa jeunesse, alors qu'on jouait encore sur des patinoires extérieures" (he was crazy about hockey, a sport he had played in his youth when it was still played on outdoor rinks).[36]

Like April's protagonist Gaston Ratté, Fournier possesses a quasi-mystical power: "chaque fois que Fernand Fournier s'éloignait de son téléviseur pour aller à la salle de bains, son équipe de hockey préférée marquait un but" (every time that Fernand Fournier left his television to go to the bathroom, his favourite hockey team scored a goal).[37] Of course, his team is the Paysans and Noël Lachard his favourite player, but he only slowly understands his gift. Barcelo characterizes Fournier as a certain type of self-destructive French Canadian underdog (much like many of the characters in the hockey film *Les Boys*, discussed in chapter 4). His position as one of the "déshérités" (disinherited) appears in his life trajectory as a downward spiral towards solitude, unemployment, and a meagre existence on welfare; it is also evident in the amount of time it takes him to realize the cause-and-effect nature of his "étrange pouvoir" (strange power).[38] Consistent with the novel's science-fictional aspects, Fernand eventually begins to record when goals are scored during each televised game and to experiment, deducing the rules governing his power. Through empirical observation, he finally "conclut que ce pouvoir n'était attaché qu'à son vieux téléviseur, qui servait sans doute de moyen de transmission pour sa volonté" (concluded that the power was attached to his old television, which no doubt served to transmit his will).[39]

Once he understands his gift, Fernand feels himself to be absolutely instrumental in the Paysans' success. He also plans to support the Panurian national team in hockey's first World Cup, which allows Barcelo to comment on the publicity leading up to the Summit Series of 1972 and on the outcomes of that series. The narrator informs the reader that the Panurian team's principal rival will be the "roussienne" (Roussian) and that what is at stake is proving that "le système sportif, économique et politique occidental était nettement supérieur au système oriental égalitaire" (the Western sports, economic, and political system was clearly superior to the egalitarian Eastern system).[40] Furthermore, the pretext of the international hockey rivalry offers Barcelo the occasion to comment on the specific political context for this post-referendum text.

The creation of a Panurian team allows the nation's two superstars, the Vieux-Paysan Noël Lachard and the "zanglophone" Bill Sulzky, to play together, uniting Hauturiens and "Zanglos"[41] in a single cause. But that team has not been assembled without controversy, and even the advertising between periods feeds into perceptions of inequality. For example, Fernand notices that a commercial message in which a Roussian player endorses the food products of a certain sponsor has been filmed only once, "pour le marché zanglais" (for the Zenglish market)[42] and then simply subtitled with an approximation of the original message. This failure to respect cultural difference and to accord the same importance to "tourtières et autres plats bien hauturois" (tourtières [traditional Quebec meat pies] and other really hauturian dishes) leaves him suddenly feeling "méprisé par ce commanditaire du tournoi" (contempt from the tournament sponsor).[43] In this way, Barcelo is targeting the commercialization of hockey, much like April does in "Fantome du Forum," a trend later decried by eminent hockey scholars like Bélanger, Gruneau and Whitson, and Harvey and Law;[44] furthermore, this sense of hurt leads to further political recriminations on Fernand's part. In his fit of pique, the fan recalls:

> Le peu de joueurs hauturois invités à se joindre à l'équipe panurienne. Les chandails exclusivement en zanglais portés lors du camp d'entraînement. Le refus des organisateurs du tournoi de laisser former une équipe purement hauturoise.[45]

> The low number of Hauturian players invited to join the Panurian team. The exclusively Zenglish jerseys worn during training camp. The tournament organizers' refusals to allow the formation of a solely Hauturian team.

Barcelo ridicules here some of the real controversy surrounding the composition of Team Canada for competitions like the Olympics and other international tournaments; in Quebec, such controversies focus on the number of French Canadian players on the roster.

Barcelo also comments directly on Fernand's political opinions, which provide him with an opportunity to directly address the 1980 referendum in his allegory, as well as deride his protagonist's weakness:

> Fernand Fournier n'était à vrai dire pas très politisé. Il avait voté « oui » au référendum demandant s'il fallait accorder plus d'autonomie politique à la Hauturie, mais n'avait pris cette décision que lorsqu'il avait été raisonnablement sûr que le « non » l'emporterait.[46]

> Fernand Fournier wasn't really very political. He had voted "yes" in the referendum asking if it was necessary to grant more political autonomy to Hauturia, but he hadn't made this decision until he was reasonably sure that the "no" would win.

Although he is not as apolitical as his namesake, Fern, in *Les Boys*, who does not vote at all and who is told that people like him are the reason why Quebec doesn't have its own country (see chapter 4), Fournier only dares to vote Yes because he thinks there is no chance the Yes side will win.

By rendering literal the superstition many fans hold that they can influence play on the field or on the ice by the way they wear their caps, Barcelo critiques fan culture in general. He then extends that critique by linking it to the national question, raising the point made by actual sports sociologists and critics that sports fandom has become an alternative form of "national" loyalty, even replacing the latter rather than serving as an occasion to strengthen it, as others suggest. While Barcelo's story is humorous in its exaggerations, the purpose of any satire is ultimately to criticize and condemn. Fournier's personal failings derail the reader's sympathy, thus forcing us to examine fandom critically as a pathetic substitute for playing the sport and even for responsible citizenship. The parallel developed between the couch-potato loser Fournier and the superstar Lachard reinforces the suggestion that the Québécois should go out and *do* hockey (or anything else, for that matter) rather than imitate this lamentable fan. At the same time, it paradoxically reveals how all Québécois have the opportunity to succeed, as Barcelo's narrator asserts:

> Curieusement, Fernand Fournier chômeur éternel se reconnaissait en Noël Lachard: tous deux étaient partis de rien et avaient fait montre de patience et de courage pour surmonter les obstacles. La seule différence entre Fernand Fournier et Noël Lachard, c'est que celui-ci avait réussi tandis que celui-là avait échoué.[47]

> Curiously, the eternally unemployed Fernand Fournier recognized himself in Noël Lachard: both had come from nothing and had shown patience and courage to overcome obstacles. The only difference between Fernand Fournier and Noël Lachard was that the latter had succeeded while the former had failed.

Indeed, Lachard lives the dream of becoming a professional hockey player. But the novel also reveals how quickly the bubble of that dream can burst: at the end of the match against Roussianie, Lachard collapses on the ice and knows instantly that "sa carrière était finie" (his career was over).[48]

Michael Robidoux, among others, has called the fantasy of making it as a professional hockey player in the NHL "the Great Canadian Dream."[49] In *Ville-Dieu*, Barcelo recounts both the dream and its nightmare with the story of Noël Lachard, invoking along the way, in a bizarre admixture of homage and parody, the tropes of the hockey biography genre. His tale opens on a Christmas Eve; the eldest of nine siblings, Noël – so named because he shares a birthday with Jesus Christ – is the last to open his gift, which is hidden well behind the tree. In this parodical image of a traditional pre–Quiet Revolution French Canadian family, Noël opens the box and finds inside it a pair of skates. The magic is so complete that not even his father's admission that "[y] a juste une chose [...]. Y sont tous les deux du pied gauche" (there's just one thing ... They are both for the left foot) can spoil the gift.[50]

Yet when Noël tries on the skates, his father also experiences pride, for his son resembles "[u]n vrai joueur de hockey" (a real hockey player).[51] His mother spoils the moment, correcting her husband's purportedly anglicized discourse, at the same time reflecting her own, colonized mentality through the petty correction:

> " – De gouret," corrigea Louisette Lachard qui n'aimait pas les mots zanglais et qui avait découvert ce mot dans les longues colonnes de la chronique "Ne dites pas ... Mais dites ... " qu'un brave prêtre plus porté sur la morale que sur la linguistique faisait paraître dans le *Journal des paysans*.[52]
>
> "Of *gouret*," corrected Louisette Lachard who did not like Zenglish words and who had discovered this word in the long columns of the feature "Don't say ... Say instead ..." that a courageous priest more expert in morality than in linguistics published in the *Paysans' Journal.*

Barcelo is referring here to the long battle waged in Quebec to maintain the purity of the French language, which is at risk of dissolving in a sea of English on the North American continent. Such efforts at times veer towards the ridiculous in the quest to avoid the anglicisms that distinguish Québécois French from that of Europe. The well-meaning priest-columnist uses the term *gouret,* which was current in the 1920s and 1930s but so defunct today as to be nearly impossible to trace.[53]

Barcelo thus sets the stage for the rise to fame of his protagonist through hard work and a large dose of innate talent. Although the elements are accelerated in order to reflect the fairy-tale nature of the brief chapter, the author draws on features of the real-life hockey biography in the fictional life of Noël Lachard.[54] The next morning he is up before dawn to begin his initiation into the world of ice hockey. First, he must improvise a stick and a puck from odds and ends found in his father's workshop: "Il alluma une bougie et parvint à se confectionner une crosse de hockey à partir de deux morceaux de bois retenus ensemble par deux boulons rouillés. Il trouva aussi un bout de gros tuyau qui ferait office de palet" (He lit a candle and managed to confect a hockey stick from two pieces of wood held together with two rusty bolts. He also found a piece of thick pipe that could serve as a puck).[55] With the continental terms "crosse" and "palet" rather than the current Quebec "bâton" and "rondelle," as well as simply "puck," Barcelo (like Louisette) parodies Quebec's rural past by resorting to antiquated terminology. Noël's initiation occurs not in a rink, but on a frozen lake whose magical quality is evident in Barcelo's description: "Une épaisse couche de nuages diffusait sur le lac une lueur blafarde" (A thick layer of clouds diffused a pale light over the lake).[56] This is the first time the sixteen-year-old has laced up a pair of skates, yet by noon he has mastered the basic skills, a passage that bears citing at length to reveal Barcelo's trademark humour:

> Il savait se tenir debout, sur place; il savait accélérer; puis continuer à peu près en ligne droite; il savait arrêter lentement (une fois sur deux sans tomber); il savait tourner à gauche mais non à droite (plusieurs années plus tard, un universitaire spécialiste du conditionnement physique remarquerait que Noël Lachard tournait 94 pour cent du temps du côté gauche et tournait mal du côté droit, sans se douter que cela venait de sa première paire de deux patins du pied gauche); et il était incapable de patiner de reculons, pour la simple raison qu'il ignorait que cela pouvait se faire.[57]

> He knew how to stand up in one spot; he could accelerate, then continue forward in a more or less straight line; he knew how to stop slowly (without falling every other time); he knew how to turn left, but not right (several years later, an academic specializing in physical conditioning would notice that Noël Lachard turned left 94 percent of the time and turned right with difficulty, without realizing that this was because of his first pair of two left-foot skates), and he was unable to skate backward for the simple reason that he did not know that this could be done.

When the others arrive on the ice to play, he joins them. Noël is such a prodigy that by the end of the day he is the third or fourth player chosen by the captains, and by the end of the following day he has become first pick.

Satire is never far away in Barcelo's discourse, yet he also traces an elegy to the pond hockey of bygone days, attributing to sport the magical power to invest its players with a sense of well-being:

> Pour la première fois de sa vie, il était heureux. Et il savait qu'il avait trouvé une forme de bonheur infiniment renouvelable. […]
>
> Il y a la passion du jeu – celle de marquer des buts, d'en empêcher, de déjouer l'adversaire, d'avoir un coup de chance ou d'en manquer soudainement, le plaisir de l'inattendu constamment renouvelé, comme si jamais deux jeux n'étaient pour être tout à fait semblables, quand bien même on jouerait jusqu'à la fin des temps.[58]

> For the first time in his life, he was happy. And he knew he had found a form of happiness that was infinitely renewable. […]
>
> There is the passion for the game – that of scoring goals, stopping them, of cheating the adversary, of getting a lucky shot or suddenly missing one,

> the pleasure of the unexpected constantly renewed, as if two games had never been completely similar, even if one played until the end of time.

Not only does Noël feel this magic, but it also brings him closer to his father – another cliché, however true, for both sons and daughters who speak about their coming to hockey.[59]

While clearly Noël has the raw talent to become a true star, the fairy tale accelerates his career. Having become the most admired player on the national team of the Continental Hockey League, the Paysans, within only a few years, the golden boy Lachard takes on the image of Guy Lafleur: "Sa tête aux cheveux blonds bouclés meublait les fantasmes de centaines de milliers de fillettes, de jeunes filles et même de femmes éminemment mariées" (His head with its curly blond hair filled the fantasies of hundreds of thousands of little girls, young women, and eminently married women).[60] Noël marries and has a son, a family whom he believes he loves, yet "il n'était pas heureux et il commençait à en prendre conscience. Pourtant, cette absence de bonheur le faisait jouer au hockey avec encore plus de rage, de courage et de détermination que jamais" (he wasn't happy and he had started to realize it. Still, this absence of happiness made him play hockey with even greater rage, courage, and determination than ever).[61] This parting image of the tormented star who sublimates his frustration on the ice concludes the first segment on Lachard in *Ville-Dieu*.

The chapter "Noël Lachard (II)" immediately follows the one devoted to "Fernand Fournier," and Barcelo picks up the hockey star's narrative precisely at the moment of his collapse at the end of the World Cup series against the Roussiens, the result of "une violente mise en échec" (a violent body-check)[62] that leaves him paralysed. In dark contrast to the earlier chapter, which describes his youth in rosy tones in spite of the hardships he faced, Barcelo makes here a pointed, incisive critique of how professional sports turn men into mere exploitable bodies, an argument made by Michael Robidoux, Jean-Marc Barreau, Varda Burstyn, and Brian Pronger, among many others.[63] Indeed, the chapter opens with a detailed description of Lachard's immobile, useless legs as he lies in a hospital bed. From the perspective of his doctor, we see

> de[s] jambes si musclées, nerveuses et puissantes. De belles mécaniques, faites pour marcher, courir, patiner, avec des muscles parfaitement développés, pour lever, tourner, allonger le pas. Et ces mécaniques étaient

> encore, cela se voyait, en parfait état de fonctionnement, sauf qu'elles n'avaient plus rien pour les commander, les faire agir, les contrôler.[64]

> such muscular, nervous and powerful legs. Beautiful mechanisms, made for walking, running, skating, with perfectly developed muscles, to raise, turn, lengthen the step. And you could see that these mechanisms were still in perfect running order, except that they no longer had anything to command them, make them act, control them.

Having learned the truth about his condition, Noël embarks on a series of ever more horrifying acts of self-mutilation, enabled by the gullible medical staff and family members who surround him.

Noël's gradual self-deconstruction begins with the simple request that he be allowed to shave himself; when the nurse returns, she is shocked to see that, Samson-like, he has removed the symbol of his power and shaved his entire head, including his eyebrows.[65] The next day, he asks for scissors to trim his nails and instead cuts off his eyelashes, explaining that they are good for nothing either. When the star returns home, Barcelo depicts – in a scene of astonishing horror – the still young but now physically disabled Lachard sawing off his own legs. Back in the hospital, when a psychiatrist attempts to understand this desperate act, Noël explains with compelling (yet obviously absurd) logic that his legs were heavy and useless and prevented him from moving around his apartment. This rationale temporarily convinces the doctors that he is not insane, allowing him to accomplish another act that is much more difficult to accept: he swipes a nurse's scissors and cuts off his penis. He follows this by performing an appendectomy on himself, again with the pretext that the organ, like his legs and penis (since no woman would ostensibly desire him in this state) "ne servait à rien" (were good for nothing).[66] Finally, in a masterful technique of "show, don't tell" – the narrator never explains the inner workings of his mental state – Noël puts a final end to his unacknowledged internal suffering by throwing himself down a garbage chute. Again in Barcelo's understated, darkly humorous manner, the chapter concludes with Noël's death among the garbage: "Il vécut encore deux jours et deux nuits dans une odeur de putréfaction telle qu'elle finit par lui briser le sens olfactif et qu'il ne sentit plus rien. Et il regretta, avant de mourir, de ne pas pouvoir se couper le nez devenu inutile" (He lived for two more days and nights in an odor of putrefaction so horrible that it ended by destroying his olfactory sense and he could smell no more.

And he regretted, before dying, not being able to cut of his nose which was now useless).[67] So, what does this dark parable tell us about the meaning of hockey in Quebec?

Both the scholarly literature on the professional athlete, for example, Michael Robidoux's *Men At Play* (2001), and hockey fiction, such as Bill Gaston's *The Good Body* (2000),[68] address the problem of the objectification of the male body. As a professional hockey player, Noël has become nothing more than a body, objectified by women for his physical beauty and objectified by men for his physical prowess. When he is injured and can no longer walk, can no longer exercise his profession, Lachard perceives himself as useless, hence his fixation on removing his unused body parts and eventually his suicide. The parable appears so dark and grim because Noël has no other resources than his body, unlike, for example, Bill Gaston's hero Bobby Bonaduce, who turns to the world of the mind and to rebuilding the broken relationships in his life when he learns that he has multiple sclerosis and will eventually reach a state even more debilitating than that faced by Lachard. The latter's gradual removal of body parts deemed useless, and the doctor's description of Lachard's body as a machine at the beginning of the chapter, together point to the systemic objectification and commodification of the male body in professional hockey as critiqued by Robidoux in his ethnography of a team in the American Hockey League (AHL), an NHL farm league.

Lachard's self-disfigurement functions as a literal deconstruction of what Robidoux describes as the "ideological representations of the body that romanticize, glamourize, and mythologize it from a Canadian hockey perspective."[69] Having removed all of the glamour surrounding his protagonist's body, Barcelo allows the injured player the ultimate act of defiance towards a system that forces young men to accept a Foucauldian "shaping and moulding" of their bodies, "which either intentionally or not, satisfy a *use* for the industry that employs [them]."[70] As Lachard so painfully learns, athletes subject

> themselves to disciplines of excellence, and are subsequently celebrated within this framework. In fact, these male figures are often turned into heroes and placed upon pedestals for everyone to see.
>
> But quite clearly, this heroic status is a delusion; outside the athletic framework its validity is undermined. [...] In the case of professional hockey, it is apparent that the heroic values placed upon players are largely superficial, and that the hockey player's ability to physically dominate an

> opponent has little currency outside the sporting arena. In fact, it is the hockey player's dependence on his body that denies him access to the very system of power that dictates his professional career.[71]

Long before Robidoux's intellectualized interpretation of professional hockey as an industry that consumes male bodies, then, Barcelo's novel essentially staged that critique, drawing upon the resources of a hybrid literary form of magical realism tinged with science fiction to do so. Furthermore, while Franco-Quebecers do wax poetic about their national game, like their anglophone counterparts, they also cast a critical eye, recognizing the flaws in the sport as an institution.

Disappearance as Metaphor for Cultural Extinction: Gilles Tremblay's *Les Nordiques sont disparus* (1983)[72]

A public official who worked for the federal government in its Quebec City offices, science fiction and Nordiques fan, Gilles Tremblay (1933–2011) contributed a fascinating but relatively obscure work to the body of hockey-themed SFQ.[73] His only published novel, *Les Nordiques sont disparus*, shares with Barcelo's *Ville-Dieu* and April's "Le Fantôme du Forum" what the latter calls "le fantasme du gérant d'estrades" (fantasy of the bleacher seat manager).[74] Whereas April and Barcelo allow their loser protagonists to realize such fantasies, Tremblay's villains wield their power for the forces of destruction. In its negative fantasy, his novel imagines the disappearance of the Québécois people as personified by their two hockey teams, the Nordiques and the Canadiens, along with their fans, all of whom vanish during a manifestation of power by the Solitonians, a group of mutant humans with telekinetic abilities. The traumatizing aspect of Tremblay's science fiction appears even more clearly once we grasp its premonitory aspects: the only Québécois franchise in the World Hockey Association until its absorption into the NHL in 1979, the Nordiques *have* disappeared. Sold in 1995, the team exists today only in the memories of its fans, having become the Colorado Avalanche. This move deprived Quebec City of a home team; according to statistical research conducted by former NHLer Bob Sirois, it also deprived francophone players of an important career outlet in the big league.[75] Yet those same fans can still hope: apparently concrete plans for a new Nordiques team were announced in February 2012, hopes fuelled by the Jets' 2011 return to Winnipeg.[76]

In Tremblay's novel, a hostile force erases in an instant, from the face of the planet, Quebec's (then) two NHL franchises, excellent symbols for the nation. At first glance we can read this work of science fiction as a simple allegorical expression of a nationalist discourse, one that has long reiterated the need for French Canadians to resist the threat of assimilation and the extinction of the French language and culture in North America. This concern is traceable back to the earliest days of the post-Conquest era, when those fears were exacerbated by Lord Durham's oft-cited *Report on the Affairs of British North America* (1839), which explicitly recommended to the Crown a policy of assimilation for a people he judged to have no history or culture.[77] This menace figured in the arguments of conservative nationalist clerics and historians throughout the nineteenth century and into the early twentieth in the work of Lionel Groulx. It also arose in the discourse of René Lévesque and the Parti Québécois as a compelling reason for holding the 1980 referendum on sovereignty-association.[78] As with many popular texts from Quebec, however, on deeper analysis Tremblay's novel expresses a certain ambivalence towards the national question – it is not simply a separatist *roman-à-thèse*. We might just as easily interpret the novel as a statement of federalist solidarity if we read Paul Jacques and his henchmen as representing sovereignists who menace the integrity of the Canadian nation by excising the Colisée, a figure for the province of Quebec. This analysis appears all the more compelling because the novel depicts the arena holding both the Nordiques, traditionally seen as more sovereignist, and their co-citizens yet rivals, the Canadiens, perceived as more federalist, and thus as representing a more complete microcosm of the divided nation.[79] Yet on further consideration, that assessment too appears overly simplistic, since the author envisions a "corrected" future in which Quebec, having negotiated independence in 1996, has been a republic for several centuries by the novel's main chronotope of 2586.[80]

Although *Les Nordiques sont disparus* does not, then, propose a clear national allegory, either sovereignist or federalist, it certainly expresses contemporary Quebec's preoccupation with history. In a province whose motto is *Je me souviens* (I remember), history has played a central role in the evolution of French Canadian into Québécois culture, and an entire body of intellectual discourse surrounds its role in the construction of such a national identity.[81] That discourse consistently differentiates between *history* and *History*, with the latter referring simultaneously to history as concept and to the established, institutionalized discourse on the province's history. Science-fictional works engaged with history often reproduce this distinction,[82] as does Tremblay's novel. The science fiction subgenre of alternate history has proved especially popular in Quebec because of its ability to explore tensions between different visions of history itself and to problematize the notion that a single definitive History exists by positing an infinite array of possible interpretations and even factual outcomes for the past, present, and future.[83]

This tension plays out via Tremblay's exploitation of the science-fictional theme of time travel being used to change history, to thwart some fateful event and thereby save humanity – or in this case, the city of Quebec and its francophone citizens. While it includes an analeptic sequence set in the 1960s, during which the Solitonians' founder Paul Jacques discovers his psychic powers, as well as chapters set in the 1990s, during which a team of commandos from the future works to save the Colisée, the novel is set mainly in the twenty-sixth century. The scientific researchers investigating the historic disappearance of the Colisée in 1993 underscore the eventual significance of the work they have undertaken, and so do Paul Jacques's team of terrorists. The former assert that "l'Histoire rendra un jour hommage à notre honnêteté" (one day History will honour our honesty).[84] Similarly, the Solitonians, who have uncovered the existence of the secret mission to thwart their rise to supremacy, assert the need to "empêcher les membres du commando de s'interposer dans le cours normal de l'Histoire" (prevent members of the commando team from interfering with the normal course of History).[85] According to them, "le 15 mars avait été l'occasion d'un grand événement dans l'histoire de l'humanité et cet événement ne devait faire l'objet d'aucune modification importante" (15 March had been a great event in the history of humanity and it must not become the object of any significant modification).[86] The twenty-sixth-century team that perfects the technology of time travel precisely in order to prevent the disappearance of the Colisée and its tenants employs a discourse that resembles the one resorted to in the campaigns for sovereignty in 1980 and 1995: "ils écriraient bientôt une grande page de l'Histoire [...] ils participaient à la confection d'une NOUVELLE HISTOIRE" (they would soon write a great page in History ... they were participating in the creation of a NEW HISTORY).[87]

Any alternate history or time travel narrative enacts a *mise en abyme* of the problem of history and the human capacity to affect or change it. Tremblay's polyvalent novel, which may be read as supporting either/neither sovereignty or federalism, expresses a generalized anxiety about the contemporary national situation, a situation that was not clear-cut at the time. Only a few years earlier, with the 1980 referendum, federalists had experienced a close call: the distinct possibility that Quebec would negotiate secession from Confederation. The novel's conclusion further clouds any clear reading of *Les Nordiques sont disparus* as a political allegory in that the author leads us to understand that the time travellers' expedition, known as Mission Québec, succeeded, but precisely because it did, the disappearance itself has become a non-event. Since the Solitonians failed to manifest their telekinetic powers by making the Colisée disappear, they were unable to organize and eventually threaten the entire continent – a threat that would have motivated the United States, Canada, and Mexico to form such a close alliance against a common enemy that, as in the novel's original timeline, they united to become a single nation. Rather, the course of history followed another trajectory: "les États-Unis sont maintenant disparus au profit de quatre pays distincts, le Québec constitue une vieille République, le Canada continue sans les Maritimes, et ainsi de suite" (the United States have now disappeared, to the benefit of four distinct countries, Quebec constitutes an old Republic, Canada carries on without the Maritimes, and so on).[88] In a bizarre twist that is possible only in the convoluted subgenres of time travel and alternate history, the erasure of two disasters with horrific impact on the province allows the author to envision the disappearance of the United States coupled with the creation of a sovereign Quebec.

In his fantasy, as the threat to the Colisée unites *all* Quebecers in their concern for the safety of the fans and players of *both* the Nordiques and the Canadiens, Tremblay erases yet another historic rivalry besides the one between anglophones and francophones in Canada: *La Grande Rivalité Canadiens-Nordiques*, as journalist Jean-François Chabot describes it in his book of that title.[89] Because of the Montreal Canadiens' large anglophone following and the metropole's greater ethnic diversity, the provincial capital often claims to be *more* Québécois and, by extension, more nationalist. The Nordiques signified their *québécitude* (Quebecness) with team colours invoking the vivid blue-and-white, along with the fleur-de-lys, of the provincial flag. Tremblay plays on this rivalry in the reproduced media banter leading up to the fatal game, having characters compare the fictional Nordiques-versus-Canadians match-up to the Battle of the Plains of Abraham,[90] Montcalm's historic loss of Quebec City to Wolfe in 1759, a battle identified as the death blow to the French presence in Canada. Later, on a radio call-in show, "un farouche partisan des Nordiques était presque en train d'accuser les partisans des Canadiens d'être les responsables de cette histoire saugrenue" (a fierce supporter of the Nordiques was almost accusing the Canadiens' fans of being responsible for this unbelievable story).[91] Here the ludic aspects of science fiction appear as Tremblay plays out elements of the "real" rivalry constructed by media and fans alike.

In addition to the rivalry, Tremblay – who obtained the permission of Marcel Aubut and the Nordiques organization to use the franchise's name in his novel's title[92] – references contemporary issues in hockey. Notably, he has the capital's fictional mayor, Eugène Paré, discuss the need for a new arena to replace the Colisée with Vincent Phaneuf, the fictional president of the Nordiques. While in the real Quebec, the Colisée had been renovated in 1979–81, Aubut consistently pushed for a new arena, for which he, of course, sought heavy subsidies from the city and the province.[93] Normand Bourgeois documents the press debate of 1989 and 1990, a debate that elements of *Les Nordiques sont disparus* appear, eerily, to prefigure. Bourgeois cites contemporary newspaper accounts of how Aubut essentially threatened – but also in a sense predicted – the disappearance of the Nordiques if a new arena was not built by 1993.[94] Fan attendance was apparently not a problem[95] – the issue, rather, was the need for more seats to boost revenue. Nonetheless, the image of the empty Colisée painted by Tremblay's fictional journalists – who arrive prepared to cover a hockey game and instead cover an uncanny phenomenon – may uncomfortably invoke images that are all too real to small market hockey teams and those in the American South: "Le Colisée est désert. Il ne semble y avoir personne ici. Pas âme qui vive. Personne!!" (The Coliseum is deserted. There appears to be no one here. Not a living soul. Nobody!!).[96] In the novel, the story takes on a life of its own, referred to as "L'affaire du Colisée" as well as "l'énigme du Colisée."[97] While the actual disappearance of more than 10,000 people would certainly be a real tragedy of epic proportions, the hyperbolic discourse of the journalists in Tremblay's novel rings with a certain level of perhaps unintended parody. Later we will discuss the tempest in a teacup caused by what would be called the "Affaire Lindros," reflective of a pattern of hyperbole in the Quebec press's coverage of hockey news; but the hysterical terms in which Tremblay describes the reaction to the mysterious disappearance of the entire human contents of the Colisée bring us back to the notion of the failure of the 1980 referendum, which is often depicted as a collective trauma. There are also aspects of the narrative that recall yet another provincial trauma, one buried a bit more deeply: the 1970 October Crisis, during which nationalist terrorists from the Front de Libération du Québec (FLQ) kidnapped British diplomat James Cross and provincial minister Pierre Laporte, eventually murdering the latter.[98]

Three days after the Nordiques and their fans have vanished, the fictional government has yet to explain to the public what happened; the provincial premier, Henri Lacombe, concerned about the upcoming elections, has holed up in a bunker in the Laurentides with his chief advisers. This scenario eerily recalls the fact that Robert Bourassa was similarly absent at the beginning of the October Crisis and that critics accused him of vacillating and possibly worsening the situation through his inaction.[99] The novel's omniscient narrator describes the public reaction to the arena's disappearance: "Le plus outrageant dans toute cette calamité qui frappait le Québec, c'était peut-être le fait que la population dans son ensemble et les médias exigeaient à toutes fins utiles du gouvernement qu'il élucidait lui-même ce mystère" (The most outrageous aspect of this calamity that had struck Quebec was perhaps the fact that the entire population and the media insisted that the government clear up this mystery itself).[100] In the face of public terror, Lacombe's cabinet head, Gilles Beausoleil, recommends not revealing the truth, but rather coming up with a plausible story to reassure the public, and, above all, "écarter toute hypothèse à l'effet que les événements du Colisée auraient pu être le fait des terroristes" (to dismiss any hypothesis to the effect that the events of the Coliseum were linked to terrorism).[101] His twenty-sixth century counterparts refer to their own "crise solitonienne" (Solitonian Crisis),[102] borrowing a label that directly references the October Crisis.

Les Nordiques sont disparus, then, expresses anxiety about a province under seige because of a terrorist threat and then offers a fantasy of empowerment via the science-fictional device of time travel to repair the damage done. By preventing the original terrorist attack on the Colisée, the aptly named expedition from the future, Mission Québec, modifies the "natural" course of History and thereby creates conditions that allow for the peaceful establishment of an independent Republic of Quebec. The ludic aspects of the local hockey rivalry between the Nordiques and the Canadiens, themselves representative of the province's internal debate between sovereignty and federalism, allow Tremblay to express such anxieties safely and provide the magic for partisans to achieve their collective dream of sovereignty. At the same time, the science-fictional discourse allows both author and readers to distance themselves from the reality of such debates, displacing them onto allegorical representations (the two hockey teams) and into a distant future (the twenty-sixth century) and parallel universe (the alternate twentieth century in which North America is all one nation). Furthermore, because of the external threat posed by the Solitonians, internal divisions between sovereignists and federalists within Quebec can be allegorically removed as they unite against the common enemy.

Hockeyeur as Worker/Robot: Denis Côté's *Shooting for the Stars* (1983) and Its Sequels (1989–90)

A similar fantasy of empowerment, in which a hockey hero becomes not just a national hero, but that of an entire oppressed underclass, appears in Denis Côté's (b. 1954) prize-winning young adult novel *Hockeyeurs cybernétiques* (1983; trans. *Shooting for the Stars*, 1990).[103] Marrying the conventions of SF with the structure of classic sport fiction, its initial chapter introduces the main character(s)/hero-player and outlines the athletic challenge that drives the narrative forward. In this case, a spoiled eighteen-year-old hockey star, Michel Lenoir, will lead an all-star team of human players against a new professional threat, a team of robots. The second chapter, "Training Camp," introduces the rest of the team and its coach, presenting the individual and collective challenges the group will face; as in many hockey films, turning a group of selfish, spoiled stars into a team is the central challenge faced by the coach.[104] This chapter also includes the obligatory outing to a bar for the team's social bonding.[105] The three central chapters each describe one of the games in the human/robot series, and the final chapter offers a conclusion that reveals the hero's growth and maturity. As a work of SF, Côté's novel departs, however, from some of the conventions of the sports narrative.

One of the basic definitions of science fiction outlined in the genre's early days by Hugo Gernsback, often called its founder, is that it combines a fictional narrative with "scientific fact and prophetic vision."[106] Later critics refined this notion, referring to the "plausible extrapolation" of current technology into the future.[107] Côté's title clearly signals both of this book's genres; *Hockeyeurs cybernétiques* – literally, "the cybernetic hockey players" – extrapolates the technological development of humanoid robots and their potential use in sport as spectacle. Jane Brierley's English translation, *Shooting for the Stars*, with its wordplay on "shooting" as both a sports term and a synonym for "targeting" or even "rocketing," also signals the hybrid nature of the novel, but it misdirects the reader towards a completely different SF trope, that of space travel (of which there is absolutely none here).[108] Côté's novel does not portray human travel to another world; rather, set in 2010, it depicts a dystopian near future for our own.

Hockeyeurs cybernétiques and its sequels couple the central science-fictional trope of the robot with the developmental and didactic aims of sports and young adult literatures; furthermore, its extrapolation of contemporary social and political trends into the future constructs a significant critique of labour practices in professional sports. As Côté develops the narrative of the hero's increased political consciousness and personal growth across the Bildungsroman structure of the series, this development occurs in the context of a collective society. The hero Michel Lenoir's growing awareness of inequity and injustice in the world around him allows for the elaboration of an ethical discourse relating to the treatment and behaviour not only of the hockey player as worker, but of all workers. In its depiction of Lenoir's exploitation, as in Barcelo's depiction of Lachard, Côté's critique of hockey as business prefigures a detailed analysis of the hockey player as worker later found in sociologist Michael Robidoux's *Men at Play*.

Elsewhere, I have discussed in detail Côté's future extrapolation of current trends in hockey and of social problems in *Shooting for the Stars* and its untranslated French-language sequels,[109] so I will simply summarize that discussion here. The author's projections about hockey's development in years to come involve technological advances that purportedly heighten the spectacle of play and reduce human error in its arbitration. They also include increased levels of fan violence in a dystopian future, in which so little offers the public escape from its daily misery that sport has come to mean almost everything to the disenfranchised masses. Côté rightly predicts the development of pay-per-view televised sports, but he mis-extrapolates the composition of actual arena attendees; only the impoverished masses risk attending the bread-and-circus sport spectacles of the future.

In terms of player status and attitudes, Côté's vision sometimes appears more accurate, and I will develop the novel's projections for the future of hockey as a profession in more detail here. His hero Lenoir represents a stereotypically selfish, privileged elite player. Injured, and thus only a spectator at the final game of the regular season, which opens the novel, he "wasn't exactly sorry that a superficial injury had kept him off the ice today. He didn't really care whether or not he missed the last game of the season."[110] Above all, since Côté wishes to cast a critical gaze upon the contemporary world of professional hockey, he extrapolates the working conditions of his players to the extreme:

> Unlike hockey moguls in the old twentieth-century system, David Swindler not only employed Michel and his teammates, he owned them.
>
> His relationship with Michel, among others, had no real equivalent in the previous century, except perhaps the last vestiges of slavery.[111]

Extrapolating attitudes from the 1980s union-busting era of free trade (discussed in more detail in chapter 3), Côté's vision of players being literally owned, purchased from their parents at the tender age of seven, completely erases the reality that the Players' Association has protected player interests to the point that the critical discourse today targets their excessive salaries, with the costs passed on to the fans rather than being deducted from owner profits. The commercialization of the sport has become so extreme that one of Côté's players is nicknamed "Trademark," signalling his exploitation of the endorsement system,[112] a phenomenon Benoît Melançon sees as already occurring with Maurice Richard in the 1950s and 1960s.[113] Through its extrapolation of the literal reification of hockey players in the form of the title objects, robotic hockey players, proposing that machines *can* play hockey,[114] the novel suggests the inverse proposition that hockey players *are* machines. That the players of the future are illiterate further dehumanizes them.[115]

After its description as the "plausible extrapolation of future trends," the second most common remark made about science fiction calls attention to its criticism of the present state of affairs.[116] SF is a discourse for social critique; as such, it is related to satire. In the central philosophical proposition of his novel, Côté successfully weds the two genres: its SF aspect explores the problem of what it means to be human through the supposedly contrasting device of the robot, while the sports literature aspect explores what characteristics elevate sport above a mere mindless pastime. These two problems are inextricably linked as owner David Swindler explains to Lenoir the difference between his human team and the robots:

> The major difference is that the machines can't make any so-called mental errors.
>
> Their performance is fool-proof, since they've been programmed with an infinite number of game plans. The other side of the coin is that they have no imagination, no instinct. That's the angle we have to exploit to win.[117]

What at first appears to be a weakness, our fallibility, is precisely what makes us human; even the most dilettante viewer of television SF will recognize this argument from *Star Trek* episodes.

For the threat to humanity to be real, the robots must *look* convincingly human, yet have identifying characteristics that set them apart. These aspects of the SF robot narrative are described as the human players watch the robots practice:

> In motion the robots looked like anything but machines. Everything seemed alive. They skated with a swift harmony, showing no trace of stiffness as they passed the puck and scored goals.
>
> What made them different was their lack of emotion. They were completely wooden-faced, displaying no feelings whatever – no sign of nervousness, no arms thrown triumphantly in the air after a goal, no friendly pat on the back of a teammate. When they returned to the bench they became statues, looking as though they'd been switched off or had died. There they stayed until the coach gave them the sign.
>
> The robots may have been inert in repose, but they never made a mistake in action – no missed shots, no bad passes, no offsides. They seemed perfect, like parts of a single, flawless organism.[118]

Of course, as it was with Team Canada when they watched the Soviets in 1972, this is the wake-up call the players need: "For the first time they realised they couldn't take anything for granted in their battle against the machines."[119] Furthermore, the notion of fair play inherent in Western sports requires that the match-up be at least somewhat equal. If the possibility of winning is too heavily weighted in favour of one side or the other, then the contest is of no interest to players *or* spectators. For this reason, T.I.L.T., the corporation responsible for the robots' design, claims to have programmed the robots to specifications for muscle strength, flexibility, speed, and so on, that precisely mimic those of human athletes. During the first game, however, the speed of the puck amazes the human players, who accuse the company of having "built the robots stronger than the Crusaders, although that's not what they told us!"[120]

Ostensibly, the robots are also incapable of one of hockey's most controversial, yet for many fans most exciting, aspects: bodychecking. For the humans-versus-robots series:

> Game rules remained the same as usual except for roughing.
>
> Body checking was out, since a robot might inflict a fatal injury or a man might conceivably break up a robot.

> In fact, all aggressive action would be subject to severe penalties.
>
> Brawling was out, obviously, although in theory such a thing was unthinkable, since a robot wasn't supposed to feel anger or frustration.[121]

However, as the human team leads in the final, third game that will decide a series tied after two, a robot does precisely what they are forbidden to do and violently checks a player, resulting in the game being suspended after just two periods, with the Valiant Crusaders leading thanks to Lenoir's brilliant comeback. When this occurs, Lenoir wonders:

> *How could that robot bump into Zedenik if he wasn't programmed to do it? Is this a breach of the rules, or are these creatures so highly developed that they can go beyond their programming? No, that's crazy; I'm letting the shock cloud my mind.*[122]

However, in its revelation that Swindler, who besides being the human team's owner and a heavy investor in the robot hockey team, is himself a cyborg, the novel's conclusion seems to be asserting that the robotic hockey players can indeed go beyond their programming. This calls into question the status and definitions of humanity and "artificial" intelligence.

Similarly, April invokes the figure of the hockey player as machine in "Le Fantôme du Forum," if we recall that the Guy Lafleur clones play the Robot Russes. The clones themselves reflect Robidoux's concern that the hockey system creates a homogenized identity. Obviously, team jerseys inject uniformity – the word "uniform" says it all. Others have pointed to the removal of identity via the use of numbers – let us recall that long ago, players' names did not appear on jerseys.[123] But Robidoux argues that the system itself creates a homogenized identity, "one informed by a physically dominant, white, heterosexual male model that has been validated through annual rituals and everyday behaviour. [...] The effect is a homogenized workforce achieved at the expense of the individual."[124]

The fictional text vividly illustrates Robidoux's notion that management views professional hockey players as mere instruments to their own goal of profit, like the machines that Côté allows to take the ice. As Lenoir wanders uncontested into the opponents' locker room, the narrator contrasts this image with what the scene should look like:

> The special post-game atmosphere, the jumble of exhausted players, their bodies streaming with sweat, their faces jubilant or downcast, depending on whether they'd won or lost. There was nothing like this here.[125]

Instead, Lenoir witnesses the sterile, inhuman scene of technicians at work:

> A technician was wiping a head before putting it into the bottom of a case along with a dozen others.
>
> The robots were no longer imitations of men, but amputated synthetic legs and arms, open thoraxes and abdomens with electronic guts spilling over the tables. It's incredible – they take them apart after the game![126]

An uncannily similar scene appears in a section of Robidoux's study titled "Producing 'Hockey Bodies,'" in which the sociologist describes an actual treatment session on a "player's leg – commonly referred to as a 'wheel' – [which] was being repaired through a series of manipulations: massage, stretching, and what appeared to be some form of electronic stimuli."[127] The damaged leg being "repaired" like a "wheel" reminds us of nothing so much as the robotic hockey players in Côté's *Hockeyeurs cybernétiques*. The genre of science fiction has allowed the author to literalize a critique that is perceived perhaps only at an intuitive level, but that the intellectual discourse can identify and discuss with the tools of observation, theory, and analysis.

While Côté's exploration of the limits and nature of humanity transcends the merely local, national allegory found in the other SFQ texts examined here, he cannot fail to address the specificity of his hero's identity – that is, Lenoir's francophone moniker and his physical resemblance to the province's biggest star of the day, Guy Lafleur. Like his nickname-sake, *le démon blond*, "Lenoir's hair was extraordinarily blond, almost white – a curious twist of fate for someone whose name meant 'black' in his mother tongue."[128] The same image recalls a central icon of the radical franco-nationalist discourse of FLQ member Pierre Vallières, *White Niggers of America* (1969). Following the Marxist discourse of decolonization found in Frantz Fanon's *The Wretched of the Earth* (1961) and *Black Skin, White Masks* (1952), Vallières drew upon the reality that working-class French Canadians were at times referred to as *nègres blancs* (white niggers) and upon a partly real and partly exaggerated parallel between the economically oppressed French Canadian majority in Quebec and the Jim Crow conditions of African Americans in the Southern United States.[129] With his onomastic markers blending the opposites, white and black (Whitey/Lenoir), this *nègre blanc* is literally a slave in the sense that his team's proprietor bought him from his parents at age seven in order to turn him into a sports star. Clearly, the power of science fiction lies in its ability to literalize the metaphors around which social tensions arise, so that in Côté's extrapolation into the future of past and current trends in professional sports, players appear as literal slaves.

Indeed, Lenoir complains about news reports on his poor performance after games one and two of the series: "*They analyse me as though I were an object. But I'm a human being! I'm not strong and invincible the way they want me to be.*"[130] Swindler tries to convince Lenoir of his lack of agency and his reification: "Without my protection you're nothing, do you hear? Not a star, not a hockey player, not even a man. An insect – that's what you are! A tiny insect at the mercy of every predator."[131] In the end, though, he stands up for himself as a free, mature individual and as a worker capable of making his own decisions, and reasserts his French origins by rejecting the childish, anglophone nicknames with which Swindler addresses him:

> "To begin with [...] my name is not Whitey [...]. My name is Michel Lenoir, do hear? Michel Lenoir!" [...]
>
> "All you care about is my performance on the ice. I'm just a toy you dangle in front of the public. A jumping-jack, a mere tool of your covert empire!" [...]
>
> "I belong to nobody. From now on I'm a free man!"[132]

The highly critical attitude towards professional hockey evidenced in the first novel of the series offers little of the elevating discourse about sport often encountered in the hockey novel. It ends, after all, not with a victory for the team, but with the hero redeeming himself and, paradoxically, demonstrating his maturity by abandoning his team to join a movement for social and political reform. This conclusion, which implies that real meaning is found in these spheres of activity rather than in the artificially constructed, ludic world of sport, clearly contravenes the conventions of sports literature. Readers must wait for such an attitude to appear in the novel's untranslated sequels, *L'Idole des Inactifs* (1989), *La Révolte des Inactifs* (1990), and *Le Retour des Inactifs* (1990).

In these books, which I discuss at greater length elsewhere,[133] Lenoir leads the people's revolt against the oppressive social conditions outlined in *Shooting for the Stars*. Because of his refusal to submit to the tyranny of his employer at the first novel's conclusion, he has been forced to live underground among the large population of the unemployed, referred to as Inactives. By the end of the series, having used hockey as a tool of liberation and freed it from the clutches of his evil capitalist boss, and having thereby restored some purity to the game, Lenoir has begun teaching hockey to young people. By the end of the series, Côté has redeemed the sport by reinstating the alternative hockey myth: the purity of pond hockey and its ability to empower young people by offering them role models. At Lenoir's hockey clinic, we hear a young girl player crying out in excitement, "Je suis Michel Lenoir!" (I am Michel Lenoir!).[134] In this way, Côté reinstates the sense of physical and mental well-being attributed to amateur sports. In Guy Bouchard's contribution to the intersection of hockey and SF in Quebec, two pioneering leaders take the values expressed by Côté as the foundation for an entirely new, revolutionary society.

Professional Sport as Dystopia: Guy Bouchard's "Au jeu" (1992)

Hockeyeurs cybernétiques appeared during the immediate post-referendum era, but its English translation and sequels were published nearly a decade later. Guy Bouchard's (b. 1942) story "Au jeu" appeared at the same time, in the aftermath of yet another crisis for Quebec sovereignists, this one over the patriation of the Canadian Constitution. Partly in response to the 1980 referendum, Prime Minister Pierre Elliott Trudeau renewed his efforts to patriate Canada's Constitution from Great Britain; he succeeded in doing so in 1982 with the Patriation Act, which was approved by Queen Elizabeth II on 17 April 1982. Quebec was the only province that failed to ratify the act (and it still has not), insisting on greater recognition of and protection for its distinct francophone society. In 1987, Trudeau's successor, Brian Mulroney, seeking to bring Quebec into the federal fold, began negotiations with the ten provinces at Meech Lake, Quebec, with the goal of amending the constitution to recognize Quebec as a "distinct society" and of granting it (along with the other provinces) greater control over immigration, Supreme Court appointments, and federally funded social programs. Even a constitutional veto was on offer. In the climate of cooperation between Mulroney and Premier Robert Bourassa of Quebec, it appeared that such an agreement had been reached, although the Parti Québécois opposed it, insisting that it offered inadequate recognition. All that remained to cement the Meech Lake Accord was for each province to ratify it. But on 23 June 1990, when Premier Clyde Wells of Newfoundland allowed the ratification deadline to expire, hopes for national agreement on the

Quebec issue died. Robert Bourassa's speech, which (apparently inadvertently) affirmed the distinct society concept and expressed Quebec's feeling that it had been betrayed by the rest of Canada, re-energized nationalist sentiment in Quebec and fed a discourse of resentment.[135] The failure of yet another agreement, this one negotiated in Charlottetown, Prince Edward Island, in 1992, exacerbated Quebec's sense of isolation and fuelled the desire for another referendum on sovereignty in 1995. That one also failed, but by a much narrower margin than in 1980: 49.4 per cent in favour of opening negotiations for independence, 50.6 per cent against.[136]

As in the 1980s, Quebec's science fiction in the early 1990s reflected a renewed nationalist sentiment fuelled by what were perceived as betrayals over failed constitutional negotiations.[137] In his sport fiction, Guy Bouchard refers not only to this political climate but also to contemporary issues in hockey. Like April, Bouchard was directly involved with the province's science fiction milieu; between 1983 and 1997 he authored a novel, *Les Gelules utopiques* (1988), and published twelve works of fiction and five analytical articles in the specialized magazine, *imagine ....* A now retired philosophy professor at Quebec's Laval University, Bouchard has also published a number of scholarly studies on feminist utopian literature from Quebec as well as a theoretical book on science fiction.[138]

"Au jeu" directly engages the matter of a utopian society that has become an authoritarian dystopia as a result of pressures to conform to a single vision of the pursuit of happiness and the good commonwealth. The story applies the format of the judicial procedure. Bouchard's narrator, a public prosecutor, addresses a jury comprised of telespectators who will vote via referendum to determine the guilt or innocence of the accused. The charge against her is not revealed until the very end of the story, which engages the notion of sport as utopia along with the view that professional sports, by creating undemocratic, privileged elites, have corrupted the primary goals of sport itself. In a thinly veiled allegory, Bouchard – a resident of the Quebec City area – also engages the then contemporary hockey controversy surrounding Eric Lindros and his relationship with the Nordiques, a controversy still remembered in Quebec as "L'Affaire Lindros."

In keeping with the stereotypical image of the trial lawyer, Bouchard's narrator is somewhat long-winded, a strategy that allows Bouchard to describe for his readers the so-called "Révolution sportive."[139] This Sports Revolution came about in two phases, the first of which was the direct result of a hockey player and his family's greed, known as the "scandale Kelly Ross."[140] Rick Ross, a talented hockey player for the "Nordiques de Québec"[141] – Bouchard does not disguise the team name at all – affected by the death of his father Lind Ross, became embroiled in a contract dispute, spurred by his mother, Kelly, and his agent. His refusal to submit to the draft stipulations that would send him to the last-place team of the prior season – namely, the Nordiques – leads to the team's bankruptcy. Bouchard's prosecutor cites a laundry list of complaints made by hockey purists across Canada about what is wrong with professional hockey.[142] Furthermore, the story ties these issues directly to the real news item: Lindros's widely publicized and politically charged rejection of Quebec and the Nordiques.

"L'Affaire Lindros" may qualify for the most ado in any sports market about a player who never actually donned the franchise's uniform. It also developed into a public relations nightmare for the Lindros family, as well as a highly politicized (and profitable?) incident for Quebec's media to jump on. In the late 1980s, Toronto native Eric Lindros had been building a major reputation with the Ontario Junior Hockey League's Oshawa Generals. His career suggests the significance of hockey for Anglo-Canadians in that Lindros had published (with Randy Starkman) the first edition of his autobiography at the ripe old age of eighteen, *prior* to playing with any NHL team; a second edition appeared only a year later. Having placed last in the 1990 season, the Nordiques were entitled to the first pick in the 1991 draft; long before the actual event, however, the team's management had clearly expressed their interest in the prodigy. Unfortunately, Lindros made it clear that he had no interest in playing in the provincial capital. The francophone media depicted this rejection as an ethnocentric, if not racist, rejection of Quebecers by an Anglo-Canadian spoiled brat. Eric's nickname quickly became "bébé Lindros," and Nordiques (and apparently even Canadiens) fans would later appear with pacifiers and other symbolic expressions of their disfavour whenever he appeared at either the Colisée or the Forum.[143] Lindros explained that his decision was not anti-Québécois; rather, it was a lifestyle, career, and business decision targeting the Nordiques organization and Marcel Aubut in particular:

> There was a lot of talk about me being anti-French. That's bull. I think it's great that the people of Quebec have a different heritage. Diversity is great. It would be pretty boring if we were all the same. I think it's great that Quebec is part of Canada.

> I just don't feel the Nordiques care about winning. [...]
> I've said publicly a number of times that I'd be very happy to play in Montreal [...]. The Canadiens organization has the will to win. [...]
> I just don't sense any of that same burning desire to win in the Nordiques' organization. Marcel Aubut cheated the fans and his players last year.[144]

Lindros went on to express his fears that the Nordiques management would keep him on a last-place team for the rest of his career, always setting the price tag too high for any potential trade.[145] While his comments had some validity (and they were reiterated by his agent, Rick Curran, and his brother),[146] those of his father were more transparently political:

> Quebec City is a hotbed of the separatist movement. If it comes down to a referendum, a Nordique who's strongly against separatism isn't going to be the most popular man in town. If Eric says that he thinks Quebec should be an integral and desirable part of Canada [...] I think there could be a tremendous backlash from perhaps as many as 65 to 70 percent of the fans in Quebec City. [...] It would be difficult for him to play in a city that would like to separate from the rest of Canada.[147]

Fortunately for Lindros and his family, the Nordiques traded him to the Philadelphia Flyers over the summer, making this a non-issue.

The Lindros Affair, if it did not directly inspire Bouchard to write this story, at least offered him a pretext for a playful nod to his readers. In a page-and-a-half-long paragraph, Bouchard excoriates rising salaries in sports, alluding to figures that were current at the time although they seem risible today. As a result of the growing insanity of the system – an insanity typified by the "geste égoïste comme celui de la famille Ross" (egotistical gesture like that of the Ross family) – professional sports eventually reached a breaking point where small market teams could not survive. Hindsight indicates that the insanity reached its peak in the case of the Nordiques.

Having outlined the negative conditions that were ripe for a revolutionary change, Bouchard describes the events leading up to the creation of the utopian society. As in many utopian narratives, there is a visionary leader – in this case "notre vénéré Lionel MacPherson" (our revered Lionel MacPherson). In Bouchard's story, MacPherson takes up the cause and sets out to completely reform professional sports.[148] The allegory extends here to the imaginary leader, whose name refers both to the once-revered French Canadian historian and cleric Lionel Groulx as well as to Lester Pearson, the Canadian prime minister who first asserted that national strength could be demonstrated in the international sports arena.[149] The "mesures draconiennes" (draconian measures) that MacPherson institutes, however, are not enough, and a second revolutionary phase is begun by "notre vénérée Marie Monsoleil" (our revered Marie Monsoleil)[150] With the reference to the Virgin Mary and the honorary term "revered," applied to both figures, Bouchard ties the revolutionary discourse to the religious. Simultaneously, he invokes the clerico-nationalist ideology of Groulx's period[151] and more recent political concerns about the role of sports in developing national pride and identity. The name Monsoleil alludes to both the French Canadian "martyrs" of the colonial era – the Recollet and Jesuit missionaries killed by the Iroquois – and the founding women in the colony's history, such as Marguerite Bourgeoys. Monsoleil's first name also invokes that of another foundress, Marie de l'Incarnation, as well as Montreal's original name: Ville-Marie, in honour of the Virgin Mary. Monsoleil is a martyr to sport, a ski accident having left her paralysed. This apparent tragedy, however, allows her to experience an epiphany about the injustice of the privileged life she led as an elite athlete, and her meeting with MacPherson leads to the creation of a collectivist society based on sport, its practice, and its values.

As is the case with many contemporary "utopias," the author's aim in establishing this ostensibly ideal society is to demonstrate how a utopia may quickly degenerate into a dystopia, becoming what Marxist critics have termed a critical utopia.[152] As the charges against Renée Laplante are revealed, however, we learn that all of this sport utopia's achievements, including the general physical welfare of all citizens, come with a price: a diminution of knowledge and of individual freedom of thought and speech. Laplante is accused of instituting pedagogical innovations without official approval, including the teaching of history, poetry, drama, and art. As the prosecutor reminds the telejurors in his concluding remarks: "Nous appartenons tous à la même ligue. Quiconque l'oublie, quiconque revendique l'art, la solitude et la misère est coupable du crime de lèse-humanité" (We all belong to the same league. Anyone who forgets this, anyone who favours art, solitude, and misery is guilty of a crime against humanity).[153] Attitudes like Mlle Laplante's, according to him, "exsude la nostalgie d'une époque révolue et barbare" (reek of nostalgia for a bygone, barbarous epoch).[154]

The text ends in suspension, unresolved, but with a description of the penalty that awaits the prisoner: "Nous enfermerons cette criminelle dans une pièce aux murs de verre, nous l'installerons devant un téléviseur à écran géant et nous la condamnerons, n'est-ce pas? – aux jeux à perpette" (We will lock this criminal up in a room with glass walls, and we will sit her in front of a giant television screen and we will condemn her to games in perpetuity).[155] Bouchard apparently imagines the ultimate punishment for this liberal humanist: to sit in a space that clearly resembles the hockey penalty box, condemned to watch televised sports for eternity.

Conclusions

To conclude these reflections on hockey, science fiction, and other popular literature genres, I return to April's seminal essay on "Sport-fiction: le hockey et la science-fiction québécoise." April offers some insightful comments on the relationship between these two ostensibly unrelated forms of popular culture, linking them through their relationship to myth. He argues that SF is naturally fed by great popular myths and collective fantasies, and that in Quebec, "le grand mythe pouvant soulever des foules nous vient de notre sport national qui, depuis des générations, fait jaillir dans la population des rêves de puissance, de richesse, de célébrité et d'indépendance" (the great myth that can bring the crowds to their feet comes from our national sport, which, for generations, has spawned dreams of power, wealth, fame, and independence) – an aspect we will see clearly in the next chapter's discussion of the television series *Lance et compte*.[156] With these givens, April naturalizes the relationship between hockey and SF in Quebec, a move that is not as astonishing as it might seem, given that SF has been called a mythology for the space age and that hockey is the stuff of legend in Quebec.[157] Haitian writer Rodney Saint-Éloi, who has lived in the province for over a decade, writes that "le hockey, dans la fiction forgée, n'aura pas été seulement un déploiement de force, de violence et de muscles, mais aussi une mythologie transformatrice où il est possible de 'regarder demain'" (hockey, forged in fiction, will be seen not only as a deployment of force, violence, and muscles, but also a transformative mythology through which it is possible to "see tomorrow").[158] The various texts analysed in this chapter offer a range of positions regarding foundational myths of national identity, including hockey's often central place in such myths.

Gilles Tremblay's *Les Nordiques sont disparus* – the fruit of a dabbler, albeit an imaginative one – offers a relatively simplistic fantasy of power, as his twenty-sixth-century heroes thwart an attack on Quebec City, a threat prefigured in the 1993 disappearance of the province's two NHL hockey franchises and their fans. The nation of Quebec demonstrates its ability to resist threats from both within itself (the Solitonians) and from outside (US hegemony, both geographical and against Quebec's and Canada's national game of hockey). Although they are works of young adult fiction, Denis Côté's novels featuring the resistance hero Michel Lenoir reveal a somewhat more complex relationship to both myth and fantasy. By combining the Bildungsroman aspects of the young adult genre with the extrapolative and fantasy aspects of SF, Côté complicates his hero's relationship to hockey as national myth. As he develops into a more critical young adult, Lenoir makes eye-opening discoveries about his status as a near slave in the (then) futuristic, dystopian North America in *Shooting for the Stars*; in this way, the reader is offered a distanced but still clear critique of the myth of the Canadian Dream of playing for the NHL. The power fantasy for Lenoir becomes displaced from the hockey arena onto the "real" world of the class struggle of the Inactives; however, the positive power of amateur sport restores hockey to its pristine state in the series' conclusion.

Jean-Pierre April's own hockey fiction, "Le Fantôme du Forum," and those of François Barcelo offer the most complex and ambivalent reflections on the "sport national du peuple québécois."[159] As Marie Vautier observes of Barcelo's *La Tribu*, texts like these "strive to destabilize the accepted workings of traditional myth":[160] "Barcelo's use of parody and of reversal techniques lays bare the inherent tensions regarding historiography that is characteristic of New World Myth narrative. Through its use of magic realist techniques in its particular reworking of events of the Québécois past, Barcelo's novel resists and challenges the European inspired totalizing systems of history."[161] The same can be said about Barcelo's and April's treatment of the national myths surrounding hockey. Both authors employ the conventions of science fiction and magic realism to actualize the sports fan's common fantasy of power: their loser protagonists truly believe they have the ability to influence play. But when both authors allow their protagonists to employ that power, it is for the purpose of ridicule rather than praise; they thereby reveal the pathetic nature of these men's existences. Again, the chapters of *Ville-Dieu* that focus on Noël Lachard invoke the Canadian Dream of becoming a player in the NHL (in "Noël Lachard [I]") precisely in order to reveal the violence and destruction at the heart of such a dream (in "Noël Lachard [II]").

April directly links these texts published in the immediate post-1980 referendum era to national politics and fantasies of power:

> Sans doute ces textes des années quatre-vingt ont-ils été inspirés par l'internationalisation récente du sport au Québec, à partir des Jeux olympiques de Montréal en 1976[162] et des rencontres entre les plus grands hockeyeurs de l'U.R.S.S. et de l'Amérique du Nord. Et comme la politique-spectacle et le sport-spectacle ont beaucoup en commun, on pourrait voir dans le Sport-Fiction une compensation par les voies de l'imaginaire à l'échec référendaire de 1980. L'indépendance du Québec n'ayant pu accéder à la scène politique internationale, ses super-sportifs fictifs réaliseront des exploits inouïs.[163]

> These texts from the 1980s were no doubt inspired by the recent internationalization of sports in Quebec, from the 1976 Montreal Olympic Games to the encounters between the greatest hockey players in the world from the USSR and North America. And since the political spectacle and the sport spectacle have much in common, one could see in this Sport-Fiction a compensation via the imaginary for the failure of the 1980 referendum. Quebec's independence unable to access the international political scene, its fictional super-sportsmen could accomplish unheard of feats.

The heated reactions and accusations of anti-French bias surrounding the Lindros Affair referred to in Brossard's "Au jeu," and the ongoing constitutional debates that occurred up through the 1995 sovereignty referendum, coupled with the real disappearance of the Nordiques, continued to feed the fires of nationalist discontent.

Coda: François Barcelo's *J'haïs le hockey* (2011)

In the decades following the publication of his early postcolonial allegories, including *Ville-Dieu* (discussed above), François Barcelo published over two dozen more or less realist novels and two short story collections, as well as a significant number of children's books. Around the turn of the millennium, however, he turned to a genre only recently developing in Quebec, but one that fit well with the darker side of his nature – "l'humour corrosif" noted very early in his career by Michel Bélil[164] – namely, the *polar* or *roman noir*. And he did so with a high degree of success, becoming the first Québécois to publish under the *Série Noire* imprint of one of Paris's most prestigious publishing houses, Gallimard. These books included *Cadavres* (1998), which was adapted to film in 2009 by Érik Canuel, director of *Bon Cop, Bad Cop* (discussed in the introduction).

We have already seen Barcelo's tendency towards black humour in his depiction of paralysed hockey star Noël Lachard's self-dismemberment and eventual suicide by garbage chute in *Ville-Dieu*. Another hockey fiction, *J'haïs le hockey*, his first novel to come out in English (as *I Hate Hockey*, trans. Peter McCambridge), sustains itself – up until its shocking and demoralizing conclusion – with just such dark humour. The reader cannot help but laugh at the self-reflections of its first-person narrator, yet another Québécois loser, Antoine Groleau, who begins and ends his short narrative with a nearly sacrilegious expression of contempt for "the most resounding expression of our national stupidity": "I HATE hockey!"[165] In between, the separated, unemployed, forty-something hockey hater experiences a potentially redemptive encounter with the odious sport as he faces the challenge of coaching his son's bantam hockey team. This unlikely candidate must do so because the regular coach, Don Moisan, has been murdered.

Since he has nothing else to do, and the bus is waiting outside, Groleau embarks on this adventure. While Barcelo fleetingly introduces the crime the reader expects to appear in a book whose spine says "roman noir," he spends most of the first two chapters establishing just what a loser Antoine is and how little he knows about hockey. The author purposefully creates the perfect anti-hockey novel as he reverses all of the tropes of that genre, while at the same time drawing on newly developing ones and, paradoxically, offering his anti-hero narrator the possibility of finding redemption through the sport, which is precisely the goal of many straight hockey novels.

The work's title and first sentence clearly establish an anti-hockey point of view – an unnatural position for a hockey-themed novel. Overdetermination reigns free as Barcelo's narrator reiterates both his antipathy for and his ignorance of the game: "I HATE hockey!" "every day it makes me hate hockey a little bit more"; "I don't know anything about hockey"; "a dad who doesn't know the first thing about hockey."[166] Rather than singing the game's praises, Antoine invokes only negative memories and his own inabilities, further reinforcing his status as a loser. Instead of a nostalgic elegy for lost father–son bonding, this text shows how hockey divides families. First, he is unable to fulfil his father's hockey dream, that of seeing his son play in the NHL, because his "lack of talent was there for all to see" with the result that "things were never the same between us after that."[167] The novel thus reverses the trope of the son fulfilling the father's dreams found in hockey biographies and fiction, including Barcelo's own portrayal of Noël Lachard in *Ville-Dieu*. It introduces, of course, the original trauma at the root of his angst, his alienation from his nation's pastime, since he subsequently "hated hockey for each of the thirty-three years that followed."[168]

Next, the cycle of hockey alienation passes from generation to generation, as Antoine recounts his experience of attending a Canadiens game in the Bell Centre with his son. Instead of describing the sacramental ritual of father–son bonding, he couches the experience of watching hockey in terms of a "misfortune" "which there's no getting around if you [...] liv[e] in Quebec," underscoring at the same time the game's omnipresence in the province's cultural life. Upon entering the Bell Centre, "so-called hockey Mecca,"[169] he regrets immediately having accepted the tickets from his former car-dealer boss. He ironically reveals his status as a non-aficionado by asserting that "the game was of no interest whatsoever. Too few goals for my liking, as is nearly always the case with hockey."[170] Antoine nonetheless offers a popular version of scholarly discourses critiquing the commercialism of NHL hockey, noting that "I hadn't expected the sport's merchandising to have reached such loud, in-your-face proportions."[171] He then spends a paragraph and a half (two-thirds of a paperback page) decrying the advertising and spectacle, lamenting that he had "expos[ed] [his] six-year-old son to such an abuse of marketing."[172]

In this way, Barcelo reverses the time-worn tropes of hockey memories as cementers of father–son (and more recently father–daughter) relationships; but he also reverses the gender roles and identification with hockey in the broken family comprised of Antoine, his ex-wife Colombe, and his son Jonathan. Indeed, the ironically named Colombe (dove) is the member of the family who "loves hockey. And she knows the game inside and out."[173] She bought Jonathan his first equipment and has brought him to the rink since peewee. This image of the hockey mom, however, has now become commonplace, a trope for the evolving Quebec family with its more open contemporary gender roles. In *J'haïs le hockey*, the sport is not the only arena in which traditional gender roles are reversed: Colombe is a dynamic professional, the wage earner, and clearly the "decider" for the family. Antoine lives a totally passive existence, pushed out of his job as a car salesman. Now unemployed, he doesn't even own a car; instead, he rides his bicycle around town like his adolescent son.

Yet as Antoine fumbles his way into the role of bantam hockey coach, the novel offers him a chance to redeem himself. He has inevitably internalized the game's basic rules and tropes; he learns the team members' names – although that of the team eludes him – and begins to care about winning. He has been told they are the best team in the league, and as Antoine witnesses the discipline with which the team members board the bus, enter the arena, suit up, and take the ice, he imagines that "their dead coach must have been a real law and order freak. Probably a retired cop or soldier."[174] Thanks to the discipline of his young players and an aphasic, nerdy assistant coach who has all the lines on note cards, the team manages to switch shifts and carry on for the first two periods.

Nonetheless, Antoine notices their lacklustre play. Somehow, in yet another hockey film and fiction cliché, the second period ends in a fight, a fight that he feels he has unconsciously sparked: "the two boys must have read my mind because they drop their sticks and gloves, fling their helmets to the ice, raise their fists, and get ready to box."[175] Accepting a certain responsibility, he gives them a most atypical rally speech before they return to the ice for the third period:

> I have a confession to make: I HATE hockey. [...] If I'm here with you tonight, it's because they couldn't find anybody else. I'm unlucky to have fathered one of you and President Beauchemin had my phone number.[176]

Not only does he have the grace not to identify "which of you is mortified at being my son,"[177] but the sheer honesty of his speech seems to relax the team. He learns at the end of the period, which he has spent alone in the locker room – ironically, he was ejected for trying to break up the fight – that they have won 6 to 3. One of their players has scored a hat trick: Kim Nguyen, the only one to smile at him on the bus, the one seated next to his son, and the one who will be in his room when they reach the hotel to overnight after this distant away game.

A redemptive potential emerges for Antoine, who even has begun to build a fantasy of hope for himself around the idea that he might become their permanent coach. Such an association, he thinks, with a winning team might lead to his future success with women, and possibly even a job, since the players' fathers will also see him as a winner. These hopes are brutally shattered in an instant, by a single sentence uttered by Kim as they both lie awake, sleepless in twin beds. Their eyes inadvertently meet, and the young player says: "I only do blow jobs."[178] Barcelo continues to relate the situation with a dark humour that further underscores the weasly character of his protagonist. However, the realization of this assertion's significance eventually dawns on him:

> My predecessor must have assaulted him in exchange for ice time. [...]
> And suddenly – horror of horrors – I remember K. Nguyen telling me Jonathan sometimes roomed with the coach too. There's only one possible conclusion: my son has been sexually assaulted![179]

This realization, coupled with a number of unfortuitously ambiguous questions and coincidences, sends Antoine reeling into a course of action that shatters all of his new-found hockey dreams and eventually leads him to the most tragic of losses.

Having introduced the issue of coach sexual abuse of young hockey players – a question recently in the media because of the Sheldon Kennedy/Theo Fleury case – Barcelo now turns from the hockey aspect of his hybrid novel to the *noir*. Now that Antoine sees a motive for the former coach's death by unnatural causes, he jumps to the conclusion that his son may be guilty. The novel's reverse logic continues to build the case for Antoine's redemption as he finally takes positive, decisive action to protect his child at all costs:

> I'm not the perfect father. You might already have noticed, whether you're a better parent than me or not. But that doesn't stop me making up my mind to do the impossible so that Jonathan isn't ever suspected let alone arrested.[180]

Finally attempting to communicate with his son, he learns that Kim is a girl, that she is pregnant (by Moisan, he immediately suspects), and that perhaps the two adolescents committed the crime together.

Before he can learn the entire truth, however, Jonathan flees with Kim. At this point, only a few pages from its conclusion, the novel's humour and the thread of hope for Antoine's redemption continue to lead the reader towards the expectation of a happy ending. This, even though it raises the horrible spectre that the abusive coach was gruesomely murdered. Antoine and Colombe, working together to find their child, arrive at their agricultural town's ridiculous monument, a giant Holstein. Instead of achieving a happy reunion, however, Antoine bungles it again: Colombe cries out as the teenagers carry out a suicide pact, their naked bodies landing head first on the oversized cow's concrete base.

This horrifying conclusion establishes the beautiful structural irony that allows the author to close his novel with the reutterance of its very first words. As Antoine concludes: "To be honest, I know diddly-squat right now. / Apart from one thing I've always known. And now I know it more than ever … / I HATE hockey!"[181]

Clearly, such a dark ending conforms to the conventions of the *noir* genre; the happy ending is the stuff of the "straight" hockey novel. This work's light-hearted nihilism perhaps expresses a general sense of late capitalist alienation. But its devastating conclusion also links this chapter to questions of gender construction and masculinity, issues that are central to Barcelo's book, discussed in greater detail in chapter 4. The novel's similarity of tone to *Ville-Dieu*, and the irony in *I Hate Hockey*, reveal Barcelo's artistry, as he exploits the power of humour to shield us from the pain of the actual realities of families impacted by coach sexual abuse – a phenomenon that has come to substitute for the priestly abuse scandals of the 1990s, it would seem. But the humour deployed to cover such pain also suggests one of the key elements of Western masculinity, which is constructed negatively, in that it denies "real" men the right to express intense emotion. In any case, after dealing with this corpus of critically engaged works of popular literature, the next chapter's examination of the highly popular – and largely uncritical – prime-time television drama, *Lance et compte*, represents something of a breath of fresh air. Yet as we shall see, this purportedly "realist" television show presents Quebecers with as much a fantasy world as these admittedly fantastic narratives.

Chapter Three

Plus ça change…: The Hockey-Themed Television Series *Lance et compte* as a Reflection of Quebec Society

With He Shoots! He Scores!, *we are creating what the CRTC says it wants: broadcasting a pan-Canadian production adopted by viewers from one ocean to the other.*

Claude Héroux[1]

By introducing the figure of the winner, Lance et compte *radically transforms the imaginary landscape of the televised drama. Personal success becomes the new panacea and Pierre Lambert is a winner who crystallizes the aspirations of thousands of viewers.*

Jean-Pierre Désaulniers[2]

On Tuesday, 9 September 1986, at eight p.m., a record nearly two million[3] Québécois viewers tuned in to Radio-Canada for the debut of what would become a cult television series in the province, the hockey-themed prime-time drama *Lance et compte* (*He Shoots! He Scores!*). By the end of the season (the finale aired on Tuesday, 2 December 1986), it had garnered 2,756,000 viewers, according to the Nielsen ratings.[4] The series featured a fictional NHL team, the National of Quebec City, explicitly modelled on the Quebec Nordiques.[5] Its blue-and-white uniforms sported the fleurs-de-lys of both the provincial flag and the Nordiques' jerseys; similarly, the series' "NL" logo was designed to imitate the Nordiques' stylized N paired with a hockey stick and puck. The National's home ice was, of course, the Colisée, where game sequences were filmed, sometimes with Nordiques audiences, players, and opponents as extras. The National even shared a sponsor, O'Keefe Breweries, with their real-life model, the Nordiques. In contrast to the often struggling Nordiques, however, the National's winning record offered viewers a fantasy of French Canadian success.

This chapter examines how the popular, privately produced television series *Lance et compte* represents what cultural critics would call an "ideological" text, that is, one that reflects and reinscribes rather than contests the dominant ideology of the society that produced it.[6] First aired on Radio-Canada for three consecutive seasons from 1986 to 1989, with an additional six made-for-television films in 1991–2, the series *Lance et compte* engages numerous themes that are relevant both to the sport of hockey and to Quebec's modernizing, post–Quiet Revolution society. Structured around the players, coaches, agents, and journalists associated with a fictionalized NHL franchise, and written by well-known sports journalist Réjean Tremblay,[7] *Lance et compte* foregrounds issues of concern to the sport and adopts many of the discourses about how hockey has changed in relation to an idealized era of the "good old days." Perhaps ironically, the same discourse reappears, often nearly word for word, in its reprise broadcast in five series from 2002 to 2012, during which it addresses the hockey-related issues of rising salaries, salary caps, rivalries, goons versus skill players, off-the-ice antics, and so on. The sport of hockey provides the series with a selling hook, but since it was meant to appeal to a wide television audience, *Lance et compte* also shows not just heroes and villains among the players and coaching staff, but also the women in their lives (as did the prime-time soap operas *Dallas* and *Dynasty*, which it emulates). Through these family relationships the series explores a broader set of social issues that are relevant to Quebec society in general during these periods.

While the Nordiques still existed, *Lance et compte* offered the illusion of an intimate view into the lives of the province's elite NHL players. The National's winning record also provided consolation for fans of an expansion franchise that often found it difficult to compete with bigger and richer markets in the recruitment of star players. The Nordiques' five worst seasons, 1987 to 1992, corresponded almost exactly with the first series' and telefilms' success. Although they did win a championship series during the World Hockey Association era (1972–79) – in 1977 against the Winnipeg Jets – the Nordiques never once reached the Stanley Cup finals; the National, by contrast, won five Stanley Cups, albeit fictional ones. Clearly, the National offered a compensatory fantasy to viewers after the Nordiques were sold in 1995 and moved to Denver, where they were renamed the Colorado Avalanche. In the words of actor Michel Daigle (Nounou, the team trainer), "comme il n'y a plus de Nordiques" (since there's no more Nordiques),[8] the producers had added reason to believe that a comeback series would be popular.

Furthermore, they exploited the fantasy of a continued rivalry with the Montreal Canadiens, a highly popular and perhaps exaggerated and mythologized rivalry, as we will see in our discussion of it in this chapter. In the context of the 1980 referendum defeat and an economic recession, *Lance et compte*'s first series provided the average Quebec viewer with a fantasy of national dominance and empowerment during an era in which the discourse of the French Canadian underdog and a lingering sense of the *colonisé* still prevailed. As suggested by television scholar Jean-Pierre Désaulniers (cited in this chapter's epigraph), viewers could tune in each Tuesday evening to follow the lives of winners. In the series' reprise, viewers are able to indulge a nostalgic fantasy about "notre équipe" (our team), a majority francophone, Quebec City NHL franchise still in existence and battling hard against both US hegemony and the Montreal Canadiens, the metropole's franchise, a team viewed as increasingly anglophone and internationalized.

Lance et compte's Place in Quebec Media History

The culture industries in Quebec and in Canada as a whole benefit from government subsidies at levels unheard of in the United States.[9] Privatization began in 1958, and in the 1980s there were further initiatives to open Canadian television production to the private sector.[10] In 1983, Canada passed laws whose intent was to boost private television production in order to counter US cultural imperialism by increasing the volume of Canadian-content broadcasting.[11] Claude Héroux, who had worked in the Canadian film industry producing the films of acclaimed director David Cronenberg, and also in Hollywood, decided at this critical moment to change his career direction, returning to his native province to develop authentic, made-in-Quebec television to compete with mass American imports.[12] Noting the success of *Dallas* and *Dynasty*, he saw a genre open for development in Quebec, a province that greatly prized locally produced content.[13] In his own legend-like account of the series' origins, he describes crossing paths with sports journalist Réjean Tremblay at a Canadiens game in the Forum. Both men dreamed of making a series about hockey[14] that would reflect the values of 1980s Quebec society: "la réussite personnelle et l'ambition" (personal success and ambition).[15]

These values united the United States, Britain, and Canada during what has been termed the Reagan–Thatcher–Mulroney era;[16] in Quebec studies, we add to that list Quebec's Liberal premier, Robert Bourassa.[17]

In his memoir about the series' development, *Lance et compte: les dessous d'une réussite* (*He Shoots! He Scores!* The Underside of a Success; 2006), Héroux's adherence to the capitalist ideology of personal success through financial gain on the free market emerges clearly in a number of ways. First, his frustration with Radio-Canada's bureaucracy and his strong efforts to obtain sponsors for the show reveal his disdain for state-sponsored industry and his acceptance that advertising is vital to business.[18] He expresses pride in the show's pioneering use of product placement and its ability to get around the laws governing advertisements in public broadcasting (e.g., the ads on the boards of the Colisée appeared on the television series).[19] He shamelessly describes the various prizes and contests used to *fidéliser*, attract loyal viewers, even before the series' debut, often in tandem with Carling O'Keefe and Ultramar, the other major sponsor of the series.[20] Within the entertainment industry, in his role as a producer, Héroux is clearly an entrepreneur rather than an artist.

Yet Héroux also takes artisanal pride in his work, situating *Lance et compte* as a pioneering effort in the Quebec-specific television genre of the *téléroman*, the telenovel.[21] Outside sources confirm the series' significance: it was Quebec's first big-budget production, and that budget allowed it to "recourir à la technique cinématographique, de renouveler la structure narrative, de dynamiser le traitement esthétique et d'être diffusé en Europe et au Canada anglais" (have recourse to cinematographic techniques, to renew narrative structure, to offer a dynamic esthetic treatment, and to broadcast in Europe and English Canada).[22] While admitting that he was inspired by American productions, Héroux nonetheless describes the series as "une émission mettant en vedette des joueurs de hockey," as a "histoire québécoise pure laine" (a show starring hockey players; a dyed-in-the-wool Quebec story).[23] He hired Louis Caron, an established telefilm writer in Quebec, to craft stories loosely based on the lives of real NHL players, pairing him with Réjean Tremblay, a sports journalist with Montreal's *La Presse,* so that the series would get the hockey right.[24] Héroux had first sought permission from the Montreal Canadiens and from the Forum, which is run by a separate corporate entity, to film scenes there. Perhaps serendipitously, given Quebec City's later loss of its franchise, Marcel Aubut, the Nordiques' president, who was directly involved in the Colisée's management, and the team's primary sponsor, Carling O'Keefe, were quicker and more positive in their response, and it was they who ultimately closed the deal with Héroux.[25]

Although he was a private producer, Héroux did rely on government subsidies from both Canada (Telefilm Canada) and Quebec (Sodec),[26] and he was selling the program to air on Radio-Canada. This meant that however strong his desire for realism (and good ratings), he had to respect certain limits. In particular, he needed to stay away from "les sujets tabous de la consommation d'alcool et de drogues" (the taboo subjects of alcohol and drug use) in the first series.[27] At that time, attitudes towards depictions of nudity and sexual relations were more open in Quebec (indeed, some naked breasts were censored for the English versions of the series); still, Radio-Canada expressed concerns about nudity and swearing.[28] As we will see in the next section, the melodrama eventually included just about every conceivable scandalous behaviour, ostensibly out of a concern for realism, although no doubt this was coupled with the desire for good ratings. Before examining how the two series – whose production spanned more than a quarter-century – reflect (or not) the evolution of Quebec society, let's look at *Lance et compte*'s treatment of the game itself.

The Hockey in *Lance et compte*

The series' producers consistently sought to keep its hockey aspects as realistic as possible so as to meet the expectations of exacting and expert hockey fans. Aware that getting it wrong could alienate their audience, Héroux obtained permission from the NHL to use stock footage, an element that both added realism and saved on production costs.[29] The series also iced a team of actors who were more or less competent skaters and hockey players, along with a number of professionals as extras, even filming them facing actual NHL franchises, such as the Bruins, early in the series.[30] In addition, of course, to the melodrama of the players' domestic lives, several plot trajectories across each season reflect issues of specific concern to the world of hockey and to professional sports in general. Interestingly, as much as or more than the social issues, the hockey-related debates engaged by *Lance et compte* reflect the adage invoked in the title of this chapter, *plus ça change, plus c'est la même chose.*

Lance et compte's sets include the central locations unique to hockey – the locker room and the arena (during practice and games) – along with ancillary, instrumental locations such as busses and planes, hotels, and various locations where players socialize (bars, restaurants, sometimes private homes). These contrast with the domestic settings of the players, although both figure as sites of personal success and fulfilment as well as stress and conflict. Each episode or telefilm features several compulsory locker room sequences involving various conceits of the sports genre, such as the coach's rallying speech or medical treatment after an injury. These sequences strive for realism, mimicking the clutter, states of undress, and beverages found in locker rooms; the latter include beer and champagne for celebrating, and water and Orangina for hydrating (*LCI*, ep. 2),[31] the latter obviously due to plans for the series to air in France. Hockey literature often highlights players' superstitions, which can be deeply rooted, as well as their love of pranks: a player might be offered a drink that has been urinated into, or find that his locker has been booby-trapped. And almost every hockey novel, biography, or memoir mentions the rookie's initiation, a ritual described as hazing by Jamie Bryshun and Kevin Young, who assert that "perhaps more than any other sport [...], male hockey players reported an abundance of initiations that tended to involve nudity, physical punishments, and excessive amounts of alcohol consumption."[32] Compared to some of the incidents they report, series protagonist Pierre Lambert's (Carl Marotte) initiation appears relatively tame: he begins to don his long johns only to find a truncated sleeve, a missing leg, and so on; he is then grappled into submission by the others, and shaving cream is lathered into his hair (*LCI*, ep. 2).

The series repeatedly exploits for their dramatic potential a number of issues relating to hockey as labour. Of course, the Canadian Dream of making it to the NHL is central to the series, and Pierre Lambert's experience with the draft represents the major narrative tension of the original series pilot. Of course, the francophone star of the Trois-Rivières Dragons wants to sign with a team close to home, and the National is his first choice. Here the "realism" of the prime-time soap opera veers into the realm of fantasy fulfilment. Although the Canadiens were allowed to draft Quebec's top two francophone players until 1967, and both the Canadiens and the Nordiques did draft more francophones than any other franchise, in reality, no NHL franchise today specifically drafts francophone stars.[33] Obviously, the hero of *Lance et comte* (and first-billed actor) must play for the team that series features; but besides that, the National's choice of Pierre as their first pick feeds into the discourse about winners and losers developed throughout the series. Winners get what they want, and Pierre wants to be on the National, so that is what he gets. This plot trajectory is repeated for Pierre's son Guy Lambert (Jason Roy-Léveillé) in the later series, when he moves up from Junior in Chicoutimi to the National.

After the draft come salary negotiations, another real-life process ripe with dramatic potential, which the series exploits. Plot lines frequently revolve around player (and coach) salaries and contract negotiations. Money is certainly not a taboo subject; indeed, it is constantly at issue in the series, reflecting the dominant ideology of the free market and the acquisition of wealth as an end in itself, which we discuss further below. The series never questions the tenet that, as with any other commodity subject to laws of supply and demand, these players should seek "what they are worth." While the figures change over time, the ideology does not. In season one, Gilles Guilbeault offers Pierre's agent a three-year contract with an escalating salary of $30,000, $35,000, and $40,000 in the minors and $90,000, $105,000, and $120,000 if he makes it into "la grande ligue" (*LCI*, ep. 1). Note that those sums are in Canadian dollars and from a period when the Canadian dollar was worth about $0.75 US.[34] The series reprise, *Le Grand Duel,* has a sub-plot about the contract negotiations for Francis Gagnon (Louis-Philippe Dandenault), the son of the original series' superstar player turned coach, Marc Gagnon (Marc Messier). Now an agent, Pierre Lambert obtains for his client some $8,000,000 for three seasons with the Canadiens (*LCGD*, ep. 1).

Should these negotiations not work out, or a player not live up to expectations, a club may decide to trade him. Such decisions and the reactions of players to the news of a trade provide narrative tension in a number of seasons. In the first series, anglophone goalie Gary Bennett (Timothy Webber) appears to be a composite of great goalies of the past, wearing number 1 (long the traditional number for first-string goalies) and throwing up before games like Glenn Hall. As his performance flags, management trades him to the Boston Bruins. Clearly distressed, Bennett tells general manager Gilles Guilbeault (Michel Forget) that he has even enrolled his children in French schools, an honest attempt to assimilate to Quebec City's dominant culture. In season three, encumbered by massive gambling debts, owner Allan Goldman (Peter McNicoll) instructs Guilbeault to trade several "expensive" players, treating them like pawns. In one episode, Goldman presents his GM with a trade he has arranged on his own as a done deal; here, owners and managers are shown trading players as if they were boys swapping trading cards. In this way, the series shines a rare critical light on an obviously dehumanizing reality of the game.

Even worse than being traded to another NHL franchise, players may be sent down to the minor leagues, either because of poor performance or perhaps to rehab from an injury or simply to change the atmosphere in the locker room, as head coach Jacques Mercier (Yvan Ponton) suggests at one point (*LCI*, ep. 6). Such is the case for both Denis Mercure (Jean Harvey) and National star Pierre Lambert in season one; each spends time on the National's minor league AHL affiliate, the Chicoutimi Saints, during injury rehab. Much of episode nine portrays the "reality" of minor league hockey, playing on stereotypes of its excessive violence but also revealing the tensions and difficulties faced by minor league players. Again, in another rare critical instance, it questions the Canadian Dream of a career in hockey. Denis has been in Chicoutimi for some weeks when Pierre arrives in the locker room for the first time, accompanied by reporters. Some players, clearly jealous of his privileged position in the NHL, resent him and see him as simply a tourist in their tougher league. Rumours fly that the AHL franchise will close because of financial troubles, the insinuation being that Denis and Pierre are being kept in Chicoutimi longer than necessary so that the minor team can make a financial recovery. Goldman has made this decision not for the good of hockey, but for the good of his own bank account and for the ill of powerless rookie Pierre, whose contract has a clause stating that if he doesn't play a full forty games for the National he will receive minor league pay. In addition to all this locker room grousing, the Saints' bus trips are contrasted with the luxury air travel enjoyed by the National. When Pierre first arrives, Denis describes the brooding atmosphere as "pourri" (rotten); many of the players, besides being jealous of Pierre, are simply fed up with losing.

The minor league episodes also allow viewers to meet some stock characters, including the good-natured team captain "Bébert" (Alain Gendreau). His bald pate an obvious sign of aging, his career reflects the sort of abjection aligned with the "losers"[35] who can't make it into the majors, but who refuse to give up the dream and move on. When asked what is waiting for him in a year or two when he can no longer play, he replies that he'll go back to delivering beer; in fact, by season three he is coaching the team. A few games later, when Chicoutimi has started to win and to fill its arena with fans, the atmosphere on the bus is completely different, but this time it swings to the opposite extreme as players sing and throw beer cans around. Since they appear drunk, the viewer at first believes they are returning home from a match; actually, they have not even played yet that night, and this serves to highlight the lack of professionalism in the minors. Finally, excessive violence also appears in *Lance et compte.* This aspect of minor league hockey was examined in *Slap Shot* in 1977 and is still the case today, as seen in the recent documentary on the Laval, Quebec, semi-pro team *The Chiefs* (2004; dir. Jason Gileno). In the reprise series, which often directly mirrors the original, Pierre Lambert's son Guy starts his career with the Chicoutimi franchise before being called up to the National. His problems revolve around another area, female fans and available sex.

To protect themselves from unfair labour practices, the players unionized, founding the NHL Players' Association in 1967. Although the NHLPA was well established by the time of the first series' premier in 1986, *Lance et compte* makes little mention of it, perhaps because of the free trade climate prevailing during the 1980s. In season three, Pierre Lambert briefly goes on a one-man strike, refusing to play until contract negotiations are finalized. *La Reconquête* (2004) develops this timely issue much more thoroughly in the context of the 2005 lockout. It depicts Jérôme Labrie (Raymond Bouchard), a former agent, now head of the union (a reflection of Alan Eagleson's similar career trajectory), trying to convince players that a strike may be necessary, invoking Maurice Richard to do so: "Maurice Richard était un esclave" (Maurice Richard was a slave).[36] When Guilbeault gives him full access to the National's books, Labrie realizes that the struggling franchise truly cannot afford to pay anything more to the players, and drops his campaign. The lockout, of course, raises the issue of salary caps for franchises, one of the few completely new developments between the original series and its reprise. This issue arises in *La Reconquête,* when the NHL finally adopts caps after the 2004–5 lockout.[37]

Another significant development in hockey reflected in both the original series and its reprise is the recruitment of international players to the major league and the inclusion of players of colour on NHL rosters. Here the series begins to address Quebec's changing demographics. The National's original 1986 roster includes a few anglophone players for verisimilitude (although few of these are *unilingues* – another fantasy aspect of the series I address at length elsewhere)[38] – and its francophone players are *Québécois de vieille souche*, old-roots French Canadians, as their surnames reveal: Gagnon, Lambert, Mercier, Couture, and so on.

The series does reflect the game's internationalization over the decades of its production. The first player who learned the game outside of

North America to be recruited into the NHL was a Swede, Ulf Sterner,[39] who played as early as 1965 with the New York Rangers. During the 1970s, more and more international players were recruited, and the 1980s – the decade in which *Lance et Compte* first aired – saw a dramatic increase in their numbers.[40] To reflect this aspect of the changing game, the National recruit a Swede in the first series; in season two, they help a Russian player defect during an international tournament. In the reprise, they recruit a Russian teenager – the son of *LCII*'s Koulikov – who arrives towards the end of *Le Grand Duel*.

In terms of racial diversity (discussed further below), apart from Haitian Lucie Baptiste and her family in seasons one and two, and a biracial teenager who helps Pierre Lambert make a comeback in the made-for-TV movie *Le Retour du Chat* (The Return of the Cat, Lambert's nickname being the cat), the original series' cast is overwhelmingly white. The reprise series also has a predominantly white cast, with very little diversity among the players and their families. On the one hand, the number of francophone players on the National clearly sets that team apart, as does the fluent Québécois French of the Anglos who play on the team (including team captain Mike Ludano [played by Peter Miller, who, in spite of his Anglo name was born in Chibougamau]). On the other, the team's Eurocentric racio-ethnic make-up aligns with that of other NHL franchises, which each seem now to hire one token black player: Jarome Iginla, longtime star of the Calgary Flames, now with Boston; the P.K. Subban on the Canadiens, preceded by Donald Brashear in the 1990s; the Winnipeg Jets' Dustin Byfuglien.[41] Following in step, the National has hired the colourful Haitian-Canadian goalie, Alex Beauchesne (Fayolle Jean, Jr.); while Beauchesne's boasting provides comic relief throughout *La Nouvelle Génération* through to *Le Grand Duel*, there are some distasteful minstrel show aspects to this characterization.

On repeated occasions during National practice sessions, when the boastful goalie, nicknamed the Black Cat, has proved his prowess, he requires the white players whose shots he has blocked to bow down to him and even to kiss his black ass (*LCGD*, ep. 1); elsewhere, jokes are made about the size of his "queue" (tail/penis; *LCGD*, ep. 2). He proclaims that "C'est ma mission sur terre. Sauver la peau des petits blancs du National!" (It's my mission on earth. To save the skin of the National's little white men! *LCRec*, ep. 7). Although the other team members laugh with Alex the Great, the sheer tokenism, the stereotypical representation of this black character (boastful, colourful, happy that women are a fringe benefit of being a hockey player) verges on the offensive.

Furthermore, there lingers a Sambo element to his attitude during the tensions over the possibility of a strike in *La Reconquête*. Indeed, this portrayal actually represents a backslide, when we contrast Alex with the educated, sophisticated Lucie Baptiste, who is a central character in the original series (see below). Her lighter skin and upward mobility as a doctor reflect an earlier wave of Haitian immigration in the 1960s; Alex's darker skin aligns him with the 1980s wave of poorer migrants associated with the waves of "Boat People." His physical ability alone has allowed for his upward economic mobility; he is simply grateful for a well-paid job with – as already mentioned – access to plenty of women, an opinion he expresses with savour.

The issue of violence – perhaps the most omnipresent theme in contemporary (and past) hockey discourse – also arises in the series, often for dramatic effect. The National has its "role players" and its "goons," like any other franchise; most notably, one of the beloved characters, faux-anglophone Mac Templeton (Éric Hoziel), both serves in this role and paradoxically denies it. *Lance et compte*'s treatment of goon hockey thus appears refreshingly sophisticated in its self-referentiality. In the first season, the Boston Bruins ice a fictional goon called Jimmy Thompson (Claude Chagnon; not to be confused with the real Jim Thomson, drafted into the NHL in 1984). Pierre points him out to Mac, who, without irony, says: "That big goon. I'll take care of him" (*LCI*, ep. 3). Later, when Pierre's younger sister Suzie Lambert (Marina Orsini) needs to be rescued from a potential gang bang/date rape, Mac is called in to help. Still playing for the National in the second series and the team's senior member, Templeton specifically shouts to Marc Gagnon, who is now the coach, "I'm not a goon, Marc!" (*LCRec*, ep. 9). Later, after he moves off the ice to serve as a coach, he teaches a young player how to fight and take a hit, skills effectively put into play during a game by that player at a crucial moment later in the series (*LCGD*, ep. 5).

In spite of producers' explicit choice of a fictionalized team and players, during the immensely popular first series, viewers and journalists sought to blur the lines between fantasy and reality as they speculated about which real-life players might be figured in the series' characters and intrigues. In particular, it was speculated that Marc Gagnon – a blond Don Juan – was based on Guy Lafleur.[42] Players were asked about their reactions to the series; while Lafleur was not bothered, a young Patrick Roy was more critical.[43] During the series, actual players and controversies are mentioned on occasion; for example, when Mathias Ladouceur (Karim Toupin-Chaieb) reveals in *Le Grand Duel* that he had been sexually abused by his peewee league coach, he says he does not want to be another Sheldon Kennedy.[44]

Much greater than the desire to connect individual characters to real-life hockey players appeared viewers' engagement in connecting the exploits of the fictional National to those of the real Nordiques. The series also became an arena to play out the fantasy of a now mythologized rivalry, the one between the Nordiques and the Canadiens, which sports journalist Jean-François Chabot has compared to the one between the Red Sox and Yankees. Indeed, when Chabot asserts in his history of that rivalry that he will tell "la saga qui fait rêver, rager, pleurer et sauter de joie tant de personnes. Que ces gens aient été ou non des mordus du hockey, nul n'y sera indifférent" (the saga that has made so many people dream, rage, cry, and jump for joy. Whether or not they were hockey fans, no one would be indifferent),[45] he might just as well be describing *Lance et compte*. Similarly, Steve Lasorsa's analysis of what the players and coaches of the Canadiens and the Nordiques meant for the people of Quebec during the 1980s also applies to a great extent to the public's love of the fictional characters who were designed to represent them: "nous nous retrouvons avec des personnages qui représentent ni plus ni moins que des héros nationaux dans l'imaginaire collectif de l'époque" (we find ourselves with characters who represent no more and no less than national heroes in the collective imagination of the era).[46]

The Rivalry, the Fantasy

Series producer Claude Héroux writes that, even beyond the realm of hockey, "une longue rivalité aussi vieille que le pays, oppose Québec à Montréal" (a long rivalry as old as the country opposes Quebec City and Montreal).[47] The provincial capital, with its smaller and more homogeneous population, vaunts its nationalism and francophilia, along with its historic atmosphere – elements that the larger, more cosmopolitan metropole disdains in the rival "village." Between 1979 and 1995, when the Nordiques faced off against the Canadiens in the NHL, that rivalry played itself out in the province's media and on the ice of the Forum and the Colisée. Two recent accounts rehearse the excitement and the significance of those years. Journalist Jean-François Chabot's *La Grande Rivalité Canadiens-Nordiques* (2009) offers first-hand recollections enhanced by contemporary accounts and recent interviews with players, coaches, and management staff. Historian Steve Lasorsa's *La Rivalité*

Canadien-Nordiques (2011) relies on Chabot's work, and on research based on contemporary print media, to explicitly (and repeatedly) link the great sports rivalry to the province's nationalist aspirations.[48] Before we explore this connection, however, let us recall the explicit connection the series' creators made between the fictional National and the real-life Nordiques.

Héroux realized quite early during the production that Quebec City, precisely because it was small and because its inhabitants were enthusiastic about a major media production, would be a much better choice than Montreal, a metropolis jaded by the omnipresence of its cultural industries: "Jamais nous n'aurions obtenu ce type de résultats à Montréal" (We would never have obtained this type of results in Montreal).[49] It is clear that the hockey and television fans of Quebec City adopted the National (the singular of their name ironically nods to that of the Canadien, however), at first as a perhaps idealized reflection of their own Nordiques and later as a surrogate for the prodigal team, by then the Colorado Avalanche. Héroux recalls that "la population de la ville de Québec collabore au-delà de nos espérances" (the population of Quebec City collaborates beyond our expectations).[50] Aubut and the Colisée management advised the film crew on how to get extras to show up for the shooting of game sequences in the arena, and indeed, the crowd that attended took on a life of its own.[51] For example, for sequences shot during an actual Bruins–Nordiques game at the Colisée, fans in the stands waved signs for the fictional National.[52] Even during the first season, although media hype about the hockey-related series had begun quite early, nine thousand extras showed up for one filming session.[53] Quebec City embraced the show as wholeheartedly as it had the Nordiques.

When we watch the various iterations of the series *Lance et compte*, the incestuous nature of the relationship between the two teams, the National and the Canadien, appears at times contrived and unrealistic, and so does the extent of exchange between them. Because of the additional challenges they face in an anglophone-dominated league, francophones in the NHL are very clannish. Thus, many of the series' fantasy-like exchanges are based on actual events. For example, Jacques Mercier seems to be a composite of Jacques Lemaire and Michel Bergeron, real-life rivals during the 1980s. Lemaire played for the Canadiens from 1968 to 1979 and then coached them from 1983 to 1985; like Mercier in *LCII*, he went to coach in Switzerland for a time.[54] Their use of anglicisms characterizes both the real and the fictional coaches.[55]

Bergeron, who was the Nordiques coach during the peak of the rivalry (and who later made many cameo appearances in the *Les Boys* franchise, discussed in the next chapter), sports a heavy Quebec accent,[56] as does Gilles Guilbeault, the National's general manager. Nicknamed the Tiger for his fiery temperament, a trait he shares with Mercier, Bergeron also went into television journalism, appearing as a panelist on RDS's sports talk show, *L'Antichambre*.

Like Lemaire, *Lance et compte*'s second star (after Pierre Lambert) Marc Gagnon moves from player to coach, a trajectory taken by many hockey players. More directly connected to the reality of the Canadiens–Nordiques rivalry is that his son, Francis, follows in his footsteps; he plays for the National before being traded to the Canadien in *Le Grand Duel*, the 2010 season, whose main plot trajectory pits the National against the Canadien in the Stanley Cup race. While the Howe and Hull families are perhaps the best-known examples of two generations of major league hockey stars,[57] the Canadiens also saw a Geoffrion dynasty. Bernie "Boom-Boom" Geoffrion played during the Maurice Richard era and married the daughter of Howie Morenz; his son Dan also played for the Habs as well as for the Nordiques. Grandson Blake Geoffrion also made the Canadiens' roster in the 2011–12 season. Other key players on the National appear to be modelled on real-life Nordiques – for example, anglophone enforcer Dale Hunter's possible avatar, Mac Templeton. The National's Paul Couture (Jean Deschênes), a born-again Christian nickenamed "Preach" or "Le Curé," may be modelled on real-life Nordiques goalie Daniel Bouchard, also nicknamed "Le Curé." And while the selection of French Canadian surnames is limited, various players across the franchise's seasons bear the names of former Canadiens and Nordiques, such as Martin (Bob Martin *LCI* through *LCGD*), Richard (Steve Richard in *Envers et contre tous*), and Bouchard (Dany Bouchard from *LCNG* through *LCRec*).

Contemporary viewers would have enjoyed such guessing games. But tracing all of these connections is not simply an amusement; it also reveals some of the devices that the creators of *Lance et Compte* used in order to inject the series with verisimilitude and familiarity and thereby hold fans' attention and loyalty. More important, though, appears the task of tracing the show's meaning as a representation of Quebec and Franco-Quebecers' vision of themselves. The National was explicitly modelled on the Nordiques, a team that represented the province's capital city and that actively appropriated franco-nationalist symbols: the royal blue and the fleur-de-lys; in this way, Héroux and his team produced a cultural product that offered an idealized reflection of the province to its audience, which took pride in this consistently winning team (albeit a fictional one). Above all, Pierre Lambert, as described by Désaulniers, came to represent a "personnage emblématique du Québécois déterminé, combatif et talentueux" (a character emblematic of the determined, aggressive, and talented Québécois).[58] By introducing the rivalry with the Canadiens, Héroux and his cohorts could count on building a loyal audience from Montreal as well, for they were essentially offering *all* Quebecers a positive self-image, one in which everyone eventually wins (except the American teams, of course).

Lance et compte astutely capitalized, then, on the real-life rivalry between the Canadien and the Nordiques, in the same way that Marcel Aubut capitalized on the historical rivalry between Montreal and Quebec City as he developed and marketed the Nordiques. Both the televised dramatization and the sports rivalry owed some of their success to their ability to tap into the attitudes of their times, particularly in the 1980s, which was a period of rising nationalism as well as disappointment over the failed referendum. Steve Lasorsa's articulation of this connection bears citing:

> La rivalité qui se développe entre les deux équipes de la province offre, par le truchement de l'imaginaire, une métaphore similaire au débat national qui divise le Québec des années 1980. Les couleurs des uniformes, les démarches des Nordiques pour s'attirer la sympathie des Québécois francophones, la guerre entre deux clans, les affrontements fratricides et, surtout, les millions de Québécois qui suivent cette rivalité avec une passion, une fougue qui va bien plus loin que le hockey. À travers cette rivalité, c'est un peuple qui s'exprime, qui crie sa fierté, dans toute sa beauté, sa complexité et ses paradoxes.[59]

> The rivalry developing between the two teams of the province offers, via the imaginary, a metaphor similar to the national debate that divided Quebec in the 1980s. The colour of their uniforms, the steps taken by the Nordiques to attract the sympathy of Francophone Quebecers, the war between two clans, the fratricidal battles and, above all, the millions of Quebecers who follow this rivalry with a passion that far surpasses hockey itself. Through this rivalry, an entire people in all of its beauty, complexity and paradoxes expresses itself, shouts out its pride.

The series drew upon the same dreams and aspirations, appealing to such a broad sector of Quebecers that episode twelve of season three, aired on 23 March 1989, attracted the fourth-highest number of viewers for any single episode of a *téléroman* between 1962 and 1995: 3,227,000[60] – over half the province's population.

Indeed, what is striking about the accounts by Chabot and Lasorsa of the real-life Nordiques–Canadiens rivalry is their repeated association of that rivalry with *all of Quebec*. In their minds, "la rivalité la plus explosive de l'histoire du sport au Québec" (the most explosive rivalry in the history of sports in Quebec)[61] engaged the population as a whole, not just its hockey fans. As Jacques Demers asserts in his preface to Chabot's book: "Tout le Québec avait embrassé cette rivalité" (All of Quebec embraced this rivalry).[62] Chabot and Lasorsa use the same vocabulary to invoke its excitement: "La rivalité a fait vibrer le Québec entier" (The rivalry excited all of Quebec); "c'est tout le territoire québécois qui vibre" (it's the entire territory of Quebec that vibrates).[63] In any case, according to Lasorsa, "une grande majorité de Québécois sont des mordus inconditionnels de hockey" (a great majority of Quebecers are unconditional hockey lovers); "le hockey a toujours été plus qu'un jeu pour notre peuple" (hockey has always been more than a game for our people).[64] This rivalry was so successful because it seemed to represent Quebec itself in microcosm, allowing the political divisions between federalists and separatists to play out, sublimated in this rivalry. To borrow Jacques Demers's phrase, this was "saine et belle à voir" (healthy and beautiful to see).[65]

As suggested in chapter 2's discussion of *Les Nordiques sont disparus*, through their symbolic rivalry between the red and the blue, the colours of the Canadian and Quebec flags respectively, the Canadien and the Nordiques reflected political divisions within the province that had been established long before the issue of sovereignty. Red has traditionally been the colour of liberals, blue that of old-guard, largely Catholic conservatives – a colour appropriated, of course, by the Parti Québécois, whose support Marcel Aubut sought during the development of the Nordiques.[66] In *Lance et compte*, the metaphor even engaged the two coaches, "deux entraîneurs francophones qui se détestent sur la place publique" (two francophone coaches who hated each other in public), who reflected René Lévesque and Pierre Trudeau, according to Lasorsa.[67] At the management level, similar comparisons revealed the Canadiens' anglophone backing and leadership, in contrast to the Nordiques' all-francophone team of Marcel Aubut (president), Maurice Filion (general manager), and Michel Bergeron (head coach).[68] Indeed, Aubut exploited the language card to attract francophone fans from the entire province – and even from Montreal if they could appeal to radical sovereignists – deciding that all PA announcements in the Colisée would be solely in French.[69]

Paradoxically, the rivalry represented a "plaisir qui rassemble et divise à la fois" (pleasure that both unites and divides at once).[70] Lasorsa presents the match-ups, which became as frequent as eight per year, and which were often scheduled during peak viewing times like the Christmas holidays or Good Friday weekend, as "un miroir stéréotypé que la collectivité québécoise se donne d'elle-même" (a stereotyped mirror that the Quebec community gave itself).[71] Chabot asserts that, regardless of the actual ethno-linguistic make-up of the teams' players, for the Quebec people, it felt during these games as if "des gars d'ici se mesuraient à des gars d'ici" (guys from here tested themselves against guys from here).[72] At any rate, whether it meant physically travelling from one city to the other to root for one's team in person at the Forum or the Colisée, or gathering with friends and family to watch on television, or listening to or calling radio talk shows, or reading and writing in to the newspaper, this rivalry mobilized Quebecers to express themselves and their aspirations.[73] During a period of political division, the 1980s and the early 1990s, the rivalry between the Nordiques and the Canadiens, and that of their fictional avatars on *Lance et compte,* offered a safe forum to experience the excitement of a major sports rivalry, all the while feeling united as Québécois, linked by a common territory and a common love of the game. The significance became so much greater because it involved hockey, "un sport inventé chez nous" (a sport invented here).[74] Notwithstanding the actual history that identifies the development of sports in Quebec, and the invention of modern hockey in particular, with anglophone elites in Montreal,[75] Franco-Quebecers have invested this sport with intense national meaning. Just as paradoxical as a rivalry that unites precisely because it divides "us," the "chez nous" here refers to the province (which for Franco-Quebecers also represents a "nation") as well as to the nation of Canada. Once again, we come back to the truism that the hockey rink represents one element of Canadian culture where the two solitudes unite. And they often unite against a common international enemy.

Although now considered a national icon, *Lance et compte* largely avoids overt engagement with the political. Perhaps part of its popularity derived from the fact that it allowed viewers an escape from the province's charged political atmosphere, given that it first aired in the context of federal–provincial tensions over the failure of the Meech Lake and, later, the Charlottetown Accord. Eschewing the nationalist question of sovereignty, the season two story arc focuses on the World Cup of Hockey. In that season, a solid federalism is expressed as three players from the National are chosen to play on Team Canada. Their solidarity and national identity – at least as it is represented to the world outside – appear clearly as Pierre Lambert rallies the team: "On joue pour notre pays, pis ce pays-là s'appelle le Canada!" (We play for our country and that country's called Canada! *LCII*: 26). So while the series remains silent on the national rivalries within Canada and Quebec, the arena of hockey does offer a venue for the playing out of various international rivalries, both explicitly in amateur competitions and even implicitly in the National's NHL match-ups against American teams.

To placate Quebec hockey fans as well as those in the Anglo-Canadian market that the series initially hoped to reach, American teams take on the less than shining roles in *Lance et compte*. Season one includes Pierre's first airplane flight to Winnipeg as well as an exterior shot of Maple Leaf Gardens in Toronto, yet there is no suggestion whatsoever that an anglo–franco rivalry is being staged when the Maple Leafs play the National. Rather, the principal rivalry in *Lance et compte* is between the National and the Bruins and Flyers (featured respectively in *LCI* and *LCIII*), traditionally the NHL's "brawler" teams. The Bruins' bad-guy status appears when goon Jimmy Thompson motivates his team with the ethnic slur, "Who's gonna eat them frogs!" (*LCI*, ep. 13). Clearly, the National must lose occasionally – at the beginning of season three, for example, they are eliminated from the play-offs by the Flyers, for whom Denis Mercure plays – but their regular victories over American teams offer some proxy satisfaction to hockey fans in Quebec, who may resent US hegemony in the originally Canadian institution of the NHL.

Much more obvious statements about international politics, and about the linkage of national identity to hockey-playing styles, occur in the staging of the World Cup of Hockey. The ideological dynamics of the 1980s late Cold War appear clearly at season two's inception when negotiations over the World Cup's creation stall because of head butting between the NHL and the Soviet delegation (*LCII*, eps. 2–3). Yet neither the Soviets nor the Americans leave the table with a clean image as negotiations conclude and the championship begins. As might be expected, the Soviet-linked plot lines across the second season involve two defections (one failed, one successful), a beautiful Mata Hari, a corrupt party official, and the politically motivated detention of a Canadian hockey player. The Russian plot line also, of course, allows the series' creators to invoke the historic 1972 Summit Series victory in a locker room rally speech (*LCII*, ep. 12).

But neither do the American capitalists leave the series with a clean reputation. Admittedly the bi-national NHL (represented by both Canadians and Americans) slows negotiations for a World Cup series because of concerns about the temporary loss of players and scheduling issues related to the mounting of the Stanley Cup play-offs. But Team USA appears in almost as negative a light as Team USSR, as it falls prey to a different sort of ambition. However, instead of spy intrigues meant to ensure the collective victory of the Soviet system over the West, we are presented with oil baron Bill Simpson (Walter Massey), who uses his wealth to achieve personal goals that ultimately hurt his national team. Bill's son Gary (John St Denis) is a mediocre NHL player who would normally not have made the Team USA roster. Bill, however, has obtained compromising photos of US coach Tom Snyder (Mark McManus) involved in a homosexual relationship, and he uses these to garner his son a slot on the team (*LCII*, eps. 4 and 9). The negative impact of his actions quickly becomes obvious: Team USA is eliminated without a single win, a position reflecting perhaps both fantasy vengeance for Canadian viewers and the reality of the United States' declining hockey prowess; after the "Miracle on Ice" of the 1980 Gold Medal in men's ice hockey, the Americans placed seventh at the 1984 and 1988 Winter Olympics.

Both the Soviets and the Americans, then, allow sex, money, and ambition to spoil Canada's game. Team Canada is not without its own challenges (which are, of course, necessary for dramatic tension), but it remains focused on the game itself, as is Team Europe. The show aligns Canada and Europe against the USA and USSR, while allowing their rivalry between the former – which is complicated by the fact that Jacques Mercier coaches the Europeans – to engage the discourse of different styles of play, aligning those styles with different national identities and ideologies. Interestingly, though, the image of Canadian-style hockey becomes somewhat mobile in the way it engages the skills-versus-roughness hockey debate, reflective of Tim Edensor's assertion of the polysemic nature of popular culture icons appropriated as signifiers of national identity.[76]

Jacques Mercier has been hired to coach a team in Fribourg, Switzerland, a post he accepts in part for family reasons: Switzerland has world-class clinics where his paralysed son Jimmy (Andrew Bednarski) can learn to walk again, as well as professional opportunities for his wife Judy (Mary Lou Basaraba), an opera singer. (Season three later reveals that both of these goals have been accomplished.) Indeed, Frédérick Tanner (Vania Vilers), the Swiss team owner, has dangled the prospect of coaching Team Europe to sweeten the deal for Jacques (*LCII*, ep. 1). Across the season, it is made clear that without this Canadian coach, Team Europe would never have done as well as it did; in spite of their scepticism, for example, the Canadians admit of Mercier that "Il est capable de former une vraie équipe" (He's capable of building a real team; *LCII*, ep. 9). To engage French viewers and to fulfil the requirements for co-production with France's national television corporation, the series' writers created a young French player, Patrick Devon (Hugues Profy). Devon tries out for the National (*LCII*, ep. 2) and later becomes the first of his countrymen to play on Team Europe (*LCII*, ep. 6). He also represents Suzie Lambert's love interest. Intentionally or not, Profy's physical appearance and the way his character has been written weaken the French player. Throughout the plot line, he appears sickly. He is eventually diagnosed with leukemia and – perhaps to free Suzie from other emotional claims later in the series – dies tragically in a motorcycle accident (*LCII*, ep. 9). While his as yet undiagnosed illness can be blamed for his lacklustre performances on the ice, it is not surprising that the series fared relatively poorly in France and that, indeed, only Télévision Suisse-Romande stayed on to co-produce season three and the telefilms. The actor Profy's slender build already suggests that Devon can only be a skill player, while his whiny reactions to his illness – he first hides it in shame from Suzie, then refuses chemo, seemingly giving up rather than fighting the disease (*LCII*, ep. 8) – contrast with the strength of the French Canadian Lamberts, whose toughness – "Un Lambert, c'est pas tuable!" (You can't kill a Lambert; *LCI*, ep. 12) – represents a recurrent theme across the series.

Sports commentators often discuss how two systems of hockey training come face to face when the Russians match up with the North Americans (*LCII*, ep. 6). Similarly, debates about European "skills" versus Canadian "aggression"[77] develop in the arguments between Mercier and Tanner. In Fribourg, Tanner tells Mercier that the European Ice Hockey Federation has expressed concern over his coaching style (*LCII*, ep. 5) – a style that includes strategic media theatrics and open insults and challenges to Gilles Guilbeault in order to rattle Canada's coach and thereby his team. Mercier makes it clear to Tanner that he plays to win, doing whatever it takes – even to an opponent he considers a friend. If Europe does not want to win, he implies, go ahead and keep telling me how to do my job. National differences between Canada and Switzerland appear in this exchange between Tanner and Mercier:

> TANNER: On est en Suisse. Le hockey c'est un jeu, pas un métier. (In Switzerland, hockey's a sport, not a profession.)
> MERCIER: Et vous. À quoi vous jouez? (And you, what are you playing at?; *LCII*, ep. 5)

Mercier, then, takes hockey seriously, while for Tanner, a European, it is only a game; furthermore, there is a certain bad faith in Tanner's gamesmanship as opposed to the implied honesty of Mercier's cut-throat competitiveness. In these exchanges, Europe signifies as perhaps more civilized, but also – and precisely because of this – as less strong and even less masculine than Canada, represented here by Mercier.

Yet Guilbeault's leadership of Team Canada contradicts the message that Canadian hockey is rough hockey. Again and again, the general manager, who has returned to the bench after seven years' absence – a fact repeated by Mercier to underscore his arguments to the press that "La faiblesse de Team Canada, c'est Gilles Guilbeault" (Team Canada's weakness is Gilles Guilbeault; *LCII*, ep. 11) – signals the concept at the heart of his coaching style: "Discipline." In what is almost a running gag, Guilbeault's ineptness or discomfort as a coach appears in his need to write on the blackboard at the beginning of his locker room speeches (*LCII*, eps. 8–10). In the end – and somewhat with the implication that it helps the team – Guilbeault's heart troubles result in his replacement by Marc Gagnon during the final match-ups between the USSR and Canada, which are played in Quebec. While Guilbeault's characterization reveals that one part of Canadian hockey may be skills and discipline, *Lance et compte*'s producers allow the discourse of machismo to win the day, as Gagnon's coaching style resembles more closely that of Mercier. During the final series, Bob Martin and Pierre Lambert rally the players more effectively than did their now hospitalized coach.

In terms of the big picture, if we average the two different messages about hockey style and national identity, one of which we derive from the National's battles against the Bruins and the Flyers and the other from Team Canada's performance and those of the two Canadian coaches in the World Cup, we see a Quebec-inflected vision of Canadian hockey that proposes a balance of brawn and brains. The Bruins and the Flyers – the latter's Broad Street Bullies image, established in the 1970s, was still fresh in viewers' minds at the time – represent

American brawn, hockey based on violence rather than skill, and thus are demonized as goons. The National's players must demonstrate their readiness to face this violence and that they are unafraid to fight fire with fire. For example, in his debut for the National, Denis Mercure's hard body-check against the Flyers, even though it results in a quick penalty, gains approval from his friends watching on TV: "Comme ça il va se faire respecter, surtout contre Philadelphie" (That's how he'll get respect, especially against Philadelphia; *LCI*, ep. 7). But at the same time, *only* roughness is not enough; players must also have skills and, as Guilbeault calls it, "discipline"; he repeatedly exhorts them not to draw "des punitions caves" (stupid penalties; *LCII*, ep. 7). In the end, the series' federalist attitude appears clearly in Gilles's assertion that "Les Canadiens sont fiers de vous autres et vous êtes la fierté de votre pays" (Canadians are proud of you and you are the pride of your country; *LCII*, ep. 7). But Pierre Lambert, "le Chat" or "Tomcat" – the cat who combines grace and speed with toughness – ultimately represents the consummate French Canadian hockey player; significantly, the National's team goon, fan favourite Mac Templeton, hails from the United States, thus associating that role with south-of-the-border hockey.

Perhaps most important, *Lance et compte* has offered Québécois an image of themselves not as "French Canadian losers" but as modern-day winners.[78] In that regard, the series has engaged with many of the issues facing a Quebec in evolution. In the next section we explore how each of the series' iterations – the original broadcasts and telefilms of 1986–91 and the reprise series from 2002 to 2012 – grapples with social change. Significantly, both iterations gained popularity in periods of the Quebec Liberal Party's dominance in provincial politics and a general social acceptance of neoliberal, capitalist ideology. Perhaps for this reason, while we observe some differences in how the two series approach social issues such as racial diversity and women's rights, an overall comparison reveals, once again, that *plus ça change, plus c'est la même chose.*

Quebec Society in Evolution: *Lance et compte* and the Social Issues of the 1980s

As elsewhere in the Western world, social mores in Quebec continued an evolution that had begun in the 1960s and that largely undid the conservative trend in the immediate post–Second World War era. Sexual freedom increased, and attitudes about the family grew more flexible.

Notwithstanding an economic crisis in Quebec at the beginning of the decade, the province saw a general trend towards prosperity marked by a dramatic rise in average salaries between 1960 and 1985, coupled with a significant but less dramatic rise in the cost of living.[79] Brian Mulroney, Canada's Conservative prime minister from 1984 to 1993, largely followed the neoconservative social ideology coupled with the liberal, free trade economic platform of the Reagan–Thatcher era.[80] Mulroney's platform as prime minister of Canada, like that of Margaret Thatcher in Great Britain and Ronald Reagan in the United States, involved an approach to government influenced by private sector managerialism; for example, it included the privatization of Crown corporations and the "sweeping deregulation" of industry.[81] Robert Bourassa, Quebec's Liberal premier for a similar period (from 1985 to 1994),[82] embraced the same free trade philosophy, viewing it as the best approach to creating jobs and fostering economic prosperity.[83] Within the province, as elsewhere in North America, a consumer society with surplus time and income to pursue leisure activities took hold.[84] Other trends included the tentacular presence of the welfare state, improved access to education, secularization, and an increasingly pluralistic society.[85]

Lance et compte clearly reflects the 1980s ideology that individual success is to be found through the pursuit of personal wealth and the search for individual well-being via love and a fulfilling career. The sets used for shooting the series show material comfort, if not outright luxury, in the homes, offices, restaurants, and nightclubs the characters frequent. The series also points to that decade's heightened interest in fads as well as to the cult of the individual reflected in the fitness craze and New Age philosophies, among other trends. It also serves as a primer on 1980s wardrobes and hairstyles; indeed, the series is easy to date by these. Although men's styles have not changed that much in the past thirty years – particularly in terms of denims – the pleated khakis and polo shirts sported by Pierre Lambert and his friends in *Le Retour du chat* and Gilles Guilbeault's and Hugo Lambert's (Jean-Sébastien Lord) enormous spectacles date the series quite explicitly. The most unintended comic relief, however, relates to women's clothing: shoulder pads, bulky sweaters, and pleated skirts contrast strikingly with the half tops, revealing leotards, and leg warmers required by the decade's newfound obsession with aerobics and the Nautilus gym. Other 1980s trends appear in the New Age ideas of Pierre's French lover, Marilou (Sophie Renoir); these include self-renewal through isolation and wave tanks (*LCI*, ep. 2), and pseudo-skydiving over a huge fan. Similarly, the music at discotheques throughout the series, the use of punks as low-level villains (*LCI*, ep. 8), and the small-time delinquency of a biracial youth (*Retour*) are attempts to reflect contemporary trends. Contrasting to the period's perceived decadence is the religious renewal of the times, exemplified by a born-again Christian player, Paul Couture, nicknamed "Preach" (*LCI*, ep 4).

In addition to these relatively quotidian elements that mark each series as a reflection of the society its spectators experience on a daily basis, the series directly engages issues of personal and corporate finance. As already mentioned in relation to hockey itself, economic issues are central to the various narrative threads of each season. The men are concerned about contracts and salaries. The women in their lives also face financial challenges, which relate in part to the series' depiction of changing gender roles in Quebec. For example, Pierre's mother Maroussia Lambert (Macha Méril), an enterprising widow, founds a co-op that sells multicultural artisanal fashions and accessories, but eventually faces bankruptcy.

Women's evolving role in Quebec society is a prominent thread throughout the series; indeed, Héroux asserts that when director Richard Martin came on board for season two, he called for the writers to develop more "femmes de tête, des professionnelles, indépendantes" (brainy, independent, professional women).[86] In the 1970s, in tandem with the nationalist movement, the women of Quebec spoke out for their own rights to full agency in an active feminist movement, which drew on theory from both French and American activism.[87] First, we see the North American iteration of the French language as more accommodating in terms of reducing the linguistic prominence of the masculine – for example, in France certain professions, including writer (*écrivain, auteur*), doctor (*médecin*), and professor (*professeur*), have only masculine variants, while in Quebec one frequently hears *la prof* and women writers referred to as *écrivaine* and *auteure*.[88] Similarly, official documents and scholarly publications will use the inclusive expression "Québécois et Québécoises," stating the masculine *and* feminine explicitly, whereas in France simple use of the masculine as the universal still holds out. Next, the practice of women keeping their maiden names has been and continues to be much more widely spread than in the United States, for example; indeed, since 1981 upon marriage the procedure for a new bride to change her name to that of her husband is identical to that for any other name change.[89] In other areas, too, such as maternity and paternity leave, Quebec's women and men achieved many practical goals from the femininst movement that remain in practice today.[90] Diane Lamoureux cites a rare instance of political unity, in which a bilateral declaration that "equality between women and men is now an integral part of 'Quebec's values'."[91]

Nonetheless, bourgeois capitalist society in Europe and North America remained largely patriarchal in its ideology throughout the 1980s. This gender imbalance appears clearly in *Lance et compte;* in this regard, there is very little difference between the two series from the 1980s to the 2000s. Since I address this issue at length elsewhere,[92] I will merely summarize those findings. As is to be expected, *Lance et compte* consistently represents the hockey industry as an almost exclusively male domain; male players, coaches, and executives circulate in the public sphere of the mediated sports entertainment industry. Men run the show, with one notable exception: female sports journalist and sometime villain Linda Hébert (Sylvie Bourque; *LCI–III*; *Envers*). Several strong central female characters are portrayed in a positive light, however, in particular the women revolving around Pierre Lambert: his mother Maroussia, his sister Suzie, and his first wife Patricia (Isabelle Miquelon).

The series seems to reflect Western civilization's ongoing battle with a fading but still lingering patriarchal ideology in its ambivalence towards both strong female characters and traditional "stay-at-home" housewives and mothers. While the viewers are clearly meant to identify with strong-minded, professional women who also lead fulfilling personal lives, such as Maroussia, female villains also fall into the category of the *femme de tête* (lit. "woman of the head," that is, intelligent and perhaps even strong-willed). The greatest ambivalence, however, appears in representations of stay-at-home women: to my mind, Pierre's first girlfriend Ginette and Marc Gagnon's first wife Nicole are painted in far less sympathetic colours, and are, in essence, implicitly condemned for their weakness and dependence, both economic and emotional, on the male hockey players to whom they are attached. So while the series reflects a lingering trace of the madonna–whore dichotomy established by Western, Christian society, its most sympathetic female characters are well-rounded, not always perfect professional women and wives, mothers, sisters, and (in the series reprise) even daughters.

Quebec during the 1980s was also coming to grips with ethnic diversity. Canada has long been conceptualized as a country that has developed through the efforts of "two founding nations," the French and the English, groups often, however, at odds. But this image elides the First Nations groups that were already on the continent when the French and

English arrived; it also fails to acknowledge Canada's long-standing image of being more immigrant-friendly than the United States (among others).[93] Especially in the Montreal area in the early 1980s, Quebec began coming to terms with its growing cultural diversity. After the failure of the first sovereignty referendum, the Parti Québécois and the Quebec National Assembly recognized the need to develop a Quebec nationalism that was not based on the still predominant assumption that the province was ethnically, linguistically, and culturally homogeneous. White Papers like *Le Pays de tous les Québécois* acknowledged as much.[94]

Jean-Claude Lord's interest in immigrant issues was a direct reflection of this developing climate of inclusion. For example, he spurred the original series to develop a plot line in which Pierre Lambert falls in love with a black woman.[95] The series' executives hired Martinican actress France Zobda to play love interest Lucie Baptiste as part of their quota for French co-production status; however, they attributed to her a Haitian background to reflect the province's immigration demographics.[96] Although Baptiste's father is a taxi driver, the family's educational level, light skin, fluent, unaccented French, and probable immigration date of the 1960s all align the Baptiste family with the first wave of middle-class, professional Haitians who fled political oppression under the first Duvalier regime.[97] A beautiful and ambitious professional, the cultivated, blue-eyed Lucie nonetheless faces all of the racist attitudes then (and still) current in some sectors of North American society, and the film takes advantage of these for dramatic effect as it presents her relationship with Pierre, from the time of their meeting in the second half of season one to their break-up the following year. Throughout this arc of episodes, the series' writers deal with the race question with surprising frankness, portraying any racism levelled at Lucie and her family in a negative light. Racially charged incidents range in intensity from the unintended social blunder of a young man who has simply never interacted with people from a different ethnic background than his own to the viciously aggressive attitude of a hateful villain. Lucie is presented as one of the most mature, intelligent, cultivated, beautiful, and strong-willed women in the series. In this way, *Lance et compte* admirably tackles a sensitive issue, even while exploiting it.

The biracial couple's mutual attraction does *not*, however, appear natural to other members of both their circles. Lucie's brother expresses clear hostility to the white man's presence during a family gathering, but his so-called "reverse racism" appears mild compared to what

Pierre and Lucie will encounter later. First, though, the relationship must deepen. After attending a National game with Lucie (thanks to comp tickets from Pierre), her father invites Pierre to their home for Christmas Eve celebrations. Pierre, the gracious guest, presents M. Baptiste (Alex Nicolas-Étienne) with a National jersey and Mme Baptiste (Lucie Guannel) with … a bottle of Chanel No. 5. The reactions to this are quite awkward until Lucie breaks the ice by suggesting, "Maman, now you can smell just like … Catherine Deneuve." Later, as they are about to make love for the first time, Lucie frankly invokes their racial difference as a possible reason why he is hesitant to touch and kiss her (*LC1*, ep. 9). While films staging interracial relationships such as *Guess Who's Coming to Dinner?* (1967, USA) and *Le Chat dans le sac* (1964, Quebec) had reached the big screen in the 1960s, and the 1970s had liberalized such interactions, on television these were much less frequent, in spite of the early popularity of *I Love Lucy* (1951–7), which placed an interracial couple at centre stage. Erica Chito Childs, in a survey of American television, observes that such relationships have long been treated with comedy and most often have involved a white man married to a black woman, as in *The Jeffersons'* Tom and Helen Willis, or have been shrouded with deviance (adultery, crime, prostitution), brief and fleeting, or simply placed at the margins of central plot lines.[98] By placing this interracial relationship at the centre of dramatic intrigue across two seasons (*LCI* and *LCII*), the Quebec series came across as relatively progressive in the face of Chito Childs's observation that even in very recent American television, "this relative invisibility and hesitancy to delve into interracial relationships for any more than a few episodes can be read as part of the representations of interracial couples as deviant or outside the norm, thereby rendering it unshowable."[99]

In contrast to Pierre's minor blunders, the result of his youth, inexperience, and provincialism rather than actual malevolent racist ill will, we see the more negative attitudes of several players on the National, including the highly popular and usually sympathetic faux-anglo goon, Mac Templeton. Indeed, writer Réjean Tremblay at first rejected the idea of having Pierre fall in love with a black woman because of his own perception, as an experienced sports journalist, that racism was endemic in the real-life NHL.[100] He felt that the storyline would simply be implausible; while the open racism expressed in several scenes may shock viewers today, this was apparently the reality in major league hockey. The most notorious racist in *Lance et compte*, however, is the anglophone player Steve Bradshaw (David Nerman), who pulls out the "n word" at a party held at team captain Bob Martin's home and physically assaults Lucie. Furthermore, several characters, including Jacques Mercier, refer to Lucie as "la Négresse de Lambert" (*LCI*, ep. 11). There is some difficulty in translating this term. While Bradshaw's use of "nigger" was a clear and straightforward attempt to harm and degrade, the French term "nègre" is somewhat more ambivalent: it can be translated as either *nigger* or *Negro,* and during a certain period, the latter was a positive term of self-affirmation in English. The major French dictionary, *Le Petit Robert*, provides a definition of the term that elides its derogatory nature; at the same time, its obvious intent to wound and insult appears clearly in expressions like "parler un français petit nègre" (to speak a little nigger French), a derogatory aspersion implying that an individual speaks a heavily accented or ungrammatical French ostensibly like an African subject in the former colonies.

This sympathetic treatment of the difficulties faced by visible minorities in a region that was until very recently ethnically homogeneous, coupled with the implied condemnation of the racism they encounter, contrasts strikingly with the first series' treatment of its Jewish-coded villain, team owner Allan Goldman (August Schellenberg, *LCI*). Jacques Mercier's hatred of management interference in coaching decisions inspires his diatribe to Gilles Guilbeault: "I don't tell him how to practice his religion, so he better not tell me how to run the team." He then closes with a request: "Dis ça en Yiddish à Goldman de ma part" (Tell that to Goldman in Yiddish for me; *LCI*, ep.3). Examples of Goldman's stereotypical cheapness include his refusal to approve a charter flight when a road trip to the West involves several early rises on game days in a row after long flights (*LCI*, ep. 11) and his exploitation of players with major league talent to make profits in the minors (*LCI*, eps. 9–10).

Double Takes: *Lance et compte* in the New Millennium

The French aphorism *plus ça change, plus c'est la même chose* (the more it changes, the more it stays the same) invoked in the title to this chapter refers to more than just the manner in which *Lance et compte* handles social issues in a similar fashion both in the 1980s and in the first decade of the 2000s. It also references explicit situations in which the reprise mimics its original, invoking the postmodern aesthetic of self-referentiality and a sense of *déjà vu*. The social and political climate of *Lance et compte*'s series reprise – and even of a big-screen film released in 2011 – surprisingly resembles that of its earlier iteration. Neatly spanning the provincial premiership of another Liberal, Jean Charest, whose mandate lasted from 2003 to 2012, the five series produced during this period eerily resemble those from the 1980s. Featuring nearly all the original cast members, although they wear a few more wrinkles, *La Nouvelle Génération* (2002) also introduced – as its title suggests – a younger group of stars, including the now adult children of Pierre Lambert and Marc Gagnon. It reflects the neoliberal ideology of the province's premier, an ideology nonetheless under attack during the student demonstrations and strikes of the spring of 2012, known as the Printemps Québécois, which may have marginally contributed to the Liberals' defeat and the election of Quebec's first female premier, Pauline Marois, and the return of the Parti Québécois to power for the first time in a decade.

Most striking of all in the various iterations of the series reprise is that its culture of wealth is specifically suburban. Unlike many big-screen films, and even the recent television series *Mirador* (2010), about a public relations firm, in which wealthy characters tend to live in downtown Montreal penthouses, members of the hockey community live in enormous mansions in American-style suburban subdivisions, often well outside the city centre. This derives partly, of course, from the fact that the team operates out of Quebec City rather than Montreal, and that some players have chosen to live closer to extended families in the province's rural outreaches. Nonetheless the opulent homes of some of the wealthiest members of Quebec society clearly reflect a capitalist ideology of consumption beyond the necessary. While some are family homes, housing couples and children who would need somewhat more space, many of these dwellings house single individuals – for example, there is the palatial home of the unmarried Mathias Ladouceur and that of Valérie Nantel (Julie du Page), a math professor who supplements her income as a high-stakes poker player.

As in the original series, in the more recent reprise writers exploit cultural trends such as the growth of the casino industry and the popularity of poker (*LCRec*, ep. 5), couples openly living together and having children outside wedlock (Dany Bouchard [Patrick Hivon] and Annie [Véronique Bannon] in *LCRec*), the struggles to recover from alcoholism (Gilles Guilbault [Michel Forget] across *LCRec* through to *LCGD*), drug use (Valérie Nantel in *LCRec*, ep. 1), Internet dating and dating for fifty-somethings (Bob Martin [Robert Marien] in *LCRec*, ep. 3), and so on. The original series occasionally framed plot elements through media reports, self-referentially showing newspaper copy about the players[101] and entering the action of the game through the television screens of viewers at home; in this vein, the reprise demonstrates the increased mediatization of daily life in the new millennium. The popularity of talk radio and cable television is featured in several episodes of *Le Grand Duel,* which opens with print journalist Lucien Boivin (Denis Bouchard) debating an obnoxious, sensationalist television broadcaster, William Jasmin (Michel Charette). Jasmin's first name reveals a new trend in the province – the increasing popularity of several traditionally anglophone first names among young francophone couples.[102]

Although the everyday dramas of adultery, alcoholism, children's accidents, and spouse's illnesses imply that wealth does not necessarily buy happiness, the series rarely makes an explicit connection between wealth and misery. One of the few such instances appears in *Le Grand Duel,* when Francis Gagnon's wife develops a compulsive shopping problem – her credit cards are maxxed out at $125,000 for Chanel handbags and a fur coat – that culminates in her arrest for shoplifting. This situation is not offered as symptomatic of a flawed society that valorizes overconsumption of elite, brand-name products; rather, it attributes Isabelle's actions to postpartum depression, the "baby blues," as Pierre calls it in English. This relatively unsympathetic portrayal of Isabelle, the stay-at-home hockey wife, mirrors that found in the earlier series' depictions of Ginette and Nicole Gagnon. Similarly, Bouchard's pregnant partner Annie appears as clingy and uninteresting. One almost understands his temptation to spend time with bad girl Valérie Nantel (*LCRec–LCGD*).

Nantel is one of the most shockingly brilliant female villains on television – she goads the young star Bouchard to play Russian roulette, and he loses. But she is not the only female nemesis in the series. Other standouts include Linda Hébert's replacement, journalist Nathalie Renaud (Catherine Florent; *LCNG–LCGD*) and the "escorte" Sabine, who pumps Jérôme Labrie for inside information (*LCGD*). Negative portrayals of strong-willed women may support arguments that a backlash against feminism has resulted in women's renewed entrenchment in traditional gender roles.[103] In society today, domestic abuse is no longer viewed as acceptable, a boss cannot ogle his female employees' breasts with impunity, and rape cannot be blamed on the victim, although defence lawyers will try to do so; yet, notwithstanding these considerable gains in terms of acceptable attitudes and behaviour towards women, issues like these remain vital social problems. Furthermore, in the public arenas of government and employment, while women's access to leadership roles in Quebec has increased, the glass ceiling remains a reality. In 2005–6, for example, only one-third of the province's Members of the National Assembly and only one-quarter of Quebec's members of the federal Parliament were women.[104] In Canada, Quebec, and the United States, corporate leaders are overwhelmingly men.[105]

In both the original series and its reprise, the hockey world is largely a male domain. However, in *La Nouvelle Génération*, the National hires a female trainer, Cathou St-Laurent (Hélène Florent). Perhaps following in Maroussia's footsteps, mothers also appear as hockey supporters. For example, in *Lance et compte: La Reconquête*, Guy Lambert is billeted with a family while he tries out for the Chicoutimi junior team; as it turns out, the mother in the family loves hockey, while the father prefers to read a book. Similarly, a running gag targets a rookie National, Michel Chantelois (Maxim Gaudette), whose mom was his hockey coach. That Quebec society continues to grapple with such issues appears in the fact that other players repeatedly tell him to quit talking about his mom since that is not macho for a hockey player.

Furthermore, Quebec's struggle to accommodate difference continues, particularly in the wake of PQ leader Jacques Parizeau's stunning comment that the Yes side in the 1995 referendum had been defeated by "le vote ethnique."[106] Throughout the 1990s, various intellectuals discussed how nationalism could accommodate diversity; one approach they articulated was a home-grown version of multiculturalism, which they referred to as "transculturalism."[107] In February 2007 the province established an official commission, the Consultation Commission on Accommodation Practices Related to Cultural Differences (CCAPRCD), chaired by two prominent public intellectuals, Gérard Bouchard and Charles Taylor, who were tasked with investigating multiculturalism and recommending policies about "reasonable accommodation" for difference.[108] Yet, as seen in our discussion of Alex Beauchesne, the token Haitian-Canadian player, the series reprise seems less comfortable with racial issues than its earlier iteration. For example, when Lucie Baptiste returns to the cast for a short-lived clandestine affair with a widowed and remarried Pierre in *Le Grand Duel*, their relationship is clearly denormalized, following the less progressive patterns in television portrayals of interracial couples outlined by Erica Chito Childs (see above).

The *Lance et compte* franchise (for more on this concept, see the next chapter, about another hockey-themed franchise, *Les Boys*) draws upon viewer familiarity with certain characters, their catch phrases and stock gags, to maintain loyalty and interest. These self-referential games become sophisticated memory games as specific situations and characters' comments refer back to other episodes or iterations of the series. The immediacy allowed by sequential viewing on DVD renders these all the more evident. I offer a few examples of this phenomenon here.

In *LCI*, rookie Pierre Lambert is pulled over for speeding on his way to the Colisée. When the officer learns that he is ticketing a National player, he expresses his admiration and lets him off with a warning. In both *La Reconquête* and *Le Grand Duel*, different players face similar situations with the opposite outcome. In the former, Danny Bouchard is late because he has spent the night with the literal *femme fatale*, Valérie Nantel;[109] he draws a female cop, who it turns out hates hockey, and when he tries to explain that he doesn't want his wife to find out about his tardiness, she expresses contempt for hockey players who fool around, leaving the wife at home to take care of the kids. Viewers' reaction to this scene is mixed. At this point in the series, Bouchard has begun to lose their sympathy, more, perhaps for his self-destructive fascination with Valérie and his weakness in the face of her manipulation of him than for his (equally weak and selfish) treatment of his wife. Yet we still find the female cop – who supposedly represents fair and equal justice in her refusal to give a rich and famous guy special privileges – somehow humourless and antipathetic.

In the series' penultimate instalment (*LCGD*), writers continue to riff on this motif, with the running gag of Mike Ludano being pulled over by a female cop, who at first also is portrayed as a humourless feminist. Our suspicions are aroused, however, when she contacts another female officer about the stop and later makes sexual advances on Mike, following him into his home after stopping him for the third time (*LCGD*, ep. 4). The writers successfully suggest that Mike is somehow being set up, perhaps for blackmail; we suspect some bizarre manipulation on the part of these two female cops, who will abuse the public trust and the power of their office to harm the popular team captain in some twisted act of feminist vengeance. Eventually this potentially sinister plot line turns humourous and then, frankly, absurd if not offensive in its mundanity. The blond, more audacious officer reveals that she has set up the situation so that her partner, a more subdued (and traditionally feminine) brunette who has a crush on Mike, can meet the player. This occurs, however, as she stages a ménage-à-trois situation – Franco-Quebecers seem to be obsessed with the *trip à trois*, which pops up in all sorts of bizarre cultural contexts. Indeed, the three lovers function well, for a while, which offers various opportunities for comic relief: other players express concerns about Mike's "legs" on the ice (drawing upon the misogynist myth that sex before battle weakens a man), and Mike offers his own interpretation of such suspicions as he plays well. Trouble starts when Mike begins to fall in love with the brunette, and she with him. The series is at its most unrealistic and fantastical while this conflict is being established and resolved. In the end, Mike gets *one* girl (because that's only normal, right?), while the more aggressive and thereby masculinized woman is excluded. By the end of the season, however, she has overcome her disappointment at this rejection and has become a sidekick to the appropriately constituted heterosexual couple.

Another double take involves a stereotypical crazy fan, of which every team has one (or many). In the show's first season, crowd scenes in the Colisée spotlight a middle-aged National fan wearing a silly hat with the team logo, a fishing vest with various team-related paraphernalia, and so on. This fan remains relatively benign, although he does verbally attack Linda Hébert (*LCI*, ep. 4). The decades between *Lance et compte*'s two iterations saw media coverage of more sinister fan activities, as well as the 1996 film, *The Fan* (dir. Tony Scott); thus we see the somewhat parodic character of "Superfan" introduced in *Le Grand Duel*. A hotel desk clerk by day, he attends numerous National games, but as a villain he roots, of course, for the Canadiens; his fanaticism – let's not forget the etymology of "fan" – includes attempting to wreck Marc Gagnon's marriage and eventually leads him to attack the beloved journalist, Lucien Bouivin, nicknamed Lulu, by throwing gasoline on him and lighting it. The depths to which the series sinks by its end appears, as with the Mike Ludano threesome situation, in the attempt to turn this horrible incident to comic effect, offensively so, by trivializing Lulu's injuries.

This insensitive treatment of a form of attack (soaking with gasoline, followed by immolation) associated with both the War on Terror and the "punishment" of women in fundamentalist Islamic nations reveals that the series and its producers have fallen out of touch with the contemporary world. Similarly, the feature film – which I saw before any of the television episodes – fails to stand up on its own; it rides largely on a pre-programmed audience that has remained loyal to the franchise's earlier iterations. These examples further support the main argument of this chapter – because they have reinscribed the same images and values as the 1980s series, the instalments produced since the year 2000 offer viewers simply more of the same. Their representation of Quebec society fails to signal significant social change in Quebec over the past thirty years, a failure attributable to a number of factors. On the one hand, although Héroux officially stepped down as producer in favour of his daughter, Caroline, the series itself maintained most of its cast and creative team. This decision offered viewers a clear sense of continuity, but it also robbed the reprise of the vital engagement with the contemporary world that we find in the original. Yet it might also be argued that Quebec itself has changed less in the past thirty years than in the previous thirty. In any case, the series maintains its popularity, and yet another season has been announced for 2014.

Chapter Four

Real Men Play Hockey: Sport, Masculinity, and National Identity in the *Les Boys* Films

If we win, they're going to say we don't have class; if we lose, they'll say we don't have balls.

Fern, *Les Boys II*

It's not like a dream that's become a reality, It's more like a nation that's become a reality.

Yvan Cournoyer, *Canada Russia '72*

In *Slap Shot* (1977), the mother of all hockey films, Québécois actor Yvan Ponton plays the secondary role of Jean-Guy Drouin, one of two token French Canadians on the Charlestown Chiefs' roster.[1] A decade later he portrayed the "castrating NHL coach,"[2] Jacques Mercier in *Lance et compte*; twenty years later, the actor found himself once again on the ice in front of the camera, as Jean-Charles in *Les Boys* (1997). This time he is a key role player in the film's eponymous "garage league" hockey team managed by bar owner Stan. Like the earlier American film, the Quebec film centre stages all of the stereotypical images of hockey and its players: they drink, they swear, they play pranks, and they hack away at one another on the ice. Most importantly for this chapter, they also talk about and interact with women, repeatedly projecting a macho image of themselves through their – real or imagined – encounters with the opposite sex. At the same time, in this all-male milieu where body contact and locker room nudity play central roles, the spectre of homosexuality must constantly be conjured away through gay bashing and displays of what R.W. Connell has termed "hegemonic masculinity."[3]

Slap Shot is as much, or more, about the changing sexual attitudes and mores (as well as the depressing economic realities) of North America in the 1970s as it is about hockey and those who play it. The objectification of women, titillation about female homosexuality, and anxiety about the increasing visibility of male homosexuality are all at the centre of that film's social discourse. *Les Boys* addresses similar issues about masculinity and male sexuality, but released two decades later, the Québécois film must offer, at least on the surface, a more progressive image of the integration of gay men into all aspects of contemporary society, including the locker room and hockey rink. Furthermore, as a text generated at the end of a decade of intense debates about sovereignty and provincial/federal relations, the *Les Boys* films and television series inevitably comment on national identity, whether that is viewed as Québécois or as French Canadian.

What happens to images of masculinity when Yvan Ponton's character Jean-Charles, the team's hero, happens to be gay? And how do such apparently compromised images of traditional hetero-masculinity then impact hockey's meaning within the construction of Québécois national identity, as discussed in chapter 1? This chapter examines these questions, teasing out the intricate relationships between hockey, masculinity, and Québec national identity in the immensely popular *Les Boys* film and television franchise in two sections with several subdivisions. After a brief discussion of the concept of the media franchise, the first section interrogates how the franchise stages questions of gender. I discuss how *Les Boys* become men, reading the franchise as a sort of Bildungsroman; then I examine how the films deal with homosexuality in a heteronormative sport/world; finally, I look at the corollary nexus of women and hockey. A second section addresses how the *Les Boys* franchise uses hockey in its constructions of Québécois and Canadian national identities. I conclude the chapter with a discussion of how the film offers a partial vision of a specifically Québécois masculinity that contests the North American norm, which overvalues hegemonic masculinity. A brief coda analyses an additional television episode of the series *Mirador* (2010), which stages the case of a professional hockey coach in a gay sex scandal.

In her 2001 essay "The Nation and the Nude: Colonial Masculinity and the Spectacle of the Male Body in Recent Canadian Cinema(s)," Lee Parpart skilfully articulates how representations of masculinity in film may reflect differences in subject position and national identity. Aligning Canadian cinema with other "nondominant" – that is, non-Hollywood – cinemas, she observes in Canadian film of the 1990s a willingness to depict male nudity, which she sees as oppositional and postcolonial in nature. Parpart invokes the concept of "colonial masculinity," which, she asserts, "has been part of the discourse of nationhood in Canada for many years," and she reads "examples of non-normative treatment of male nudity" in recent Canadian cinema as reflective of "the experience of colonial masculinity, and a willingness to reveal the nude male body in contexts that either tend to interrogate phallic power or express anxiety about its loss."[4] For the analysis that follows, Parpart's work establishes the connection that I wish to make between conceptions of national identity and representations of masculinity in film in the Canadian context; it also provides me with a basic assumption:

> Many English Canadians and Quebeckers (white and nonwhite) do experience themselves as colonized on some level, either in relation to central Canada, Britain, France, the United States, or all of the above, and that this subject position works its way, forcefully at times, into discourses on masculinity as well as representations of the male body. What interests me here is how we can begin to understand the various manifestations of colonial experience in Canada as inflected by conditions of socioeconomic heterogeneity, and how both factors might be helping to lay the foundation for a range of approaches to male sexual representation in Canadian movies.[5]

The films I have chosen to interrogate here reveal themselves as particularly apt subjects for an examination of a specifically Canadian approach to masculinity, for they foreground that purportedly definitive marker of Canadian national culture: the sport of hockey. The following analysis differs, however, from Parpart's federalist approach in two distinct ways. First, I take a more nationalist approach, examining my corpus of films largely for markers of a specifically Québécois masculinity. Second, in contrast to Parpart's corpus of Canadian, Québécois, and Acadian art films, I examine the most successful film franchise ever produced in Quebec, one whose success has in some sense launched the spate of popular, near-Hollywood-style films produced in the province since 2000.

The *Les Boys* Franchise[6]

Louis Saïa's blockbuster hockey comedy *Les Boys* (1997) was followed by three sequels (1998, 2001, 2005) and a television series (2007–10). Their success led to their individual release on DVD, as well as a boxed set, soundtrack CDs, and other merchandise, most notably hockey jerseys with the fictional team's logo. Its popularity rivalled only by that of another hockey-themed visual fiction, the immensely popular *Lance et compte* (1985–2010; see chapter 3), *Les Boys* has achieved the coveted – from a commercial standpoint, in any case – status of the film franchise. From a critical standpoint, however, such a status may often be less desirable; as Shilo T. McClean points out, "franchises often are sparked by an excellent originating premise that deserves further development but winds up being milked of its originality and promise over the course of the franchise's exploitation."[7]

While we might agree that a definite decline in artistic quality and originality does occur across the *Les Boys* franchise from the first film to the television series, such popular success is highly significant here, indicative of hockey's power to draw audiences in Quebec. In addition, while there were certainly precursors,[8] *Les Boys* played a key role in initiating a growing trend in Quebec cinema to produce, in addition to the independent art films typified by the work of Denys Arcand and Denis Villeneuve,[9] successful popular genre films, most particularly comedies, but also dramas and thrillers.[10] After *Les Boys*, a number of other hockey-themed films premiered, including the documentary *Junior* (2007), *Pour toujours les Canadiens* (2009) – a homage fiction that has little to do with the actual Montreal Canadiens other than the cameo appearance of Jean Béliveau – and *Lance et compte: Le film* (2010). Of these, Érik Canuel's action/comedy/mismatched-buddy film *Bon Cop, Bad Cop* (2006), discussed in the introduction to this book, represents the greatest success both financially and artistically, breaking box office records across Canada.[11]

In addition to referencing the earlier *Lance et compte* television series, in which the National's players chanted "Boys, Boys, Boys," as a rallying cry, Saïa's franchise reveals its engagement with notions of masculinity and with notions of *québécité* (Quebec-ness) in its very title. *Les Boys* codes itself both as French, with the article "les," and as North American, with the *québécisme* "Boys"; significantly, I refer to this appropriation of an English word into French Canadian popular discourse as a *québécisme* and not as an anglicism. Paradoxically, *Les Boys* is a group of men, but as we shall see, these men *are* boys, who form a sports team that may be read as a microcosm of the nation. At the same time, the sports team itself becomes a venue for constructing and reflecting on masculine identity(s), as sport sociologists like Varda Burstyn, Michael Messner, Brian Pronger, David Whitson, and others have asserted.[12] Finally, they do not play just any sport, they play Canada's game, the national sport of hockey.

Real Men Play Hockey

Boyz 2 Men: Les Boys *as Bildungsroman*

The original *Les Boys* directly and immediately establishes its dialogue with representations of male (hetero)sexuality as the opening credits play to the sounds of a song (in English), "I Got a Crush on You," and a tracking shot that follows the curvaceous waitress, Sonia's (Maxim Roy) rear-end through the bar (established from an initial exterior) and into the owner's office. It then depicts a confrontation between good and evil, framed within a discourse of masculinity as being tough, clearly in keeping with the film's hockey theme. The hero, a bar owner and amateur hockey coach named Stan (Rémy Girard), and the villain, gangster Méo (Pierre Lebeau), face off in a game of poker. In this sequence, Méo refers to his "réputation" as a tough guy and his need to maintain a macho image; he asserts that if Stan refuses to pay his gambling debt, "je vas être obligé de te casser les jambes" (I'll be obliged to break your legs; 4:55–57). However, this symbolic castration will be carried out not by Méo himself, but by his younger henchman. Clearly, these middle-aged men suffer from a certain crisis in virility, and both will need the proxy of younger men in order to perform.

The central conflict of the film is established: to fulfil his obligations, Stan bets his bar that his "ligue de garage" hockey team, Les Boys, will beat Méo's. This rivalry of elders to be decided on the symbolic battlefield of the rink allows for the film's universe to be read as a microcosmic allegory of the nation, with Stan and Méo as middle-aged heads of state and the younger men as the armed forces they will send out to settle their differences. Drawing upon the clichéd metaphor of the hockey rink as a battlefield,[13] the film underscores the nearly exclusively male nature of sport as war; for instance, Léopold explicitly states between periods: "Moi, je retourne à la guerre" (I'm going back to war; 1:21–28). While women characters are not entirely absent from the film, they are clearly secondary, ancillary figures: girlfriends (Karine), wives (Brigitte and Lisette), and servants (Sonia the barmaid).

The scenes that follow introduce the viewer to the team's players, and we quickly see that indeed, most of these men are still boys – that is, they have not reached a level of maturity that one would associate with an adult male. The diminutive used in the name of Patrick Huard's character Ti-Guy speaks for itself, "ti" being an abridgement of "petit" (little), analogous to "Junior" in English. In the case of the relatively older players, who ostensibly should represent adult responsibility, hockey reinforces the illusion that they have stayed in touch with their youth, offering the fantasy of lingering boyhood.[14] The discourse of comedy allows for exaggerated situations revealing that hockey is more important than professional or familial responsibilities; for example, the barrister Jean-Charles (Yvan Ponton) accepts a plea bargain for his client so that he can leave for the game. Similarly, the surgeon François (Serge Thériault) appears distracted throughout a surgery and actually relieved when the patient dies on the table so that he can make it to the rink on time for that night's match. This lack of responsibility as adult males suggests that, at least initially, *Les Boys*'s masculinity may fall short of the expectations placed on them by the dominant society, for which "being a man" means meeting social and economic responsibilities in addition to any sexual or competitive activities. This French Canadian popular culture text, then, in some ways reflects images of hockey also found in American and Anglo-Canadian hockey discourses – hockey as war, hockey as nostalgia for childhood – while at the same time breaking with the dominant image of the hockey rink as a locus where men – often specifically Canadian men – are allowed, expected, and even pressured to express a hegemonic form of masculinity.[15]

Of the various terms proffered by gender theorists to describe the dominant type of masculinity privileged in Western (and many other) civilizations today and throughout history, I prefer that of Robert W. Connell, "hegemonic masculinity," for its suggestion of an encroaching aggression that seeks power and control over others.[16] Nick Trujillo offers a compact synthesis of the concept, citing Connell and others:

> *Hegemonic masculinity* is "the culturally idealized form of masculine character" ([Connell 1990] 83) which emphasizes "the connecting of masculinity to toughness and competitiveness" as well as "the subordination of women" and "the marginalization of gay men" ([Connell 1990] 94). [...] Media critics and scholars of gender ideology have described at least five features of hegemonic masculinity in American culture: (1) physical force and control, (2) occupational achievement, (3) familial patriarchy, (4) frontiersmanship, and (5) heterosexuality (see Brod 1987; Connell 1990; Jeffords 1989; Yaufman 1987; Kimmel 1987a).[17]

As we will see, *Les Boys* initially (indeed, throughout the series) seem to be lacking in all of these areas. They are often bullied on the ice by bigger and tougher teams. Although some appear superficially successful, exercising liberal professions (Jean-Charles and François) and practising entrepreneurial capitalism (Stan, followed by his son Léopold, Bob, and Ti-Guy), several work in subordinate positions of marginal authority (Boisvert and Marcel), while the employment status of others is unclear (Fern and Julien). They have failed as fathers (Stan) or have not yet accessed that status in their lives. *Les Boys* being a completely urban narrative, the question of frontiersmanship seems absent and perhaps inapplicable, although the myth of the frontier has its own particular Québécois iteration in the figures of the *voyageur*, the *coureur de bois,* and the *défricheur* (fur trapper/trader, woodsman and settler-farmer). Finally, their sexual prowess appears limited or undermined, and one of the leader figures is gay.

Even the introductory scenes featuring the two players who are generally associated with male sexual potency and attractiveness, and thus, the most masculine by the standards of a heteronormative society, establish that for these men hockey is more important than sex. First, Bob (Marc Messier; not to be confused with former NHL star Mark Messier), quickly characterized as a Don Juan, blows off a blow job so that he can get to the game. Then, the handsome young husband and garage owner, Mario (Patrick Labbé), rushes out on his amazed wife, who wants to celebrate their first anniversary in sexy lingerie. He hollers over his shoulder: "On va faire ça après la game à soir, okay?! [...] Maintenant tu vas fêter toute seule la première fois que je te dis non, okay?" (We'll do it tonight after the game! Now you can celebrate all by yourself the first time I say no to you! 15:00–01; 16:25–28). Later in the film, the waitress Sonia tries to seduce Mario; once again, hockey is more important to him than sex, as their following exchange, which reinforces the sex/hockey simile, demonstrates:

SONIA: L'amour, c'est comme le hockey, c'est un jeu d'équipe, tu veux dire ? [Love is like hockey, it's a team sport, you mean?]
MARIO: C'est la première fois, là. [It's the first time.]
SONIA: Que tu trompes ta femme. [That you cheat on your wife?]
MARIO: Non, non; que je manque une game de hockey. [That I miss a hockey game. 1:14:27–36]

In a later scene in a strip club, the stereotypically crazy goalie, Fern (Paul Houde), recites historical hockey statistics instead of enjoying a lap dance. Scenes like these, in which various members of *Les Boys*, but mostly the married ones – Mario and Fern – eschew sex in favour of hockey, recur throughout the film franchise and into the television series, becoming a running gag. This reinforcement through repetition of the notion that these men find hockey more exciting than sex infantilizes them, situating them at a pre-pubescent stage of development prior to when "boys" develop an interest in "girls." The notion that they would rather play with *Les Boys* than with their girls sheds light on the homosocial aspects of sport, discussed below.

Bob and Mario are attractive to women, and their virility does not seem to be explicitly questioned; rather, it is their prioritization of hockey over sex that reinforces their status as *Les Boys* rather than *Les Hommes*: as immature but not inadequate in terms of their masculinity. Other characters, however, present clearly problematic relationships both to women and to their own virility. Already Stan has been threatened with symbolic castration by Méo and the wager; placing his bar in jeopardy if his team loses is clearly an act of bravado, a misplaced attempt to portray himself as still "a man." His status as a post-sexually active father figure appears through his relationships to both his son Léopold (Michel Charette) and his employee Sonia.[18] When she offers Stan comfort as he is reeling from the enormity of what he has just done, she tells him she loves him "like a father"; needless to say, he was hoping her warm embrace meant something else. Stan does find a lover (in France) in *Les Boys II*, but *Les Boys III* undoes this image of a sexually mature and fulfilled man, thus positing his return to a state of sexual inadequacy by implying that he returned home because Violette broke up with him.

Similarly, the policeman Boisvert (Dominic Philie) sports a Freddie Mercury moustache, looks like the cop in the Village People, and is a hen-pecked, divorced husband with a woman's first name, Carole. He overcompensates for a masculinity that has been impaired by his ex-wife's dominance by making inappropriate and unwanted advances – basically a form of sexual harassment – to women he meets outside the home. On a lunch break at a burger drive-in, he heckles a female diner, who retorts that 'j'aime pas les saucisses à cocktail' (I don't like cocktail wieners; 19:12), undercutting his sexual adequacy by casting aspersion on the size of his penis. The cross-eyed Marcel (Luc Guérin) is not even a real cop: he's a metre reader for the city of Montreal and is depicted as such a nerd with his slicked-down, centre-parted hair that he doesn't dare to even approach a woman; he is thus desexualized altogether and feminized by his profession.

Each character's introductory sequence focuses on some aspect of his masculinity or sexuality to establish his inadequacy as an adult male in a heteronormative, patriarchal, capitalist society; nevertheless, by the end of the film each character has grown and matured in a manner appropriate to his situation – some more than others. We can thus read the *Les Boys* franchise as a sort of Bildungsroman, a fictional genre first described by German critics in the nineteenth century. Its goal is "to portray the hero's *Bildung* (formation) in all its steps and final goal as well as to foster the *Bildung* of the readers."[19] The genre of sports fiction often reflects a Bildungsroman-type narrative progression, as Jane M. Stangl asserts: "The hero born of the sport fiction genre offers readers an insightful rendering of the making of American males; a boys-to-men developmental process."[20] In spite of their chronological ages, *Les Boys* are depicted as just that, boys; and as with other sports fictions, the franchise's various instalments allow each of them a certain amount of development. The element of Bildungsroman becomes even more overt in the sequel films, which place greater focus on the father–son relationship of Stan and Léopold, with the latter first showing his increased maturity and independence by making a vital contribution to the team in the hockey rink. Later, the beginning of *Les Boys III* portrays Léopold as financially competent, as successfully running Stan's place during his father's absence in France. His transformation from the cowering, overweight, overgrown teenager at the beginning of *Les Boys* is complete; now his confident demeanour appears in his bleached hair and loud T-shirt; he rocks out in his green VW Beetle, racing along the highway to pick up his father at the airport. The serial nature of each instalment requires some backsliding, so that by the end of the return trip to Montreal, "Popold," as he is childishly nicknamed, has regressed to a state of boyish submission and Stan has resumed his former role of paternal bully. Yet in *Les Boys IV*, Léopold explicitly states his desire to leave his father's shadow and be his own man, telling Stan: "Moi, je veux vivre ma vie, père, okay?; pas vivre la tienne" (I want to live my life, okay? not yours; 23:53–55).

As in the Bildungsroman, then, various players develop in maturity through the narrative trajectory of each film and of the series as a whole. The conclusion of the first film in the franchise thus restores the shaky masculinity of a good number of its characters. Mario learns that he is going to be a father, and he and his wife (Rosie Yale) return home after *Les Boys* win the game that allows Stan to keep his bar. Similarly, Bob realizes the shallowness of his woman hopping and accepts the attentions of one woman, Karine (Annie Dufresne); by *Les Boys III*, Bob has learned that he has fathered a child and wants to be involved in her life, revealing further steps in the process of self-development.[21] Finally, once Stan re-establishes his virility by winning the wager with Méo, in *Les Boys II*, the widower can meet an appropriate mate – in France.

As with *Les Boys*, although many of the team members appear initially to have done some backsliding in their development toward mature manhood, *Les Boys II* concludes with similar markers of their growth. Mario is now a father, and his children are more important than hockey, as revealed by his refusal to play in France because of a child's illness back home. Similarly, *Les Boys III* begins by signalling Léopold's developing maturity, just mentioned. Even the villain of the first film, Méo, having undergone a personal crisis in prison, expresses his failure to find pleasure in his criminal activities in *Les Boys III*, which suggests that he wants to embrace a more responsible, law-abiding lifestyle. *Les Boys IV* does not seek to undo this personal growth; indeed, it adds further layers to it, even in its opening scenes. In a reversal of *Les Boys*, which infantilized the team members, its opening sequence catches viewers up with developments since the last film, indicating that they have accepted greater responsibility as men. Marcel is now teaching the next generation of metre-readers; Julien is working in a day care centre (one assumes he has given up drugs); Méo has become an honest businessman as a florist; Stan now owns a hockey equipment shop; and Léopold is running the new, updated restaurant-club (rather than the dingy neighbourhood bar of the first film). Finally, Jean-Charles, depicted as something of a playboy in *II* and *III*, has settled down and is preparing to marry his partner.

In the introduction to their study of the Bildungsroman, Giovanna Summerfield and Lisa Downward attribute to Wilhelm Dilthey the understanding that "the typical Bildungsroman traces the progress of a young person toward self-understanding as well as a sense of social responsibility."[22] To the superficial extent that a popular comedy film can do so, this is precisely the trajectory taken by the various protagonists of *Les Boys* across the film series. In addition to the personal growth discussed above, the team members must learn to pull together as a team in order to face challenges both on the ice and off. In particular, in the first film, *Les Boys* face the possibility after the first period that Stan will lose his bar to Méo. Two of the team's most immature and self-centred players, the egotistical mama's boy Ti-Guy and the cokehead rocker Julien, return to the locker room and rejoin the team for the third period after having abandoned them during the second in fear that serious physical harm will be inflicted on them by Méo's team of ringers. They realize that they must put their individual, selfish fears aside and fulfil their responsibility to Stan, who represents a father not just to Léopold but to the entire team. In *Les Boys III*, Mario's house has burned down and the team sells tickets and plays a benefit game to help him, but that instalment's central dramatic tension revolves around individual members' recruitment to another team, Les Champions, run by the insidious Phil (Alexis Martin). Once again they come to understand the value of loyalty to the collective over the childish pursuit of individual needs. This reinforces the notion of the hockey team as a microcosm of the province; it also likens the team to the unit on which patriarchal, capitalist societies are based: the family.

In her pioneering discussion of the nexus of hockey, masculinity, and national identity in Quebec, Anouk Bélanger discusses how discourses about masculinity emerging in the late 1980s and 1990s were influenced strongly by Guy Corneau's best-seller, *Absent Fathers, Lost Sons* (1989; trans. 1991).[23] A Jungian psychoanalyst, Corneau developed his study from a workshop involving twenty-one men, both straight and gay, aged twenty to fifty, ranging from professionals to unemployed, held in spring 1987 at the Jung Centre in Montreal. His first question to the group was, "Do you feel like a man?" Not a single participant answered yes.[24] After the one-day workshop, all of the participants wished to continue analysis, and their sessions would substantiate Corneau's general observations about "the fragility of masculine identity" in contemporary Quebec society.[25] From these subjects, Corneau has created a typology of personalities, all of which suffer from a sense of crisis in terms of a mature, adult male sexuality and many of which clearly resemble several characters in *Les Boys*.[26]

Corneau identifies the absence of ritual marking the passage from adolescence to manhood as one element in this crisis.[27] Others have described sports as providing a form of initiation that is lacking for young men in contemporary, urban, industrialized society, a rite of passage that is necessary if they are to access adult male individual and sexual identity – in other words, manhood.[28] Organized hockey provides such rites, both through its explicit identification of stages to traverse, from Peewee to Bantam to Midget, and through the frequently cited initiation of rookie players on a team, particularly at the professional level. Furthermore, hockey provides an outlet for the repressed aggressiveness Corneau observes; in "their quest for a challenge, for something to struggle for. By tiring themselves out with these drives and quests, men can find moments of peace and tranquility."[29] Hockey thus serves a positive function with regard to this dysfunctional aspect of society; according to Bélanger, "Corneau hypothesizes that hockey in Québec serves as a surrogate family to men and boys, and that teams fulfil a need to belong as Québécois males."[30]

The all-male camaraderie of *Les Boys* in the locker room, on the ice, and at Stan's brasserie after each match certainly offers these man-boys a sense of belonging; the team logo on their sweaters openly signifies a common identity. As I have suggested, across the films a certain amount of development occurs towards their internalizing the characteristics expected of an adult male in contemporary North American society. Yet in many ways, and for reasons that have to do with the nature of the franchise film, which requires an open ending on which the next instalment can be built[31] and thus necessarily precludes the type of narrative closure with the hero's accession to adulthood and adoption of a socially approved vocation found in the classic Bildungsroman,[32] like Corneau's subjects, *Les Boys* remain fixed in an eternal adolescence. In many ways, their antics resemble those of the filmic bad boys in the essays collected by Murray Pomerance and Frances Gateward in *Where the Boys Are: Cinemas of Masculinity and Youth* (2005). Their description of the "bad boy" in adulthood fits most members of this fictional hockey team to a tee:

> The end product of screen boyhood, the screened man, is either a grown-up continuity of what he always was – blithe rogue, tongue-in-cheek and lovable criminal, awkward adventurer, all of these adamantly presexual and Panic – or a cop-out, a prisoner of the culture he had once fought in the mud puddles but could at some crucial point of transference and surrender resist no longer.[33]

The fact that serious Quebec films offer similar developmental trajectories for their protagonists either supports Corneau's thesis or simply demonstrates the extent to which it has been internalized by Québécois writers and filmmakers. The protagonist in *Un crabe dans la tête* (2000) struggles to develop an authentic adult male identity;[34] similarly, we see both types of boy-men in each of the brothers featured in Sébastien Rose's *La Vie avec mon père* (2005). Happily, *Les Boys* avoid copping out and remain what they always have been. We might simply interpret the scenes in which Bob, Mario, and even Fern privilege hockey – playing with the boys – over sexual relations with women as the continued expression of their "adamant presexuality." Perhaps their masculinity is not so much compromised as simply not yet developed, as I have noted earlier regarding Bob and Mario. Nonetheless, as Pomerance and Gateward suggest, film portrayals of boys' "coming of age" – essentially examples of the Bildungsroman – often elide crucial early steps towards a fully sexual adult identity, such as experimentation with masturbation or with the only partners available in an all-male environment (such as the boys' school, the group of male friends, or the sports team). This topic also appears taboo in the serious sports film, but hockey comedies like *Slap Shot* and *Les Boys* can raise this issue, perhaps precisely *because* of the distancing that occurs in an "unrealistic" genre like comedy.

Breaking the Code: Homosexuality in Les Boys

Discussions of masculinity in sports inevitably address the paradoxically homosocial nature of sports, which is coupled with the contingent exclusion of homosexuality and even the active cultivation of homophobia in some forms of hegemonic masculinity. Dayna B. Daniels uses the locker room chatter in *Slap Shot* as a fictional exemplar,[35] while Brian Pronger documents the presence of queer bashing in real-life locker rooms via interviews with (sometimes closeted) gay men. Pronger explains the reasons for the discourse of homophobia, which are seemingly endemic to sport culture:

> In our culture, male homosexuality is a violation of masculinity, a denigration of the mythic power of men, an ironic subversion that significant numbers of men pursue with great enthusiasm. Because it gnaws at masculinity, it weakens the gender order. [...]
>
> That a man can prove his masculinity in the boxing ring or weight room, on the football field, hockey rink, track, or basketball court, is a well-known dimension of the myth of gender. [...]
>
> The most masculine sports are the violent ones – boxing, football and hockey.[36]

Theorists like Pronger and Donald Sabo explain homophobic chatter as serving to counteract any sexual charge that might exist in what Bélanger terms team sports' "predominantly homosocial environment."[37] Happily, *Les Boys* largely eschews the homophobic comments that riddle *Slap Shot*; this leaves one hopeful that progress towards tolerance has occurred over the intervening decades between these two sports comedies. In his analysis of masculinity and representations of queer identities in Quebec sports films, including those about hunting and boxing, Thomas Waugh concludes of *Les Boys* that "this 'gang de losers' may be crude and sexist, but they're no homophobes."[38] On several occasions throughout the franchise, however, *Les Boys* expresses rather ambivalent attitudes about homosexuality.

In terms of this aspect of my analysis, the most interesting scene in *Les Boys* is the craftily sequenced outing of Jean-Charles as gay. A middle-of-the-night phone call from one of the team members wakes the relatively responsible barrister, who has gone home to bed instead of carousing after the game. Ti-Guy has been arrested for drunk driving and needs legal assistance; during the phone conversation, the viewer sees only the wavy blond, shoulder-length hair of what we believe to be the barrister's wife. As she rolls over, we realize that *she* is a *he*. We then witness Guy Jodoin's stereotypical portrayal of Pierrot – his very name refers to a clown, the Harlequin of Commedia dell'Arte theatre – staging a scene, acting like an over-the-top, hysterical queen, what Pronger terms a "screamer."[39] Jealous, like the film's other "wives," of the time his lover spends with the team, Pierrot threatens to leave Jean-Charles if he goes to help Ti-Guy. Neither Jean-Charles nor the viewer takes his threats seriously as it's made clear that Pierrot has made them before.

Notwithstanding this distastefully excessive stereotype, which is played for comedy, Jean-Charles even after being outed remains an integral and even leading member of the team. Between periods in the first film's critical match against Méo's team of ringers, who all wear black in a blatant coding as the bad guys, Jean-Charles confronts Méo himself in the men's room and physically assaults him. This is not the first time they have met: Jean-Charles has seen this goon in court, reinforcing the notion that Méo, the gangster, has iced a team full of literal "hit men" – in hockey jargon, players who specialize in hitting their opponents' key players hard enough to knock them out of the game (ironically, such players are also called "enforcers," placing them on the side of the law).[40] As he forces Méo into submission, Jean-Charles says: "A partir d'à soir [he adopts here the populist discourse rather than the standard French's 'ce soir'], je vais être sur ton cas à temps plein" (After tonight I'm going to be on your case full-time! 1:33:00–02). We also learn at this point why Pierrot appears to be missing a finger in the bedroom scene discussed earlier: Méo had one of his fingers severed for an unpaid debt, a form of symbolic castration that Jean-Charles seeks to avenge. While Méo may be unaware of the double entendre, the audience is not. Armed with our knowledge of Jean-Charles's homosexuality, we easily read the scene as one of male rape, particularly in the context of the men's room *cum* cruising spot. Put in his place, effectively feminized by Jean-Charles's threat and forced to change out of his business suit, which has been dampened by the urinal's flush, Méo receives a wolf whistle in response to his feminine bright red trousers when he returns to the rink. By the same token, Jean-Charles proves his manhood through this hegemonic display of male violence.

Ultimately, Jean-Charles becomes the team's hero when he scores on a penalty shot near the match's conclusion. He has been depressed because Pierrot actually did carry out his threat to leave him after Ti-Guy's phone call; his teammates know that "à cause de toi que je suis séparé depuis une semaine" (because of you I've been separated for a week; 1:03:53–55), but they do not know that the other half of his couple is a man. Well, at this very moment, as Jean-Charles prepares to carry the puck down the ice, Pierrot arrives – like the other wives and girlfriends present – to cheer on his man. Finding the courage he needs, Jean-Charles scores on the penalty shot, saving Stan's bar. Setting aside the politically incorrect portrayal of Pierrot as a risible travesty of a man masquerading as a woman, the film seems to be offering an important message of tolerance. As Thomas Waugh concludes, "in *Les Boys* the spectre of anal abjection is enacted and named throughout but finally exorcised in its spectacularly comic, politically correct denouement, this sudden parachuting in of the redemptive queer hero and the implausibly affirmed homosocial community that results."[41]

In the subsequent films of the series, various players engage in banter with Jean-Charles in their apparent efforts to accept their friend for who he is. And clearly, Jean-Charles's gayness does not hamper his masculinity. In fact it is he, of all the men on *Les Boys*, who proves himself to be a real man. He successfully employs a form of hegemonic masculinity with Méo, fulfilling the macho ideal of using force to make others submit; he is also consistently portrayed as the most mature, well-rounded, responsible adult male on the team.

Ti-Guy will also finally grow up and find a love interest, but not before another comedic scene engages the question of sexual preference. Consistently portrayed as a self-centred real estate agent and as one of the youngest members of the team, as his diminutive nickname indicates, he is treated like a boy. This immaturity extends to his sex life: Ti-Guy, despite his clean-cut image and the good looks and (albeit later in his career) sex symbol status of actor Patrick Huard, has yet to show interest in women. The film proposes two explanations for this as Ti-Guy dines with his dominating mother in *Les Boys III*. First, he is a mama's boy, protected from other women by his mother (Rita Lafontaine). Second, if you believe his mother, he must be gay. Dating to 2001, the film reflects the official stance of the dominant secular culture of tolerance and multiculturalism in North America; instead of expressing the shame and intolerance that many might associate with a stereotypical middle-class, middle-aged Québécois woman, Guy's mother encourages him to come out:

> MÈRE: Écoute, Guy, j'suis ta mère. [...] Pourquoi tu t'acceptes pas comme t'es ? Ton père pis moi on est ben capable de comprendre ca ? [...] Il va ben falloir que tu sortes du garderobe à un moment donné. [...] Arrête de faire semblant. Trente-deux ans, pas de blonde ..., tout le monde le sait dans la parenté que t'es homosexuel. Nie-le pas.

> Listen, Guy, I'm your mother. Why can't you accept yourself as you are? Your father and I, we're able to understand it. Eventually you'll have to come out of the closet. Stop pretending. Thirty-two and no girlfriend ... everybody in the family knows that you are a homosexual. Don't deny it. (31:30-32:08)

Guy fails to understand her until the final sentence of this speech, when she states explicitly what she thinks. At that point, he stands up in the crowded restaurant and adamantly denies it. In spite of the mother's expressed acceptance and understanding if her son should be gay, the scene's ultimate message remains ambivalent, which is often the case in popular culture texts that appeal to a broad section of the public. It is also perhaps an endemic trait in comedy. That notwithstanding, we are confronted with the expression of society's complicated attitude towards homosexuality. Ti-Guy's protests and horror that she would think he is gay undermine the "official" message of his mother's understanding. While he subsequently proves himself to be straight – instead, he is simply slow to develop an interest in women – those protestations reveal a lingering discomfort among straight men with being identified as gay, something still viewed as undermining their masculinity. We can also laugh at the mother's false stereotyping of her own son; that is, she is applying society's predominant images of straight and gay men to her image of her son. Since he is a successful thirty-two-year-old man who still doesn't have girlfriend, he must be gay. Yet another layer of complexity appears when we learn of Ti-Guy's choice for a love interest: a female hockey player. We'll return to that image in a moment.

Also in *Les Boys III* there is a scene in which Bob, growing visibly concerned about his appearance as he ages, consults Jean-Charles. Presumably (and stereotypically), the gay man will know more about how to maintain masculine attractiveness than any of his straight friends. Boisvert, seeing the two men tête-à-tête in the men's room, asks:

> BOISVERT: Quess vous faites-là? [Whatcha doin' there?]
> BOB, visibly annoyed: Rien de spécial; on frenchait. C'est-tu correct? [Nothing special; French kissing. Is that okay? 55:02-06]

Once again we are confronted with an ambivalent popular culture text that can be read in several ways. Boisvert is insecure in his masculinity, and the implication of his protest-too-much attitude is that he is a closeted or repressed gay man who is overcompensating by harassing women; thus, he feels threatened when he sees two of his teammates, one of whom is now openly gay, having an intimate conversation. In contrast to this, Jean-Charles throughout *Les Boys* and *Les Boys III* offers an admirable image of a gay man who is a "normal," well-rounded member of society. Bob, for his part, fully accepts his friend for what he is, and he is fully confident in his own masculinity since he has no problem being cloistered in a men's room – gay cruising spot par excellence – with Jean-Charles. Bob's viper-like tongue – a trait he shares with Messier's other hockey avatar, Marc Gagnon of *Lance et compte* – castigates Boisvert for his narrowmindedness.

Les Boys IV propagates a mix of progressive and reactionary representations of homosexuality. One of its central scenes is the wedding of Jean-Charles and his much younger companion, Christopher. The former's ability to attract a much younger man reinforces our sense of his masculinity as hegemonic: he remains physically fit and strong; his charismatic personality exudes power over others, as demonstrated when he overhears two of *Les Boys* questioning more the idea of a marriage between partners of an unequal age than a gay marriage. Jean-Charles puts an arm around each one of them in a gesture of faux-friendship and, in a relatively menacing tone meaning "drop it now," explains: "le sacre de mariage, c'est pour Christopher que je fais ça" (the wedding ceremony – I'm doing it for Christopher; 28:50–51).

Comedy allows us momentarily to express taboo thoughts and feelings; it serves, perhaps, as a healthy evacuation of repressed frustrations and hostilities. But to be funny, it often has to go too far, to be tasteless. *Les Boys IV* certainly achieves that as various characters react to the same-sex wedding ceremony. As the priest calls for the couple to kiss at the end of the vows, Fern and Méo wonder alouad what it would be like to kiss another man. Méo thinks it would be like kissing himself; as Jean-Charles and Christian approach their lips, Fern looks away, grimacing, in a clear expression of horror. The camera momentarily cuts away, then cuts back to Fern, who is now peeking at the kissing same-sex couple. His reaction of mingled disgust and fascination recalls Michael William Saunders's discussion of homosexuality in horror films, where he asserts that "the visibility of gay people is what makes them dangerous. [...] As long as *they* don't insist that we see them, *we* can pretend that they don't figure in the shaping of society. [...] the visibility of gay people is a *monstrous* thing."[42] By publicly showing their affection and codifying their sexual relationship through the ritual of marriage, Jean-Charles and Christopher have violated that unwritten rule. Conversely, *Les Boys* and its sequels' repeated and open depictions of Jean-Charles flirting subvert the very taboo Saunders proposes. Such is the ambivalent nature of the popular text, especially that of the major motion picture, which refuses to take too big a risk by alienating an audience whose views will be mixed. At the same time, it reveals a society in transition, in which one sector has internalized the progressive values of tolerance while another continues to reject images of difference.

During the wedding scene of *Les Boys IV*, in addition to the various fumblings about how to refer to the happy couple, since there is no bride, during the receiving line after the ceremony, Léopold puts his foot in his mouth by asking Christopher's parents if they would like to be grandparents. The gracious mother-in-law stops his stuttering apologies by stating that they already are grandparents, which again causes confusion until she mentions that Christopher has a sister. The crowd's obvious relief demonstrates a continuing unease when the boundaries of gender roles appear to be violated. While they can at least on the surface appear to accept a gay couple, they cannot yet accept the idea that a gay man can be a father. Moments like these across the series reflect the film's expression of Québécois society's attempts to come to grips with new social realities, realities that it can only partly embrace at this point in time.

"Who Let the Girls Out?" Playing with Les Boys

Ti-Guy's infatuation with the woman hockey player, Chantal, introduces an interesting dynamic of attraction and brings us to the question of women's place in organized sports in *Les Boys III*. Dedicated to Maurice Richard, who had recently passed away and received state funeral ceremonies, the franchise's third instalment stages a benefit match between *Les Boys* and Team Canada – the Olympic women's hockey team, that is. The film capitalizes on at least two recent developments for women in hockey that would have been widely publicized: the case of Manon Rhéaume, the first woman to play in an NHL game in 1992,[43] and the introduction of women's hockey as an Olympic sport in 1998, followed by a silver medal for Canada. The film comically announces the stakes in a men-versus-women competition, comparing this game to the tennis match between Bobby Riggs and Billie Jean King in 1973. Acknowledging the shame of a possible female victory, Fern makes the comment cited in the epigraph to this chapter: "Si on gagne on va dire qu'on manque de classe; si on perd on va dire qu'on manque de couilles" (If we lose, they're not going to say we don't have class but that we don't have balls; 24:55–58).

As Michael Messner cautions in his landmark study of gender in sports, "it is crucial to recognize that sport's role in constructing and legitimizing a male homosocial world, masculine power, and masculine heterosexuality has continually been contested."[44] Even before sports sociologists like Messner, Pronger, and Burstyn began examining sport's role in the construction of masculinity in North American society, feminist scholars had been denouncing the exclusion of women from the sporting world; in the United States, this led to the 1972 Title IX legislation requiring equal access for girls to sports in the educational sector. This led in turn to the development of professional team sports for women, including the Women's Basketball League (1978–1981), followed by the WNBA, founded in 1996 and still operating.[45] Women's hockey took much longer to be accepted precisely because of the gender stereotypes identifying the sport, in the words of Gordie Howe, as "a man's game."[46] A National Women's Hockey League lasted less than ten years (1999–2007), but a Canadian Women's Hockey League may prove more viable, perhaps fuelled by the growing popularity of Olympic-level women's hockey. However, Julie Stevens's analysis of the unequal press coverage of Canadian men's and women's ice hockey at the 2002 Winter Olympics – where both teams won gold – reveals that equal recognition for women in hockey remains an uphill battle.[47]

As recently as 2006, Mary Louise Adams reiterated the status of hockey as a largely male domain: "If hockey is life in Canada, then life in Canada remains decidedly masculine and white."[48] A recurrent debate in women's sports revolves around a "room of her own" – that is, all-female leagues, which some view as ghettos that fail to acknowledge full equality, versus "playing with the boys," which would entail full inclusion in the world of amateur and professional league sports at the highest levels for women with sufficient ability. One extraordinary woman had achieved full inclusion only a few years before the first *Les Boys* film. Nancy Theberge, who also authored a sociological study of women in this man's sport titled *Higher Goals: Women's Ice Hockey and the Politics of Gender* (2000), recounts Québécoise goaltender Manon Rhéaume's journey to become "the first woman to play in a regular season game in a men's professional league": she dressed for a game as a substitute in 1992, and played a full game in April 1993.[49]

As with its treatment of homosexuality, *Les Boys'* treatment of female *hockeyeurs*, or rather *hockeyeuses*, remains ambivalent upon analysis. Reflecting the need to accept homosexuality as part of a contemporary, tolerant, and pluralistic Québécois society, *Les Boys III* seems to work through the issue of women's presence in a workplace that was once a man's domain. At first, the film denaturalizes the discourse of hegemonic masculinity and male dominance as it ridicules *Les Boys* for their hubris: they quickly fall behind in their exhibition match against the Canadian women's Olympic team. I should note that, except for actress Geneviève Néron in the role of Ti-Guy's love interest, Chantal, the film ices a Women's Team Canada comprised, with only a few exceptions, of the French Canadian contingent of the actual team.[50] Humorous situations arise after Stan tells his players to "jouer galant" – to play like gentlemen (37:09). Marcel takes him literally, and rather than fight for the puck tells his opponent, "Après vous, mademoiselle" (After you, miss; 40:52). The tables are turned, though, as these skilled women play hard. Indeed, they go on the offensive, thus appropriating the traditionally masculine prerogative to be the aggressor; for example, one female player pins Boisvert against the boards, repeatedly hitting him from behind. The women also use dirty tricks, such as dramatizing minor contact ("taking a dive") so that the opponent draws a penalty; one of them even accuses an opponent of sexual harrassment, calling the linesman's attention to it: "Hey, ça va faire, là, l'harcèlement sexuel" (Hey, that's enough there with the sexual harassment; 41:49). These young women dominate the largely older men, thereby openly questioning their manhood; reversing the roles, one woman heckles Fern after he allows a puck through the five-hole: "Ça se peut-tu que t'as une petite faiblesse entre les jambes?" (Have you got a little weakness between the legs? 42:34).

While we know that Boisvert, as the most misogynistic member of the team, deserves the hit he received, the film's depiction of these women as aggressive and dominant violates gender expectations. An obvious corollary to locker room homophobia is the discourse of misogyny, above all accusing teammates and opponents alike of "playing like a girl" to motivate more aggressive play.[51] Indeed, a long-running image of women athletes, as Michael Messner points out, "stereotyped [them] as unwomanly, as unfeminine, [...] 'mannish lesbians,' no matter what their actual sexual orientations."[52] The courtship of Ti-Guy, the mama's boy, and Chantal, the *hockeyeuse*, rides a fine line between offering an alternative vision for the heterosexual couple that escapes the stereotypes of hegemonic masculinity and ultra-feminine passivity and objectification and simply reinscribing those stereotypes by reversing them.

The first spark of romance flies, actually, on the ice, when Ti-Guy loses a face-off because he is entranced with Chantal's beauty. Here, she uses her sexual attractiveness – something that Stan has perhaps warned against, telling *Les Boys* in the locker room to "garder la tête froide" (keep a cool head; 37:33) – as she compliments Ti-Guy, taking the man's role and objectifying him:

> CHANTAL: T'as ben des beaux yeux, toi. [You have beautiful eyes.]
> TI-GUY: Merci. [Thanks.]
> CHANTAL: Ben, garde-les su' l'puck. [Well, keep them on the puck.] 39:28–33)

She wins the face-off, and the women score on this first shift of the game.

The film further characterizes Chantal as a non-traditional woman, in contrast to Ti-Guy's arrested development. Again, in a role reversal, he asks her what she thinks of marriage; she replies unsentimentally that "je pense que c'est comme 20,000 piasses directement dans la poubelle" (I think it's like 20,000 bucks right into the trash; 1:24:39–40). When they go to a make-out point, Ti-Guy seems distracted; as so often happens, hockey-related activities pre-empt sexual ones, when he notices

François's car and goes to chat with his teammate, leaving Chantal alone and frustrated. Chantal's subversions of traditional gender roles are of course clichéd – as is Ti-Guy's infantilism – for the sake of the comedy; her actions simultaneously acknowledge and make room for variations in those gender roles within the framework of the compulsory heterosexuality of the dominant society; but at the same time, they lampoon individuals who differ from those norms.

Québécois Are *Real Men: Trickster Masculinity in* Les Boys

The climax, if you will, of each film, is, of course, a battle on the ice between *Les Boys* and an apparently stronger team. In the first instalment, they face the team of ringers that Méo has brought in so that he can unfairly win Stan's bar; in the second, they must face a Russian team to win an international amateur tournament; in the fourth, they face the Toronto Barristers, an anglophone amateur team that wears suits and rides a chartered bus like semi-pros. Only in the third film does the final match fail to end in an on-ice victory for *Les Boys*; however, the suspension of a game in which half the gang is playing for the rival Champions represents a clear victory for Stan's team as a national microcosm when they are reunited in adversity because Mario has broken a leg.

In their staging of such uneven matches, these Québécois hockey films adopt a discourse similar to that of many sports films, invoking two major tropes: the victory of the underdog and the importance of teamwork. Where *Les Boys* differs from most Hollywood sports films is in *how* they win. As outlined by Aaron Baker, the American sports film genre typically reinforces the bourgeois capitalist values of individual effort, teamwork, and fair play.[53] Sheer talent may be shown as an asset, but usually that talent must be tamed – in *Miracle* (2004), for example, Jack O'Callahan (Michael Mantenuto) must harness his ego and his talent, submit to the coach, and work with the group. In Québécois films, the amateurs rely on a different combination of factors to win, but most frequently their trickster natures come into play.

I invoke the trickster at the risk of a superficial application of a trendy and overused concept; yet, precisely because of the social function I attribute to popular culture texts like *Les Boys*, the term seems compellingly accurate here. Variants of the trickster are found in an array of cultures, from the classical Greek Hermes and Prometheus to the African spider Anansi to numerous Native American tales of Raven and Coyote; this figure represents, if not a cultural universal, then at least a powerful archetype, as Jung has argued.[54] As the term suggests, a trickster plays tricks; but as anthropologists, folklorists, and literary critics like Gail Jones point out, the trickster also plays a significant and even serious cultural role: "A figure both profane and sacred, foolish and clever, absurd and profound, marginal and, yet central. In whatever incarnation, trickster shakes up the status quo, rearranging boundaries and reordering our reality with amusement and laughter. The transforming, transcending trickster operates along boundaries, borders in flux."[55]

In their overview of the trickster figure, William J. Hynes and William G. Doty similarly assert that "[trickster] stories provide a fertile source of cultural reflection and critical reflexivity that leaves one thoughtful yet laughing; and what a culture does with laughter reflects its vitality, flexibility, and creativity."[56] This is precisely what I am arguing about the *Les Boys* franchise: like trickster stories that recount the clever ruses of an apparently weak and marginal figure to cheat the gods, these films all stage the victory of a group of clownish underdogs over an ostensibly indomitable opponent. And, just as trickster stories are told again and again around the evening fire, so, too, the *Les Boys* films and television episodes repeat and re-enact a victory that empowers the audience, which identifies not with the powerful gods but with the naughty but comical trickster figure represented by various team members.

Hynes identifies six characteristics of the trickster, most of which apply directly to *Les Boys*:

> (1) the fundamentally ambiguous and anomalous personality of the trickster. [...] as
> (2) deceiver/trick-player,
> (3) shape-shifter,
> (4) situation-invertor,
> (5) messenger/imitator of the gods, and
> (6) sacred/lewd bricoleur.[57]

The caricatural nature of each member of *Les Boys* leaves these personalities riddled with contradictions, particularly across the series of films. One moment they are capable of the most vile self-interestedness, the next they sacrifice themselves for the good of the team; one moment they accept Jean-Charles as a fully integrated member of the group, the next they make a tasteless joke about gays; one moment Stan expresses pride in his son's achievement, the next he chides Léopold as an "innocent" (dummy); one moment Méo helps an old lady cross the street, the next his ingrained gangster nature kicks in and he smashes her walker over the hood of a careless driver's car. In addition to the typical locker room tricks, like urinating or putting out a cigarette in a beer bottle and offering it to a teammate to drink, *Les Boys* engage in a number of on-ice ruses, besides deceiving wives and girlfriends. We might even read their transformation from ordinary citizens into unorthodox superheroes when they don their bright red-and-gold uniforms as a form of shape shifting. They repeatedly invert situations, particularly gender roles, and they certainly seek to imitate the gods of popular culture, the *real* hockey stars of the NHL. While their lewdness can pass nearly without comment for anyone who has seen at least one of the films, they also touch upon the sacred, invoking in particular the hockey-as-religion metaphor in the funeral sequence that begins *Les Boys II*.[58]

In many situations, instead of employing the violence associated with hegemonic masculinity, *Les Boys* resort to other, unorthodox trickster tactics to ensure their victory. In the first film, Bob's girlfriend uses her sex appeal to distract the opponents' goalie to allow an undefended goal to score. Julien – who pushes the gender boundary envelope with his spandex-band rock star look, wearing leopardskin print underwear and his hair long – has scored some cocaine, and he and Ti-Guy use their high to advantage on the ice. And when *Les Boys* do attempt to use violence, the strategy often backfires. In the final match against the Moscow Sputniks in *Les Boys II*, the opponents score on a power play because Fern has tripped an opponent and sits in the penalty box. And when *Les Boys* do resort to violence to win a game, that violence – the attack on Méo in the bathroom, discussed above – occurs away from the ice and is perpetrated by Jean-Charles, thus involving homosexual undertones rather than classic hegemonic masculinity.

In engaging with the problem of hockey violence – a key debate in the sport in both popular media and scholarly analyses – the *Les Boys* franchise repeatedly adopts, of course, the stance of supporting the underdog French Canadians against a monolithic and seemingly indomitable foreign force. Violence in hockey is thus wrapped up in debates about national identity, which we will address below; here, it seems that the film accepts, on one level, the stereotype that French Canadian hockey players are physically smaller than Anglo-Canadian ones and therefore less able to "dominate" the ice – that is, to exert the hegemonic masculinity associated with winners. Economist Marc Lavoie has found some slight statistical basis for this stereotype in reality, although only for forwards, not for defencemen;[59] but he also decries how such a perception has led to endemic discrimination against the recruitment of French Canadians in the NHL from Canada's provincial junior hockey leagues.[60]

On the one hand, the films appear to reinscribe this stereotype, as again and again the viewer can clearly see a size differential between *Les Boys* and their opponents, from Méo's ringers to players from the Ivory Coast and the near-giant on the Moscow Sputniks in *Les Boys II*. On the other, the franchise offers an alternate discourse to enable the victories necessary for the feel-good happy endings that audiences require of a hybrid genre like the sports comedy. Since violence – and its corollary, physical size – are largely problematized or eschewed here, the standard hockey discourse would hold that strategy, skill, and courage must win out. As with violence, few of *Les Boys* demonstrate any consummate skill on the ice, although Bob and Mario are coded as the team's most skilful players. They must rely on strategy, their brains, to win, and at times this is a very unorthodox strategy, letting coyote loose and using trickster tactics. However, the *Les Boys* films simultaneously lampoon and value brains. Stan's catchphrase is a formulaic anglicism, "[d]ans mon livre à moé ..." (in my book), which is typically followed by a silly or inappropriate piece of folk wisdom. So it is hard to take him seriously, and indeed, in several films Bob takes over the coach's role to make the rallying locker room speech, a requisite of the sports film genre. In the match against Méo's ringers, he explicitly invokes this aspect of the game. Obviously outmatched in size, Bob knows his team must look elsewhere; he asks: "C'est quoi notre force à nous, Les Boys? C'est pas entre les oreilles?" (What's our strength, Boys? Isn't it between our ears?). He then tells *Les Boys*, pronouncing the English phrase with a stereotypical French Canadian accent, that "the mental, le mental; mental toughness, la dureté du mental," is what will carry the day for them (1:22:58–23:08).

What this has to do with masculinity, as I interpret it, is that masculinity can be defined in other ways than simply who has the biggest stick, so to speak. Size doesn't matter. French Canadian men have often had to combat the notion – found in Anglo-Canadian discourses – that the French in general are foppish, effeminate, and less virile, partly because of their association with intellectuality, but also perhaps because of another major sign of weakness, the military defeat of France – in

North America and in the Second World War, to cite only two examples. Because *Les Boys* do not have the physical size to defeat their opponents, they must rely on the mental aspect of the game, defeating their opponents by subterfuge.

Much of this chapter has argued that *Les Boys*, to a man, fail to live up to the dominant society's expectations about responsible adult masculinity. I would like to nuance that argument here to propose that instead of condemning them for this failure, the films propose an alternative form of masculinity, one that allows an individual to be recognized fully as a man, without constraining him to the rigid, hegemonic definitions set by heteronormative, capitalist, bourgeois society. This "trickster masculinity" offers new possibilities for men in a postmodern, postcolonial world in which multivalence, difference, and resistance have become increasingly valorized. Anouk Bélanger connects Corneau's hypothesis in *Absent Fathers, Lost Sons* to the mentality of the *colonisé*, the "colonized" subject, an image borrowed from the discourse of decolonization in the Third World and then applied to Quebec during the Quiet Revolution and after, as further undermining masculinity in Quebec. This discourse has been increasingly decried by Quebec intellectuals as belonging to a bygone era and as no longer pertinent to the contemporary conditions of a flourishing francophone society.[61] On the one hand, it does reproduce the images of the crisis in masculinity identified by Corneau in the 1980s; on the other, *Les Boys'* irreverent and celebratory (rather than condemning) depictions of alternative masculinities demonstrate that perhaps that crisis has subsided to a certain extent. Hockey, traditionally identified as an exclusively male domain, appears to provide a buffer for the safe exploration of alternative visions of male identity.

This suggestion that a "trickster masculinity" is present in *Les Boys* brings us full circle, back to Lee Parpart's discussion of "colonial masculinity" in Canadian art film mentioned in the introduction to this chapter. While segments of Quebec culture still partly or completely embrace the dominant (albeit slowly evolving) North American valorization of hegemonic masculinity, the popularity of films like *Les Boys* reveals the acceptance of a postcolonial, trickster masculinity that resists that norm by both lampooning it and by offering other models. Like the pan-Canadian art films analysed by Parpart, films that seek to undermine what Thomas Waugh describes as the "thesis of Canadian masculinity as colonized loser-dom,"[62] *Les Boys* resists this image by celebrating these French Canadian "losers" and turning them into winners on the ice.

Appropriating Canada's Game: Quebec National Identity in *Les Boys*

As a hugely popular cultural text,[63] *Les Boys* cannot express overtly politicized statements either for or against sovereignty, lest it lose half its audience. But with the first film appearing only two years after the second sovereignty referendum, neither can the *Les Boys* series completely ignore contemporary issues. Its most explicit reference to Québécois nationalist angst is when François reminisces about exactly where he was on the night of 20 May 1980; in contrast, Fern cites hockey statistics, admitting, "J'ai même pas voté" (I didn't even vote; 53:13). Stan chastises him: "C'est à cause des gars comme toé qu'on n'a pas de pays!" (It's because of guys like you that we don't have a country! 53:15). Bart Beaty reads this comment as revealing that "the real nation here is a hockey nation. In this regard the non-voting Fernand is the ideal citizen. Highly informed and deeply committed to his ideals."[64] Others have similarly articulated that a fan identity has come to replace a national one,[65] and although it rarely comments overtly about Quebec's political situation, *Les Boys* nonetheless constructs a certain image of Québécois national identity that is inextricably linked to depictions of masculinity. The clearest opportunity for engaging such questions occurs when the team goes abroad, to the neutral territory of the Franco-Swiss border in *Les Boys II*.

Throughout the first film – and this was one of the reasons for its success, which led to the franchise – *Les Boys* offers the viewing public a cinema of recognition.[66] Its populist portrayal of comically exaggerated but nonetheless "typical" Quebecers provides an authentic form of popular culture that can compete with the imported Hollywood films that are as much blockbusters in Quebec as they are in the United States and anglophone Canada. As stock types, these characters represent a cross-section of society, from the irregularly employed musician Julien, to the blue-collar entrepreneur Mario, to the beat cop Boisvert, to the liberal professionals Jean-Charles and François. They all speak authentically Québécois French, from the professionals' near-standard discourse to Stan's rolled r's and Mario's anglicisms; above all, they know how to swear in Québécois *and* in English, with "Oh, shit!" and "Baptême" leading a roster that includes Boisvert's apparent hybrid neologism, *cibarnaque*, a combination of *ciboire* and *tabarnak*.[67] The film's musical score consists of songs composed by Franco-Quebecers but generically influenced by American rock and blues, and sometimes sung in English. Rather than artificially attempting to exorcise the American demon, the franchise consistently acknowledges the hybrid nature of North American French-language culture. Mario's anglicisms, like "back up" and "let's go," as well as the anglicized names of Bob and Stan, and the archetypically French Canadian nickname of Fern (pronounced with an American type "r"), for Fernand, all territorialize the film with these markers of Québécois identity, which are immediately recognizable to the domestic target audience.

As I have already suggested, *Les Boys* can be read as a national allegory, in which the underdog Quebecers take on a team of bully ringers (i.e., foreigners) and win. Also, *Les Boys II* openly raises the question of Québécois identity in opposition to a Metropolitan French identity, as the team travels to Chamonix (which Fern mispronounces, demonstrating their homespun, populist character) for an international amateur hockey tournament. This film not only depicts the French according to certain stereotypes but also plays irreverently with the 1972 Canada–Soviet Summit Series, a significant nation-building moment. Giving it the label "La Série du Siècle" (the Series of the Century), for once, Quebec viewed this contest between West and East in the same light as English Canada. For example, Montreal Canadiens star Serge Savard described it as "l'événement le plus important de ma carrière, plus encore que les dix coupes Stanley que j'ai remportées a titre de joueur ou de directeur général du Canadien de Montréal" (the most important event of my career, even more than the ten Stanley cups that I have won as player or general manager of the Montreal Canadiens).[68]

Les Boys II reveals the French to be everything the Québécois are not; above all, Stan's counterpart in Haute-Savoie, Laurent (Daniel Russo), is the portrait of inauthenticity. Laurent enters the picture driving his Renault like a madman through the narrow streets of Chamonix, pulling up to a screeching halt in front of the sidewalk café where *Les Boys* are sitting. He wears a cowboy hat, signalling a stereotypical French love of what they call the "Far West." When asked if he's been to America, he admits not, but still arrogantly claims to know the country very well. The oversexed – although not physically attractive – Frenchman has, of course, both a wife and a mistress. His self-image as macho, however, is just that – an image, for it comes out that he cannot satisfy his wife Corinne (Cécile Auclert), who has a wild sexual affair with Bob (who has apparently forgotten Karine, to whom he had pledged fidelity at the end of the first film). Revealing how neurotic yet how abnormally – by a puritanical North American yardstick – open about sex the French are, Corinne compulsively calls her husband before and after having sex with Bob to taunt him about her infidelity. The post-coital scenes and references to a sexual move referred to as the "toupie québécoise" (Quebec top; 1:29:40) all reinforce the Quebecers' virility as opposed to that of the French. To add to continentals' perversity, later on, after Bob has taught the move to Laurent, the latter thanks him for saving his marriage. Their relationship is in direct contrast to Stan's shy, honest, authentic desire for Violette (Anne-Marie Pisani), a café owner whom he courts and wins (staying with her for three years, until he returns home for *Les Boys III*). Of all the instalments, precisely because of the external threat of the French, *Les Boys II* presents its characters as the most traditionally masculine and sexual – even the overweight Léopold finds love.

The populist Québécois are not ashamed of their down-home, North American, agricultural roots. *Les Boys II* lampoons French sophistication as *guindée*, overly formal and precious, in contrast to the French Canadians' authenticity, which appears in their lack of cultural sophistication (e.g., Stan's beer drinking versus his French girlfriend's wine). A plot twist allows for a visual codification of their simple, old-fashioned natures in the team's hockey equipment. Innocents abroad, *Les Boys* have been duped by a con man offering better lodging for the same price (there is an extended gag about their seedy discount French hotel); he loads them in a van, drives them into the mountains, and steals all of their belongings. For this reason, they must play in hand-me-down, antique hockey gear. While they look ridiculous, this image also makes the connection between hockey's Canadian roots and the fact that *Les Boys* plan to play "old-time hockey."[69] *Les Boys* then receive penalty upon penalty playing a stereotypically Canadian rough game of heavy hitting against European "skill" players.[70] In an interesting reversal, Méo has made up with Stan and joins them as a player for the rest of the films; his background as a gangster helps out on the ice, as he cries out "On n'est pas des losers!" (We're not losers! 1:28:05), hitting as many opponents as he can as hard as he can, using dirty manoeuvres like tripping, slashing, and high-sticking. Incidentally, the middle-aged Méo is also the one who quickly masters French slang, using it and gangster techniques to recover their equipment from the thieves for the film's final match.

One of the most obvious markers of *québécitude* – the quality of Québec-ness – is the film's engagement of linguistic differences between Vernacular Quebec French (VQF) and French from France. Not only does Standard International French (SIF) – used in the French media, by service personnel in the tourist industry, and so on – differ from VQF, but so does French slang. As roommates Fern and Marcel settle down for the night, they are disturbed by excessively loud sounds of sex from the room next door – yet another opportunity to make fun of the overly sexed French. They knock on the wall and are immediately visited by an irate middle-aged Frenchwoman, who verbally abuses them with the term "tantouse" (a pejorative term for a male homosexual). When Marcel asks what that means, Fern speculates: "Je pense que ça veut dire 'Canadiens' en joual français" (I think that means "Canadians" in French *joual;* 24:32–35). Not only is his explanation ridiculous in its naivety, but so also is the reference to a specifically Québécois dialect, *joual*, as a general term for slang. Other linguistic misunderstandings arise, often as a result of VQF's practice of cannibalizing English expressions. When Stan uses his catchphrase, "dans mon livre à moi" (in my book ...), his French interlocuter takes this expression – which has no equivalent in French – literally, asking "Vous écrivez aussi ...?" (You write, too? 38:15–20). Later, he comes to help in the kitchen of Violette's café, asking: "Alors le fromage le coupes-tu en slice ...?" (To achieve the effect, I would translate this as: So, you cut the cheese in *tranches*? 48:35–40). The French are clearly at a loss when faced with the anglicism that would be understood by most Quebecers.

Not only does North American French differ from that of France, but so does its music. Although the tradition of the *chanson française* has led to the international popularity of now deceased artists like Édith Piaf, Jacques Brel, and Maurice Chevalier, contemporary French pop/rock is notoriously derivative. When rocker Julien sits in on a set with the bar band, he brings *real, authentic* rock'n'roll to the French. There is a hint of gender politics here as well; even a Québécois who looks like a girl – let us recall that Julien is a long-haired glam rocker, the inside of whose luggage looks like a woman's with its leopard-print underwear – is more masculine than these wimpy French cabaret singers. Further cultural differences appear in food staples. A publicity trailer at the beginning of the *Les Boys III* DVD makes it obvious that Pringles® negotiated a product placement deal; in *Les Boys II,* Fern brings the potato snacks to France with him and later offers Marcel "une bonne petite chip canadienne" (a nice little Canadian chip; 1:01:13–14).

As this garage league hockey team of amateurs begins to play in the *Tournoi International de Hockey Amateur de Haute-Savoie*, the film repeatedly nods to the well-known details of the 1972 Summit Series between

Canada and the Soviet Union.[71] One of the teams they face will be the "Sputniks" – an obvious reference to the satellite that placed all Westerners on alert that the Soviets might defeat the West in the Cold War space race. A slippage in references occurs, however; *Les Boys* will play the Ivory Coast first. Their disrespect for their opponents and their cocky attitude before what they obviously believe will be an easy win remains, however – a reference to Canadian attitudes prior to the 1972 series.[72] The film puts the Soviet team's words in the Ivoiriens' mouths as their captain tells Ti-Guy, "Nous sommes venus pour apprendre" (We are here to learn; 32:15–20)[73] – words that would obviously be out of place falling from Russian lips in the 1990s. To this, Ti-Guy replies without a trace of humility: "Vous êtes à la bonne place" (You're in the right place). They exchange gifts, respectively presenting each other with a beer mug – symbolic of Canada – and a stereotypically large-breasted African statue.

Increasingly frustrated by their lack of success against an opponent they have clearly underestimated and then against the home team, Laurent's Saint-Bernards, and finally the Sputniks, *Les Boys* resort to on-ice violence in a parody of the stereotypical image of "Canadian" hockey. This performance also nods ironically back to the Summit Series, one reason for which, according to Brian Kennedy, "was to heal the image of Canada abroad, which had been damaged by violent play in earlier international hockey events."[74] In spite of the franchise's overall message that these Québécois should *not* rely on brawn to win, that such violent, Canadian-style hockey is unnatural to them, they defeat Italian and French amateurs before saving national honour against the Russians. That they begin the tournament with a 6 to 1 upset by the Africans, however, allows the narrative to preserve the underdog status that is essential to the representation of *Les Boys* as Québécois trickster heroes.

The time eventually comes when the team must face off against the Moscow Sputniks. The throwback Méo toasts the prospect, "Aux Boys contre les Communistes" (To the Boys against the Communists), invoking some of the symbolic valence of the earlier, Cold War era Summit Series, which was repeatedly touted as an ideological contest. The humour here lies in part, of course, with the fact that Méo seems not to realize or accept the fall of the former Soviet Union, that he still reads the Russian team as equivalent to the Soviet one (which itself is an ironic reversal of the common erroneous assertion in the 1970s and 1980s that the Canadians, or the Americans as portrayed in *Miracle* [2004], faced off against the "Russians" rather than the Soviets). The division between European skills and Canadian roughness disappears in this match, and here, as in the first film of the series, *Les Boys'* advantage appears in their brains and heart, not in their brawn.

Brian Kennedy identifies the Summit Series as a defining event in contemporary Canadian identity: "By quite unexpectedly threatening Canadians' presumed mastery over the sport of hockey, the Russians created a situation that came to have lasting symbolic value. Thus, it might be argued that the events of September 1972 helped to create the Canada of today through giving a generation of people a touchstone moment with which to mark their participation in a shared culture."[75]

The integration of references to this historical event for comedic effect certainly suggests that its impact was truly national; indeed, *La Série du Siècle* was as closely followed in Quebec as elsewhere in Canada.[76] French Canadian players on the team, like Marcel Dionne (who never even saw ice time during the series), cite it as a major influence in their careers.[77] Kennedy's analysis invokes a contemporary account of the series by writer and journalist Jack Ludwig. Significantly for this discussion, Ludwig explicitly connects the Canadian team's performance to the nation's masculinity. Ludwig describes the staggering 7 to 3 loss in game one as a "national castration," asserting that "Canada, had so much wrapped up in this series that the experience on September 2, 1972, all but did its *macho* in."[78] Simon Richard cites journalists comparing the defeat to Napoleon's at Waterloo;[79] Jerry Trudel laments that "Hier soir, un mythe a été détruit et une leçon a été servie. Le mythe détruit, c'est celui de la suprématie du Canada au hockey; la leçon, c'est que l'intelligence a sa place même au hockey" (Last night, a myth was destroyed and a lesson given. The myth destroyed is that of Canada's supremacy in hockey; the lesson is that intelligence has its place even in hockey).[80]

Les Boys do address nationalist tensions at home. They perform their identity abroad as being specifically French *Canadian*, although at home in Canada, they would stress their identity as *French* Canadian. At one point in *Les Boys II*, Ti-Guy tries to explain Canadian politics to the Frenchman Laurent, who at first is dismissive: "C'est pas la Bastille, Québec, ça va pas si mal que ça [...]" (Quebec's not the Bastille; it's not that bad; 56:35–37). But he eventually admits: "Ça chez vous au Canada, c'est compliqué votre histoire" (At home for you in Canada, your history's complicated; 56:56). A foreigner commenting on Canadian politics sends Ti-Guy into a crisis of loyalty; family members, after all, may insult one another all day long, but when an outsider does so they join together to bring him down a notch. An increasingly drunk Ti-Guy replies: "Laisse-moi t'expliquer mon Canada dans toute sa complexité" (Let me explain my Canada in all of its complexity; 1:02:08–11). He then takes a shot of vodka for the name of each province, concluding: "Ne touchez pas à mon Canada, sinon, je te fracasse!" (Don't touch my Canada, or I'll break your neck!). The message here may be to the outsider: "Don't mess with Canada!"; but it is also a clearly federalist discourse, as Ti-Guy names Canada rather than Quebec and includes all ten provinces.

Les Boys II allowed a discourse of identity to be elaborated about differences between the Québécois and the French; *Les Boys III* engaged gender issues, pitting *Les Boys* against a women's team. *Les Boys IV* explicitly tackles the intra-Canadian national rivalry of Anglos versus Francos. Reflecting the highest production values of the franchise, the final big-screen instalment begins with a dream sequence in which Stan envisions *Les Boys* leaving the locker room and taking the ice with the likes of Martin Brodeur, Guy Lafleur, Ray Bourque, and other great francophone Canadiens players and even the token anglophone, Steve Shutt. As the film's opening reveals, if *Les Boys* can win the garage league championships, which means defeating a bigger, better-looking, more talented team from Toronto, they will play an exhibition match with the Montreal Canadiens Legends team.

Before the first game in the series, Méo – rather than Stan or Bob – gives the initial locker room pep talk, explicitly couching the rivalry in the discourse of *la Conquête,* Quebec nationalists' repeated invocation of the traumatic loss of New France to England. The communist-hating gangster-turned-florist first invokes the fall of the Berlin Wall and then brings up the national rivalry: "On joue, les gars, contre des Zanglais de Toronto. C'est un peu comme nos Plaines d'Abraham à nous autres. On va venger l'honneur de Montcalm une fois pour toutes" (We play tonight against the Zenglish from Toronto. It's a bit like our own Plains of Abraham. We're going to avenge the honour of Montcalm once and for all; 17:52–18:10). Méo is referring here, of course, to the Battle of the Plains of Abraham, on 13 September 1759, when the English general Wolfe defeated the French under Montcalm outside the walls of Quebec City. This has long been viewed as the definitive moment in Québécois history, for it led directly to the Treaty of Paris in 1763, under which New France was ceded to the English.

Les Boys are the clear underdogs in their match with the rival Toronto Barristers, who arrive on a chartered bus, wearing business suits like a pro team. This alludes strongly to the economic disadvantage long faced by French Canadians, who before the Quiet Revolution were largely blue-collar workers, while Anglos filled management positions.[81] Language games, this time between English and French, rather than North American versus European forms of French, support the film's humour. Above all, the pretension that Franco-Quebecers believe they can speak English is self-deprecatorily mocked. As the Barristers arrive, two of them comment on the appearance of Méo and Julien: an overweight, chain-smoking man with a bad combover and a skinny, long-haired glam rocker. When one calls out to Méo, "Hey fatso, ready to lose?", Méo pretends to understand, nodding and laughing, but asks Julien what he has just said. Julien admits, "J'suis pas sûr, mais je pense qu'il avait dit que t'avais l'air d'une grosse saucisse de Toulouse" (I'm not sure, but I think he said you look like a big Toulouse sausage; 15:35–38). Invoking Bob's famous speech about *la dureté du mental*, Méo, ever the tough guy, threatens the anglophone professionals in a code-switching polyglot of Canada's two official languages: "You know your mental is fucké. Anyway, I'll fix it on the glace [ice]" (15:56–58). Julien ironically compliments him: "Tu parles aussi bien l'anglais que le français" (Your English is as good as your French; 16:05). Later, during the match, Stan yells in English at the ref who fails to call a penalty against the Torontonians: "What's the matter with you!" Julien duefully cheers on: "Go Stan, tu parles anglais!" On both sides, insults are shared: an Anglo player shouts, "You're a frog, kiss me!", while Stan insults the English, calling them a "Gang d'habitants" (Bunch of peasants).

The word "frog" brings us back to the common association of French Canadians with the French. The British, of course, have long used that word to insult the French, and anglophone hockey players continue to use it to intimidate and insult their francophone opponents. Certainly, we expect that term to arise in depictions of Maurice Richard's struggles on the ice, and perhaps we are not too surprised when we hear a French Canadian player referred to as a "frog pussy" in *Slap Shot* (1977) – here, once again, Frenchness is being associated with a lack of masculinity. The term lingers in Frank Orr's novel *Puck Is a Four Letter Word* (1983), which he explains – ostensibly for American readers – as "a euphemism for French-Canadians."[82] Its longevity in today's atmosphere of political correctness astonishes me, yet former NHLer Bob Sirois, who played five seasons with the Washington Capitals in the 1970s, attests to its persistence. In *Discrimination in the NHL: Quebec Hockey Players Sidelined* (2010), he asserts that "in Canada, a supposedly bilingual country, hateful remarks can still be heard in 2010 from a clown cum sports commentator dressed in red [Don Cherry] who gets his thrills insulting French-speaking players on a government-owned national TV network. The National Hockey League has remained silent all too often or has studiously ignored racial slurs about 'Frogs,' especially when they are made by star players."[83]

Clearly, in Sirois's mind, this expression represents more than the "euphemism" that Frank Orr describes, and he cites incidences of its use continuing into the present. Perhaps ironically, hockey signifies for Franco-Quebecers as "one of the many cultural practices used to construct this national subjectivity,"[84] practices that distinctly differentiate Québécois from the Frenchmen with whom the slur aligns them in the first place. By playing hockey in a certain manner, the men of *Les Boys* perform their identity as Québécois. Similarly, the popularity of the *Les Boys* franchise reveals how hockey plays a central a role in the construction of a Québécois identity, a role just as significant as the one it plays in cementing the imagined community of the Canadian nation as a whole.

Any discussion of national identity in contemporary Quebec must address the issue of accommodating the increasingly diverse "cultural communities" in Montreal, the setting of *Les Boys*. In this area, the franchise comes up short in terms of progressive values, for it reinscribes Quebec as a land of ethnic French Canadians. *Les Boys* is an all-white team, and their last names (when we are told them) are French Canadian: Boisvert, Tremblay, and so on.[85] Only rarely do they encounter ethnic or cultural difference, and when they do, it is through the lens of stereotyped images, such as that of the Ivory Coast team they compete against in France: its players' uniforms are made of leopard print, and many of them sport afros. The one film that explicitly addresses the presence of ethnic Others in Montreal is *Les Boys III;* in it, a running gag involves surgeon François's (Serge Thériault) success with the ladies now that he has hair implants instead of a toupee. When he appears at Champions Club with an African Canadian date, Mario puts his foot in his mouth, asking the black woman, "Vous êtes sa blonde?" (Are you his girlfriend? 53:17). His awkwardness hinges on the Quebec-specific term for girlfriend, *blonde*, which also, obviously, refers to a blond woman. Mario tries to recover, next asking: "Vous êtes d'origine québécoise ou ... noire?" (Are you of Québécois or ... black origins?). The sequence indicates his clear discomfort with difference, his inability to process the anomaly of this woman's presence. The fact that François is wearing kente cloth further aggravates the violation of political correctness, as does his reappearance throughout the film with other visibly ethnic women of Asian and Latin American descent. In this respect, *Les Boys* follows the pattern of the sports film genre, which, in the words of Richard C. King and David J. Leonard, "clears a space to simultaneously reiterate taken-for-granted racial stereotypes and reasserts common sense racial hierarchies."[86]

Les Boys, La Série

While I was always cognizant of the problematic aspects of the franchise's treatment of women, minorities, and gay men, I must admit that I greatly enjoyed all four of the *Les Boys* films. The ritualistic repetition of various gags and individual catchphrases became part of that enjoyment: I "knew" *Les Boys* as characters and found their antics comical and endearing. In contrast, I was disappointed by the initial episodes of the television series and, frankly, relieved that they were twenty-two-minute rather than full-hour episodes.

Shilo T. McClean explains our anecdotal experience of the perceived decline in quality and originality from the first film to the last in any sequel or franchise experience with the assertion that "unlike genres, which start with a fresh story within an established generic style, franchises must work within the boundaries set by the original story."[87] This appears very clearly in the basic structure of a *Les Boys* film: the introduction of the central conflict that will drive the narrative forward (*I:* Stan's bet; *II:* negotiating international travel and playing in the European tournament; *III:* raising the funds for Mario's burnt-down house via the exhibition game with Team Canada Women; *IV:* winning the right to play the Canadiens Legends); sequences that introduce each character-player or that catch the viewer up on their lives since the last instalment; from one to three build-up hockey matches, with the attendant pre-game and period break locker room sessions, as well as post-game meals and partying; and finally, a climax hockey match in which the initial problem is resolved against all odds in favour of *Les Boys*.

Hockey plays a more peripheral role in the *Les Boys* series. Like each film, each season of the series poses, develops, and resolves a problem, while introducing mini-issues in each episode. The narrative conflict in season one (2007) involves *Les Boys'* desire to enter a $1,000,000 tournament in Las Vegas and the need for them to raise $10,000 each in registration fees. Several of the players take sideline jobs, around which humour will evolve – Marcel assists Méo in the latter's new funeral parlor; Julien signs on as a guinea pig in a pharmaceuticals company lab – instead of around hockey-related antics. Given the brevity of each episode, choices have had to be made regarding how much and which hockey-related settings to involve. The length of each film allowed the entire hockey-related sequence of rituals to be staged: pre-game and period break locker room antics (pranks, chatter, pep talks), ice time (occasionally even including the warm-up skate and national anthems, but at least one and sometimes all three periods of a match), and post-game time in Stan's bar or other venues. The brevity of each television episode means that viewers are treated to only a handful of hockey-related sequences. Often these are limited to a single, brief locker-room speech. In the first season, the team actually takes the ice only a handful of times. The development of Fern's private life in season one, episodes five, six, and seven, does offer a peripheral hockey-related theme for the series, as we learn that he works as a security guard at the old Bell Building in which the NHL offices are housed. When the Stanley Cup is held in the offices for a brief period, Fern thinks up a scam to charge people $100 to have their picture taken with the cup; everything goes wrong when it is stolen, with episode seven playing out as a parody of an array of crime dramas.

The franchisization of *Les Boys* ultimately undermines our reading of the films as Bildungsroman. First, with the gap of ten years between the initial film and the television series' premier in 2007, the disconnect between the actors' real ages and the immature attitudes and behaviours they display stretches beyond the plausible, even for the fantasy world of television comedy. More importantly, though, we are ultimately disappointed that none of the lessons the characters learned in the films "took" – that any personal development they might have experienced in the course of the films has completely disappeared. (Granted, each film itself had to stage some form of backsliding in maturity around which to develop the film's gags and comic aspects.) Viewer engagement with a novel, film, or television series, however episodic its plots may be, is largely invested in perceiving the characters as "real" people who grow and develop across the series. *Les Boys, La Série* fails in this respect. I invoke McClean again to understand this shortcoming; she asserts that "one of the main criticisms against the franchise film is the issue of the open-ended narrative. Such a structure is considered to be contrary to the classical narrative structure, which traditionally requires narrative closure."[88] The original Bildungsroman genre developed precisely as a classical narrative and ended with closure on the hero's maturation; the franchise, by its very nature, cannot close. Because *Les Boys* never grow up, the viewer remains unsatisfied in this regard.

So, what does this ridiculous and often very politically incorrect comedy franchise tells us about the meaning of hockey in Quebec? And more specifically for this chapter's arguments, what messages do *Les Boys* and its big- and small-screen spin-offs send to viewers about Québécois national identity and models for French Canadian masculinity? As Daniel A. Nathan points out in his critical analysis of the Marx Brothers' college football spoof *Horse Feathers* (1932), while we cannot read such popular texts as "a cogent, carefully documented critique"[89] of society, we can nonetheless draw a number of conclusions about its representations of how men, identity, and hockey interact in the Québécois imaginary. On the one hand, we have a progressive message of acceptance: friendship and loyalty trump difference, including alternatives to the dominant image of heteronormative, hegemonic masculinity. On the other, we see the reinscription of a patriarchal social system dominated by white men; women and minorities remain sidelined throughout the franchise, Pierrot and Jean-Charles's other lovers with them. The sport of hockey allows French Canadian men to assert a form of collective dominance and to differentiate and distance themselves from any perception of continental French effeminacy and intellectualism; furthermore, they can do so without fully embracing all aspects of an American-based image of sport as the venue par excellence for the assertion of a hegemonic form of masculinity. At the same time, it is clear that the French trait of using one's wits, of defying the system if necessary, is valorized and embraced. It is by "la dureté du mental" as well as their trickster natures, that *Les Boys* defeat the bad guys.

Coda: *Mirador*, "Nourrir la Bête"

A hockey-related scandal forms the central plot thrust of *Mirador*, a recent dramatic television series produced in Quebec. It addresses directly the question of homosexuality in hockey and somewhat indirectly the real-life coach sexual abuse scandals that have recently come to light. Most famously, former NHL player Theo Fleury went public with charges that his junior league hockey coach had abused him.[90] Episode three of *Mirador*'s first season, "Nourrir la Bête," opens with a sensationalistic portrayal of a hockey coach verbally abusing what we believe to be a hockey player, suited up in the locker room, a sequence that concludes with highly charged sexual contact between coach and player. It eventually becomes clear that this anglophone, Tom, was not a player but a prostitute helping professional coach René Duval play out one of his fantasies. When a video of the two men kissing goes viral, Duval's team, the fictional Cavaliers, hires Mirador, a public relations firm, to perform damage control. In a conversation with Patrick Labbé's character, Philippe Racine, who perpetually invokes the need to tell the truth and to toe a moral line in the face of his less ethical boss (Gilles Renaud) and jealous younger brother (David La Haye), Coach Duval asserts the gravity of the stakes for his career: "Un coach fif au hockey, c'est pas très bien côté" (A fag coach in hockey just doesn't sell).

The episode underscores the persistence of negative attitudes about homosexuality in the hockey world; indeed, it participates in such discourses through its demonization of Duval. He is shown to have secret, sadistic sexual fantasies about chastising young men, since Tom portrays himself as a minor to the press. Also, Duval is not openly gay and has a wife and children whom he fears losing. The situation is first portrayed as if the young man – who turns out to be nineteen and so legally an adult – had been blackmailing Duval for money; but as it turns out, his actions were motivated by " love" – he was trying to force Duval to leave his family.

The episode's opening sequence, which couples forbidden sexual acts with verbal abuse, echoes much too clearly the horribly damaging reality of such cases, the best-known of which in recent times involved, as noted, Theo Fleury.[91] He filed charges against Graham James and further publicized his battle for justice and closure in public appearances. For example, he competed in the CBC reality series *Battle of the Blades* (2010–11), for which he served as a guest judge the following season.

However interesting we find this discourse about the taboo against homosexuality in hockey, the episode of *Mirador* further engages questions of alternative masculinities in its characterization of bad boy Luc Racine (La Haye). Racine is very much the trickster, albeit a highly destructive one, with no redeeming traits. La Haye plays him up as a narcissistic dandy, to the extent that his impeccable suits, gelled hair, and primping strut lead the company's female employees (Catherine Trudeau and Marie-Ève Milot) to think he is gay. His vile nature appears in his method of setting them straight, so to speak, about his sexual orientation: he corners the young and innocent Geneviève (Milot) in the washroom and kisses her on the lips. She responds by clearly expressing her sense of violation. Indeed, another PR firm's president misreads Luc's manipulative behaviour as homosexual interest and kisses him on the lips – a karmic payback for his own aggression towards Geneviève. This ruins Luc's plans to betray both his brother and Mirador by selling their files to a rival: his horror at being perceived as gay is so great that he abandons the lucrative deal. Once again we face mixed messages about masculinity, packaged in a clearly hegemonic, heterosexual individual who does not present overtly as such. On the one hand, the series depicts the full integration of homosexuals into Quebec society, where they hold positions of power and prestige, as is the case with the head of the rival company. On the other, the women mock Luc because they believe him to be gay, and he himself is horrified by the notion that others would perceive him as such. Furthermore, the characterization of the series' villain as a non-normative heterosexual male contrasts clearly with that of the hero, Philippe, with his good looks and his traditional heterosexual masculinity. (Following Richard Dyer's "star" theory,[92] viewers would likely remember Labbé's previous role in *Les Boys* – the relatively macho Mario.)

These and the other popular culture texts discussed in this book repeatedly demonstrate hockey's wide appeal in Quebec; clearly, hockey draws viewers to the cinemas and to their living room television screens. But hockey also serves as a platform for exploring problems in Quebec society, whether this involves presenting a somewhat nostalgic image of the ethnically homogeneous but professionally diverse microcosm of the nation, or ambivalently handling the integration of gay men into contemporary Quebec society, or addressing the threat of sexual predators. Such portrayals confirm that in Quebec, as Aaron Baker asserts of the United States, "sports are of interest to filmmakers because they are hardly apolitical and they serve as an arena in which the 'contested process of defining social identities' regarding race, class, gender, and sexuality takes place."[93]

Chapter Five

Rock and Roll, Skate and Slide: Hockey Music as an Expression of National Identity in Quebec

In Montreal, the Canadiens matter! *In Quebec, the Canadiens* matter! *In Canada, the Canadiens* matter!

Bob Gainey[1]

Québécois music [is] seen as the very symbol of modern Québécois culture, and hence one of the driving forces behind the survival and development of le fait français *(the French factor) in the Americas.*

Line Grenier[2]

Through the Mist (2009) tells the brilliant and tragic life story of André Fortin, nicknamed "Dédé," the outspokenly nationalist lead singer of the extremely popular 1990s group Les Colocs. The biopic opens with a broad establishing shot of a wintry rural landscape; before we see him, we hear the unmistakable swish of skates on ice; an instant later, a lone hockey player crosses the pond, approaches a goal that we now see, shoots, and scores. This is followed by a series of cuts to a reverse shot of a house on the hill above the pond and then of another man coming towards the ice and calling out: "Dédé! Come on man. J'suis pas ici pour jouer le hockey! [*sic*]" (I'm not here to play hockey!). The stubborn player continues his game while his bandmate, Mike Sawatzky, returns, frustrated, to the house; he complains to a third collaborator, André Vanderbiest, "I can't work like this, man!" Vander replies, "C'est son rythme [...]. On force pas un type à créer; c'est contre nature" (It's his rhythm. You can't force a guy to create; it's against nature.)

The film's ability to deploy the imagery of hockey to signify a rock star's intense relationship to a distinct national identity and culture, linking these to the "natural" creative forces of the northern landscape, may well be an artistic decision only possible in Quebec. Even given the strong meaning of hockey in English Canada, the sport's connection to popular music remains more tenuous. Granted, the Tragically Hip's "The Lonely End of the Rink" (*World Container*, 2006) powerfully exploits the nation's love of the game in its homage to the position of goalie, but can we imagine a film about them introducing its subject's core identity with a hockey sequence?[3] In this chapter, we explore how contemporary popular music has become yet another vehicle for expressing the province's love of the game, while at the same time hockey itself serves as a signifier of national belonging in popular lyrics and music videos.

The roots of "hockey music" can be traced back to the beginning of the twentieth century, in "Halte-là, halte-là, halte-là, les Montagnards sont là," the anthem of the Montagnards, the first French-speaking hockey team in Montreal; they also played lacrosse.[4] This was adapted to "Les Canadiens sont là," which along with "Envoyons d'l'avant" – "an old Habitant lumberjack song," according to Herbert Wind – was sung in the Forum at early Canadiens games, as well.[5] Maurice Richard inspired a number of songs during his career, including "Maurice Richard" (1951), performed by Jeanne d'Arc Charlebois, and "Rocket Rock and Roll" (1957), by Denise Filiatrault, both of which eroticized the star.[6] Here, however, I must limit my analysis to the role of hockey in contemporary popular musical genres. First, I will lay the groundwork with a brief discussion of the development of the contemporary French-language popular music scene, examining in greater detail the sport's presence in *Through the Mist*. The core of this chapter, though, analyses the hockey-themed music of the now iconic nationalist rappers, Loco Locass, and the sport's presence in the work of Mes Aïeux, a group that expresses its local identity through the marriage of traditional French Canadian folk music and alternative rock. Finally, I examine two acts that have incorporated hockey into their very identity as musicians, the post-punk rock group Les Dales Hawerchuk and the ex-minor league hockey pro turned singer/songwriter, Bob Bissonnette.

Quebec Pop: Popular Music as Signifier of National Identity

Without rehashing the entire music history of the province, some introductory background comments will serve to contextualize the analyses that comprise this chapter and, indeed, to justify the inclusion of texts arising from a popular culture genre that many, at first glance, might consider apolitical, derivative, or an expression of teenage angst, sexual desire, lost love, and other universal sentiments. According to François Yelle, the field of Cultural Studies has been slow to develop in Quebec;[7] however, a handful of scholars from a range of disciplines have begun to examine the ups and downs of Quebec's French-language music industry and the role played by popular music as a reflection of contemporary life and a contributor to young people's sense of belonging as Canadians/Quebecers. Speaking of the entire federation, Roger Chamberland argues that "listening to music is one of the most important cultural practices in Canada";[8] while Line Grenier asserts for the province that "Québécois music [is] seen as the very symbol of modern Québécois culture, and hence one of the driving forces behind the survival and development of *le fait français* (the French factor) in the Americas."[9]

Contemporary Québécois popular music is often described in terms of a paradox:[10] its musical forms are often derived largely from rock and its subgenres as these have been developed in the United States and (to a lesser extent) Britain. But at the same time, since the 1960s, French-language popular music has been at the forefront of both cultural and sovereignist nationalist movements. Line Grenier and Val Morrison contend that the diversity and vibrancy of popular sounds produced in Quebec today resulted from an acrimonious debate that raged from the 1960s through to the 1980s about the kinds of music that could authentically represent a contemporary Québécois identity in development.[11] In what has become known as the *yé-yé versus chansonnier* debate, proponents of Anglo-American-style rock'n'roll – referred to (disparagingly) in French as *yé-yé*, a gallicization of the phrase "Yeah, yeah," found in French-language songs performed by Petula Clark and Dany Logan[12] – faced off against those arguing for the more obviously French-inflected form, *la chanson* (song). A tradition long developed in France, *la chanson* values the words as much as the music – indeed, the poetry of Jacques Prévert (1900–1977), for example, served as the basis for many *chansons*.[13] Félix Leclerc played a seminal role in the development of the *chansonnier*, the singer/songwriter, even influencing Metropolitan French performers like Georges Brassens and Jacques Brel.[14] During the highly politicized 1960s, Gilles Vigneault (b. 1928) came to typify the role, with songs like "Gens du pays" (People of the country), which has become the province's unofficial anthem since its presentation at the 1975 Saint-Jean-Baptiste Day celebrations. According to Grenier and Morrison, the opposition between *chanson* and *yé-yé* had resolved itself by the 1980s, so that today, for a number of reasons, the primary – indeed the sole – marker of authenticity in Québécois popular music has become the language in which it is performed: French.[15]

Quebec's contemporary popular music scene also owes some of its dynamism to Canadian federal initiatives and to the province's own franco-nationalist politics. Both Canada and Quebec have generated significant discourses about the development of a national popular culture in the face of the perception (and reality) that the United States's hegemonic culture industry has flooded Canadian markets and drowned out authentic domestic products. The state has for decades taken measures to counter this activity by promoting cultural production. Initially, this meant "high" culture, after the Massey Commission in 1951, but later it came to include popular cultural media like television and radio. Specifically for our purposes, federal and provincial subsidies have directly helped Québécois artists produce records, and in addition to that, Canadian and French-language content regulations for broadcast media have guaranteed a market for those productions. In his examination of the construction of Canadian national identity through cultural forms as diverse as visual art and folk music, Robert Wright informs us that as early as 1971, the Canadian Radio-Television and Telecommunications Commission (CRTC) ruled that "30 per cent of the radio programming in Canada must qualify as 'Canadian content' (or 'Cancon'), that is, it must be written, performed or produced in Canada."[16] Nearly three decades later, in 1999, "the CRTC quietly raised the Cancon quota for commercial radio from 30 per cent to 35."[17] For Quebec, the additional concern of language prompted government intervention, and the promulgation of a related CRTC policy governing "French-language vocal music (FVM) [...] which forces radio stations to devote at least 65% of their programming to French-language music."[18] To fulfil these quotas, government subsidies for production, marketing, and distribution were developed in the 1980s.[19] And although radio has begun to decline as a source for contemporary music – particularly alternative forms of it – other media have stepped in to facilitate its dissemination, including music television in the 1980s, the CD and now MP3 markets, streaming on the World Wide Web, and free music sharing on sites like YouTube.[20]

Government subsidies permitted independent record producers to thrive. This financial boost, coupled with the resolution of divisive internal debates over *yé-yé vs. chansonnier*, and franco-nationalism's renewal during the fervour leading up to the 1995 referendum, contributed to the development of a thriving French-language music scene by the late 1990s. The groups discussed below, most of which formed in the mid to late 1990s, benefited in one way or another from these conditions. Openly nationalist groups like Loco Locass and Mes Aïeux also found inspiration in the work of Les Colocs, led by André Fortin, which tapped into Quebec's folk music tradition (for example, in "La Comète," *Il me parle du Bonheur*, 2009) as well as that of world music (found in the participation of Senegal's Diouf brothers on *Dehors novembre* [1998]). All of this helped generate the type of "glocal" contemporary music that combines the global with the local and appeals to a range of Quebec age groups and listening audiences.

André Fortin, Hockey Star: Constructing the Quebec Rock Icon in *Dédé, Á travers les brumes*

The sequence described in this chapter's opening paragraph establishes one of the film's central dramatic conflicts. It also uses the imagery of hockey to introduce viewers to its central figure, who according to Audrey Messier is not just a Québécois rock icon but a figure of nationalist myth.[21] On the ice, Dédé – who will be depicted throughout the film alone in winter landscapes – enjoys the freedom of man in his natural environment. The filmmakers invoke viewers' nostalgia for the pure, unspoiled, "natural" form of the sport, specifically depicting him playing pond hockey. In tune with nature, the artist draws upon and renews his creative energies, which cannot be forced, according to bandmate Vanderbiest. In contrast, the house and Mike's interpellation from it represent the bonds of society and responsibility – specifically, Dédé's duty to work with the band on the album Les Colocs are supposed to be writing and recording there. The shot–reverse shot images of Dédé on the pond, cutting back to Mike and the house, set up the tension between individual freedom and the natural creative forces of musical genius – a genius also plagued by madness, as Dédé's tragic death by hara-kiri eventually reveals. Those same shots also highlight the constraints imposed by our relationships to others.

Francis Daniel argues that "like nothing else, hockey allows us to celebrate our northernness [...] it speaks of winter, Canada's season."[22] Thus, André Fortin's identity is partly revealed by the film's association of the northern landscape of rural Quebec in winter with the national sport of hockey. The sequence that follows reinserts the natural man of the frozen fields and ponds back into society. Dédé (Sébastien Ricard) has joined Mike (Joseph Mesiano) and Vander (David Quertiniez) inside for supper, and this communal meal signifies a renewal of the social bonds the artist had temporarily rejected by ignoring the call to work. At this point, the musician explicitly establishes his social identity as a nationalist. The Belgian Vanderbiest asks, "Qu'est-ce que tu dirais que t'es? Un francophone, un ...?" (What would you say you are? A francophone, a ...?). Dédé immediately replies, "Un Québécois." In contrast to this franco-nationalism, Mike retorts, "Depuis que j'suis au Québec tu parles que de ça. Moi, je suis un fucking Indian de Saskatchewan. Independence? We had it. We lost it" (Since I've been in Quebec you've been talkin' about nothin' but that). While the film fails to develop this controversial assertion, Mike's role as Dédé's Others – Anglos and Indians – represents his inclusive attitude. At one point, he asserts in English, "Hey, I don't refuse to play with the other loneliness," his quirky wordplay on Hugh MacLennan's now clichéd concept of Canada being comprised of *Two Solitudes* (1945).

The film reiterates Dédé's sovereignist position throughout the flashback sequences. These trace his arrival in Montreal from the northeastern region of Lac Saint-Jean, his encounter with his first love, Nicole, and the group's formation in 1990. Again, during a dinner conversation with a large group of friends, Dédé challenges Mike, whom he has only recently met; he speaks English since the latter has not yet learned the colloquial French he speaks by the winter of 1998, the film's primary chronotope. "There's a problem," Dédé tells him. "I'm a nationalist, sovereignist, separatist. Whatever you want to call it. I'll talk about it. I'll talk about it loudly. And you're an Anglo and an Indian. So will you be able to deal with that?" Ultimately, by depicting Dédé's intense excitement on the day of the 1995 referendum and his deeply felt disappointment with its results, the film appears to be suggesting that this loss figures among a series of tragedies, including the AIDS death of group co-founder Patrick Napoli (Dimitri Storoge), which may have sent the fragile genius over the brink, leading to his suicide in 2000.

Additional hockey sequences and several winter exteriors, in which Dédé appears running barefoot through the snow and later hallucinates an encounter with his dead father while cross-country skiing, contribute to the notion that the artist is in a downward spiral. After the flashbacks reveal Napoli's death, Dédé struggles with his grief on the ice, which no longer offers him the pleasure it once did. A shot captures the frozen pond, empty but for the lone goal net; then an overhead shot reveals Dédé no longer skating, but instead prone on the ice with his hockey stick gripped tightly across his throat, almost as if it were choking him, the puck positioned above and to the right at two o'clock. The film's final hockey image shows the pond's ice melting, the goal akimbo, partially submerged, signalling the *déchéance*, the decline of the artist it represents, the beginning of his engulfment by the imbalance that will result in his dramatic suicide by *seppuku*. A new recurrent image takes over, that of Dédé flying an enormous kite, revealing that in some sense, he has lost his footing in the natural world – a footing perhaps already precarious, balanced as he is on his skates on the slippery ice? – and that his soul is preparing to leave this world and ascend to the heavens. The genius's curse was foreshadowed during the bitter break-up with Nicole, who cried out in anger, "Dédé, tu vis pas dans la réalité!" (Dédé, you don't live in the real world).

Although the title invokes hockey, Les Colocs' song "Passe-moé la puck" (*Les Colocs*, 1993) actually tells the story of a homeless person being interviewed for an exploitative television news report. The song's title refers to his suggestion that if someone would pass him the puck, give him an assist, then he *could* score, could succeed in life. Here, the catchy hockey line may lure listeners to heed the song's social message. As we will see in this chapter, the hockey reference is almost ubiquitous in Quebec popular music today; indeed, the role of André Fortin in *Through the Mists* (as the biopic was titled in English) was cast with another artist in whose work hockey has taken a central role: Sébastien Ricard, better known to Quebec music fans as Batlam of the group Loco Locass.

The Habs as Signifier of National Unity: Loco Locass "Le but (à la gloire de nos Glorieux)"[23]

Through the Mist concludes with title cards making explicit that André Fortin took his own life using the samurai ritual of *hara-kiri*, that the band broke up, and that its surviving members went on to solo careers. The final title before the closing credits asserts that "l'énergie festive des COLOCS, leur volonté de chanter en français et leur engagement social et politique aura ouvert la voie à toute une génération de groupes francophones québécois" (the festive energy of the Colocs, their desire to sing in French, and their political and social commitment will open the way for an entire generation of francophone groups in Quebec). A major success in the wake of Les Colocs were the nationalist rappers known as Loco Locass, and *Through the Mist* capitalized on that success by casting Ricard in the role of Dédé. Ricard, joined by Sébastien

Fréchette (Biz) and Stéphane Dionne-Farhoud (Chafiik), began to rap in French in the mid-1990s; their overtly nationalist agenda contributed to their popularity, as the title of their first big hit, "Libérez-nous des Libéraux" (*Amour oral*, 2004), suggests.

The young men, noticing the popularity of American hip hop in the province and of the new, French-language rap coming from France,[24] believed that francophone rap had the potential to "agir sur le Québec, l'influencer, prendre part au destin de cette nation" (act on Quebec, to influence it and take part in the destiny of this nation), as one group member told Christopher M. Jones in a 1996 interview.[25] First using a standard spelling, "Les Locos Loquaces" (The Loquacious Locos) asserted the specificity of their Québécois rap both linguistically, as seen in titles like "Sheila, ch'us là" (Sheila, I'm here; *Manifestif*, 2000), and musically, in their willingness to include "de la turlutte, de la cuillère, du tapage de pied, du folklore québécois dans une chanson hip hop" (traditional Quebec song forms, spoons, foot tapping, and folklore in a hip hop song).[26] Their appearances at the Montreal Francofolies musical festival since 1999, their 2001 Félix award at the ADISQ gala (the Quebec equivalent of a Grammy), and their inclusion in "Fête nationale," the annual Saint-Jean-Baptiste Day celebrations in the early years of the new millennium, all established Loco Locass as representing not only contemporary Quebec music, but Quebec national culture itself.

In her recent monograph, Marie-Claude Tremblay legitimates the group's use of the term "rapoèmes" to describe their work, analysing the recurring themes of their lyrics and identifying their poetic aspects, such as the use of alliteration, enjambment, wordplays, and rapid shifts in register (from formal discourse to the highly informal).[27] A love for language, both as a vehicle for a message and as an end in itself, marks the group's work, according to Tremblay, who observes the inevitable connection between nationalist politics and the promotion of French, which represents the group's central theme.[28] The very title of "Langage-toi," for example, plays on the French term for language (*langage*) and the imperative of the verb describing political engagement (*engage-toi*); that song appeared on a CD titled *Manifestif* (2000), another wordplay combining the French terms for manifesto and civil demonstration (*manif*, short for *manifestation*) with the adjective *festif*, a cognate for the English festive. The message appears to be: have fun, but also get involved and express an opinion. For the group, the nationalist nature of that message is undeniable, as Tremblay demonstrates in her analysis of their lyrics;[29] but it is also indicated visually in their use of the provincial flag's royal-blue and fleur-de-lys motifs on stage. Jones describes the group as sovereignist and *engagé* (politically engaged),[30] a stance they reconfirm in *Le Québec est mort, vive le Québec* (2012). It thematizes the 2012 student demonstrations, referred to as the "printemps québécois" or "printemps érable," thus riffing on the "printemps arabe." Its first track, "[wi]," a bilingual wordplay on the phonetic spelling of "oui," references the Yes vote needed for Quebec sovereignty to pass and the English *we*, the union of the collectivity similarly necessary; it is also probably a reference to the *wi* of wireless communications. Yet the album also includes a surprisingly uncritical homage to the Montreal Canadiens, released as a single in 2008, in which the group's usually critical stance appears buffered.

As franco-nationalists, Loco Locass are inevitably hockey fans, and two of their recent hits, "Hymne à Québec" and "Le But (à la gloire de nos Glorieux)," honour the national game. Hockey makes cameo appearances in their other songs as well. For example, the group inserts a clever hockey reference in "La Paix des braves," a collaboration with Samian, the first person to rap in French and Algonquin; this work celebrates the positive exchanges between French colonists and Native people in the colonial period long before hockey's codification in the last quarter of the nineteenth century. Referencing an actual historical event in which Samuel de Champlain's crew were treated for scurvy with the indigenous, vitamin C-rich tea made from white spruce (*arbor vitae*) bark,[31] they colourfully assert that

> La maladie du scorbut scorait droit au but
> Et, c'est aux Premières Nations que je dois ma guérison.
>
> The illness of scurvy [*scorbut*] scored right in the goal
> And it's to the First Nations that I owe my recovery.

Unfortunately, my translation fails to transmit the wordplay's humour. Of more direct interest to us here, the group's "Hymne à Québec" was used as the team song for the province's capital in a recent television reality series, *La Série Montréal-Québec,* in which each city iced a team of amateurs – which included two women and one man over forty and another over fifty – to train and compete for hometown supremacy.[32] Although the anthem largely focuses on praising the geography, topography, history, and cultural aspects of the provincial capital, the song devotes a verse to hockey: "Au hockey on s'prend contre n'importe qui mais j't'avertis: / Ça barde le long des bandes à l'aréna Bardy" (In hockey, we'll take on anybody, but I warn you / Sparks fly along the boards at Bardy Arena). The group's most thorough treatment of hockey, however, praises the Montreal Canadiens as a *lieu de mémoire*, a site of memory, as conceived by Pierre Nora (a concept linked to Maurice Richard in chapter 1).

Nora describes the site of memory not only as a place but also as an item. Thus, the red, white, and blue of the French flag is a site "where memory crystallizes and secretes itself ... where a sense of historical continuity persists."[33] Loco Locass's "Le But (à la gloire de nos Glorieux)" (2008) clearly invests the Canadiens as a site for French Canadian, then Québécois national identity. The song's very title invokes a sense of history; it is a frank homage that infers a relationship between the team and glorious heroes of the French Canadian/Québécois past like René Lévesque and Louis-Joseph Papineau. The hockey context appears immediately through the prelude, which is composed of faint organ music accompanied by the unmistakable sound of a hockey puck sliding across the ice; it is then recoded to indicate a Québécois specificity in the title's use of "nos Glorieux," with the collective "we" and the use of the French-language nickname for the Canadiens. Furthermore, the goal – literally, to score in the game – may be read polysemically in the context of Loco Locass's reputation as nationalist rappers, as referring to a wider goal of recognition for Quebec's distinct francophone society.

The lyrics begin with a direct invocation of the province and its natural features. Here, the group's French is loaded with *québécismes* (in my italics):

> *Icitte* au Québec *y* fait pas froid, *y* fait *frette*
> C'est *de même* parce que c'est *de même pis* c'est *ben correct*
> On a de la place en masse
>
> Here in Québec, it's not cold, it's colt
> It's like that because it's the same and it's correct
> We've got tons of space

These linguistic choices signal the immediacy of Quebec, through its language as well as its climate and geography; the cold, wide-open spaces reflect the discourse of the naturalization of hockey as a metaphor for Canada critiqued by Gruneau and Whitson,[34] Brian Wilson,[35] and others. With the ice of the rink standing in metonymically for the ice of the North, the hockey-for-Quebec metaphor appears ever more clearly: "Et nos face-à-face on les fait sur la glace" (Our face-offs, we do them on the ice). This is finally made explicit: "c'est la métaphore de notre sort" (it's a metaphor for our fate). Playing on a sense of their audience's shared, collective knowledge, Loco Locass refer to Maurice Richard by first name only. The hero inspires subsequent generations, as the lyrics invoke a collective "we" (*on/nos*), likening it to him:

Alors, on lace nos patins pis nos casques
Et comme Maurice, on glisse dans l'arène avec la haine de la défaite
Et le feu dans les yeux
En fait, quand on veut, on peut / Gagner!

So we lace up our skates then our helmets
And like Maurice, we slide in the arena with hate for defeat
and fire in the eyes
Indeed, when we want to, we can
Win!

"Gagner" (to win) becomes a refrain, repeated again and again throughout the song; if hockey is a metaphor for "our" destiny, then of course the goal of winning here refers not only to the game, to the Stanley Cup, but also to winning the larger battle of national sovereignty.

Collective memory, which plays an essential role in the song's establishment of community focused on the shared love of a team and its heroes, reaches further into the past, recalling a time when the term "Canadiens" referred to French Canadians, and Anglo-Canadians were called *les Anglais:*

En des temps si lointains qu'les francos s'appelaient Canadiens
À une époque où les pucks étaient faites de crottin
On a réuni des hommes dont le destin commun est comme un film sans fin
En Technicolor et tricolore

In times so long ago that Francos were called Canadiens
An epoch when pucks were made of turds
We got together men whose common destiny is like an endless film
In Technicolor and the tricolour.

This sense of common destiny, "linking the history of its ancestors to the undifferentiated times of heroes, origins, and myth,"[36] invokes the quasi-mythical past of the *Anciens Canadiens* and earlier generations of nationalists like l'abbé Lionel Groulx, who asserted that the mission of the French-Canadian people was to populate the continent and to spread Catholicism.

That sense of destiny and the linkage of hockey to the physical geography of the continent recur in the lyrics' recitation of the three colours of the *lieu de mémoire*, linking the bodies of the hockey team to the body politic:

Bleu comme le Saint-Laurent
Blanc comme l'hiver
Rouge comme le sang qui nous coule à travers
Le corps de l'équipe c'est le cœur de la nation.

Blue like the Saint Lawrence
White like winter
Red like the blood that flows through us
The body of the team is the heart of the nation.

This common past unites those of the present, and although so far the song refers to a traditional, ethnic nationalism, we soon see that it includes not only francophones but all Montrealers, if not all citizens of a new, postnational, transcultural Quebec:

le tissu social de Montréal
C'est de la Sainte-Flanelle ... C'est ça qui nous ressemble
C'est ça qui nous rassemble.

The social fabric of Montréal
Is made of the Holy Flannel ...
It's that which resembles us
It's that which unites us.

While the Canadiens represent a specifically French Canadian contribution, they also stand as synecdoche, the part for the whole, of Quebec, and the lyrics operate a constant slippage in reference from Montreal to the entire province and back: "les Canadiens pour une fois / Rallient tous les Québécois" (the Canadiens, for once / Rally all Quebecers). Of course, during the existence of the Quebec Nordiques from 1972 to 1995, first in the World Hockey Association and then in the NHL, the Canadiens could not claim to represent the entire province. Indeed,

Jean-Claude Simard associates the two teams with "deux formes de nationalisme, l'un fédéraliste, l'autre indépendantiste" (two forms of nationalism, one federalist, the other independentist).[37] In the same way that the provincial government asks as a condition for inclusion that new immigrants learn French, so Loco Locass dubs as authentic citizens *all* Quebecers who partake of the holy wine of Canadiens fandom:

> Anglo, franco peu importe ta couleur de peau
> Si tu détestes Toronto le sang qui bouge dans tes artères
> Est aussi rouge, mon frère, que les chandails de nos
> Vingt cœurs de vainqueurs.
>
> Anglo, Franco, whatever the colour of your skin
> If you hate Toronto the blood that moves in your veins
> Is as red, my brother, as the sweater of our
> Twenty hearts of Conquerors.

As these lines erase the precise markers of belonging to an ethnically based national or racial group, of differences in "blood" and skin colour, they create a community founded on a different basis, but still drawing on a shared past and a present rivalry, in order to achieve a future goal. Inevitably, it would seem, this collective unity is depicted as built through opposition to a common foe, Toronto, a potential metonymy for the Rest of Canada, as Olivier Bauer observes,[38] but one that excludes the Western provinces and their NHL teams. Sport appears ambivalently, both as an icon of a specifically French Canadian/ Franco-Québécois national identity and as a unifying force that melts away difference to allow for contemporary civic, non-ethnic notions of either or both urban and national identity. As Jonathan Cha compellingly demonstrates, although such significance may be built through popular and administrative efforts, it often results from entrepreneurial publicity campaigns.[39]

Cha describes the *hockeyisation* of Montreal as "propageant 'la bonne nouvelle'" (propagating "the Good News / the Gospel").[40] Loco Locass's "Le But" exploits such religious imagery, which harkens back to the Catholic tradition of pre–Quiet Revolution Quebec and compromises the desire to include diversity within that community, revealing ambivalence and nostalgia for a community that is homogeneous if only in its sports loyalties. Comparing that rivalry to a Crusade, the Stanley Cup to the Holy Grail, and so on, the group intones:

Nos chevaliers sont en cavale pour ramener le Graal à Montréal
Le tournoi est un chemin de croix parsemé d'émois
Mais la Coupe on y croit, comme autrefois, on a la foi
Pis si c'est pas c't'année, ben comme dirait René
"À la prochaine fois."

Our knights are mounted to bring the Grail back to Montreal
The tournament is a Way of the Cross sprinkled with emotion
But the Cup, we believe in it, like before, we have faith
But if it's not this year, well, like René would say
"Til the next time."

The sufferings of the patient fan, steadfast in the belief that victory will return, resemble those of Christ on the fourteen Stations of the Cross. And like the Catholic tradition, so, too, the nationalist is again invoked, with the reference to René Lévesque's famous speech after the defeat of the 1980 referendum.

The *lieu de mémoire*'s association with ritual appears in the rituals of the hockey game, but also in its treatment as religion, itself a recurring metaphor in hockey discourses. At various moments throughout the song, the ritualistic aspect of the game appears in the exhortation "Gagner!" It also appears in the final chorus: "Allez, allez, allez, allez Montréal." At one moment, the group literally chants the name of the Canadiens great Guy Lafleur: "Guy! Guy! Guy!" Loco Locass do not forget another obligatory element of the hockey liturgy, the litany of great stars remembered: "Jack Laviolette, [Elmer] Lach, [Didier] Pitre et Pit Lépine en passant par Newsy Lalonde et Joe Malone, Aurèle [Joliat] et [Howie] Morenz, [George] Hains[worth], [Jacques] Plante, Gump [Lorne Worsley]" and so on. The importance of inclusion is signalled as a group member calls: "Oublie pas les anglos, yo. Toe [Hector Blake],[41] Dickie [Irvin], Doug [Harvey] et Scotty [Bowman], [Steve] Shutt, Larry [Robinson], Ken [Dryden] et Bobby [Smith]" (Don't forget the Anglos, yo).

Canadiens like Maurice Richard, Guy Lafleur, and the entire recitative of past stars inspire the present because of their excellence, yet at the same time, the song serves to rally courage in hard times – the current hard times the Canadiens are experiencing:

Mais quand ça va mal, quand on cale ou on dévire
Que je voie pas un sale quitter le pont du navire
C'pas à matin qu'on accroche nos patins

Un Flying Frenchman, franchement! Ça franchit sans flancher.

But when it's going bad, when we stall or stray
I don't want to see a single one leave the bridge of the ship
It's not in the morning that we hang up our skates
A Flying Frenchman, frankly! He crosses without quavering.

The hard times for which the true fan needs faith did not occur during the 1950s, when "Montreal ruled hockey."[42] Rather, they date back to 1980: they have won the Stanley Cup exactly twice since then (in 1986 and 1993). In contrast to Loco Locass's unquestioned goal of rallying enthusiasm, particularly in a season like 2008, at the end of which the Canadiens nearly touched the Grail, Mes Aïeux's "Le Fantôme du Forum" takes a more critical approach to the commercial aspects of hockey, directly linking that lack of success to the Canadiens' controversial move out of an established *lieu de mémoire* and into a contemporary facility designed specifically to make more money for the team's owners.

Lieu de mémoire or *lieu du dollar?* Mes Aïeux's "Le Fantôme du Forum"

The Canadiens' success over the decades offered francophone fans an image of themselves as winners, while anglophone fans felt a sense of pride as they conquered teams from the south as US hegemony in the NHL grew over the years. That success may seem linked to the team's home ice from 1924 to 1996, the Forum, since they have failed to bring a Stanley Cup to their new abode, the Molson Centre, rechristened the Bell Centre in 2002 when naming rights were sold. Olivier Bauer claims today that for the 2008 finals, "Montréal n'avait plus à ce moment-là mille clochers, mais un seul temple, le Centre Bell!" (Montreal no longer had one thousand bell towers, but a single temple, the Bell Centre),[43] but at the time, the move was highly controversial. Anouk Bélanger argues that Molson exploited existing senses of collective identity and memory in the development of a hegemonic discourse that controlled such expressions as a buffer for a move motivated by commercial rather than collective goals.[44] Similarly, Robert H. Dennis describes Molson's attempts to control the discourse surrounding the move in terms of Eric Hobsbawm's "invented tradition."[45] Dennis establishes with clarity the Forum's status as a *lieu de mémoire*, tracking its history not only as a hockey arena but also as a venue for major religious gatherings in the pre–Quiet Revolution era, and then later for rock concerts. True to the Latin origin of its name, it represented not merely a site of private enterprise, but truly a public place, so that "the events that it housed reflected Québec society, and their changing nature ultimately mirrored the province's political development as a modern nation state."[46] Those arguments notwithstanding, Lisa Anne Gunderson reminds us that the Forum, like the Bell Centre, was always a private, for-profit enterprise.[47]

Written to counter the commodification and capitalist exploitation of local identity and collective history (much like Jean-Pierre April's 1981 science fiction story of the same title, discussed in chapter 2), Stéphane Archambault's lyrics for "Le Fantôme du Forum" (2008), performed by Mes Aïeux, exploit the widespread role of superstition among athletes and fans through the intervention of a phantom haunting the storied arena. Mes Aïeux, which formed in 1996, offers a blend of Quebec folk sounds, including a good bit of fiddle, with a contemporary alternative rock attitude. Their fifth album, *La Ligne orange* (2008), pays homage to Montreal's Metro; each of their songs on that album is ostensibly linked to a metro stop, although they take creative licence with the concept, offering a song about another famous Montreal sports monument, the Olympic Stadium (which is located on the Green line).[48] As one might expect of a group touting itself as "néo-trad," the past is often a point of reference in their music; those references include traditional icons such as La Corriveau, *les coureurs de bois*, and *la chasse-galérie*; at the same time, they address contemporary identity crises in "La Dévire" and "Notre-Dame-Du-Bon-Conseil." "Le Déni de l'évidence" offers a pointed critique of present-day apathy and wait-and-see attitudes; the lyrics suggest a concern about the environment, but they remain open-ended enough to apply to other issues, such as the national question. Mes Aïeux's songs often feature a biting wit, and the ballad discussed here is no exception.

The CD's liner notes pay the group's respects to "numéro 7 du Canadien de Montréal, Howie 'The Lightning Man' Morenz," and "Le Fantôme du Forum" begins with the chiming of seven bells in his honour. Like Loco Locass, the pop group recognizes the importance of history to contemporary Montrealers/Quebecers, and the first lines mark the historic date. In a stylized manner reminiscent of a priest chanting the liturgy, singer/composer Stéphane Archambault intones:

Le mois de janvier 1937
Marqua la fin d'une grande carrière

Howie Morenz, le fameux numéro 7
Quitta le match sur une civière.

The month of January 1937
Marked the end of a great career
Howie Morenz the famous number 7
Left the match on a stretcher.

The text begins with a tragedy from the past, the individual's demise perhaps mirroring the national, with only a shadow of a remaining presence – the ghost of Howie Morenz, who returns to haunt the stadium.

Retelling the story of an actual historical event, during which Morenz's body rested in state in the Forum, where 50,000 fans paid their last respects,[49] Archambault's lyrics call upon the imagery of religion and invoke the supernatural, transforming the fallen hero into a sort of Holy Ghost of hockey. The arena explicitly appears as a church where fans have come to worship:

Le Forum converti en cathédrale
Tous les éléments étaient en place
Pour un phénomène paranormal
L'esprit de Morenz dans son tombeau glorieux [...]
Pendant qu'son corps partait au cimetière [...]
Son âme retraitait au vestiaire pour enfiler la sainte Flanelle
Le spectre revêtit l'uniforme

The Forum converted into a cathedral
All the elements were in place
For a paranormal phenomenon
The spirit of Morenz in his glorious tomb ...
While his body left for the cemetery ...
His soul retreated to the locker room to don the Holy Flannel
The spectre put on his uniform.

Thus the legend of the "fantôme du Forum" was born. The pseudo-religious nature of the shrine appears further coded in the song's lyrics, which mention the chant "*Go Habs Go!*" heard in this "temple du hockey," and refer to the "flambeau glorieux" (glorious flame) of the Canadiens' motto. The ghost of Morenz inspires later players, Rocket [Maurice Richard], the Pocket Rocket [Henri Richard, Maurice's younger brother], Jacques Plante, Ti-Guy [Lafleur], [Ken] Dryden, the Big Three

[Serge Savard, Larry Robinson, and Guy Lapointe], and Casseau [Patrick Roy], whose exploits the group recites in litany. His inspiration becomes supernatural intervention, as he returns to make assists, playing as the "septième homme sur la glace" (the seventh man on the ice):

Les mauvais bonds, les buts chanceux
Quand la *puck* roulait pour nous autres
Pis quand l'arbitre fermait les yeux
C'était Howie Morenz, qui d'autre?

The bad hops, the lucky goals
When the puck rolled for us
Then when the ref closed his eyes
It was Howie Morenz, who else?

The final chorus abandons the metaphorical register to state explicitly: "Le hockey, c'est notre religion / Ah oui! Prions, allumons des lampions" (Hockey, it's our religion / Oh yes! Let's pray, light the votives).

Like religion, hockey is a communal activity, a unifying force, and Mes Aïeux acknowledge this in their choice of subject. Instead of the *pure laine* French Canadian icon Maurice Richard, they lament the passing of Howie Morenz. Born in Mitchell, Ontario, of Anglo-Swiss heritage[50] – nothing of the *Québécois de souche* here – he speaks English to the mixed crowd: "I will be back for the series." Besides the anglicisms that enrich the vocabulary of hockey (like *puck*, cited above), the lyrics include other English words (their foreignness nonetheless signalled in italics in the liner notes' text); for example, Howie's ghost makes "l'adversaire *shake* dans ses culottes" (his adversary *tremble* in his pants). In the song's refrain, the group laments in chorus: "*How many seasons before it ends / The curse of the Lightning Man Howie Morenz?*"

The curse is, of course, the result of crass commercialism infiltrating the hallowed ground of the national sport, as Jonathan Cha asserts: "Les 'fantômes' du Forum n'ont pas encore trouvé leur niche au Centre Bell et la population ne lui accorde pas une valeur symbolique" (The "phantoms" of the Forum have not yet found their niche at the Bell Centre and the population doesn't give it a symbolic value).[51] Archambault's lyrics echo Cha's and Bélanger's critique of the financial aspects of the monument's conversion. The team moves from the Forum, a true *lieu de mémoire*, a site of authentic memory, to the Bell Centre "au nom du dollar tout-pui$$ant / Au nom de la modernité" (in the name of the

Almighty dollar / In the name of modernity). The print lyrics' playful use of the dollar sign highlights the song's critical attitude. From this moment, the great ghost begins his "descente aux enfers." Because the trip has now become a "longue distance" – a ludic reference to the communications function of the company that holds the current naming rights – Morenz's ghost remains to haunt "le Cinéplex Pepsi-AMC," an allusion to the Forum's current function. What was a blessing has become a curse. A final verse exhorts fans to pray there is truth to the rumour that Morenz's ghost has been seen wandering, looking for the Bell Centre at its "rue de La Gauchetière" address: "Peuple, à genoux dans vos salons / Pour que le Saint Graal revienne à la maison ..." (People in your living rooms, fall to your knees / So that the Holy Grail may return home ...). The hero has died, but hope has not; the fans' true faith will procure victory for the team. Such recognition of the hockey player as hero is elevated to a whole new level by the post-punk rockers from Roberval, Les Dales Hawerchuk.

Les Dales Hawerchuk

Les Dales Hawerchuk have based their entire image on an Anglo-Canadian hockey player from Toronto who crossed over to play in the Quebec junior leagues before joining the NHL with the Winnipeg Jets. Although slightly overshadowed by Gretzky and Lemieux, Hawerchuk was an icon of a generation, described by Patrick Roy's father as one of the best players in the league at the time.[52] Like Terry Sawchuk and many other Western Canadian hockey players whose surnames end in *-chuk*, Dale Hawerchuk claimed Ukrainian, not French Canadian, origins. Nonetheless, brothers Sylvain and Sébastien Séguin, working with Charles Perron and Pierre Fortin, honoured him when choosing their band's name. They released their first self-titled album in 2005, another (with a similarly original title), *Les Dales Hawerchuk 2,* in 2008, and a third that follows up on the group's hockey thematics, *Les Dales Hawerchuk – Le Tour du chapeau* (the Hat Trick), in 2011. The music video to their break-out hit, "Dale Hawerchuk," engages many of the issues covered in this book, including the young fan imagining himself to be the hockey star he idolizes, the hockey text's need to invoke the game's history, the "beer-hockey synergy,"[53] the overly masculinized homosocial nature of the sport, and, finally, its violence.

The group's musical style – raw, fast-paced, guitar-and-drum-driven rockabilly inflected with punk – mirrors the speed and energy of the athlete to whom it is paying homage. Its video (produced by C4 Productions) has a simple storyline: the guys in the band get together to drink beer, eat pizza, and watch hockey! Two essential twists give both visual and narrative interest to the brief clip: instead of watching a televised, contemporary NHL game, they watch a videocassette – decidedly not a DVD – of an old game, and their living room decor, littered with beer bottles, invokes the 1980s, Hawerchuk's own heyday. A locker room atmosphere prevails as the attractive young male band members appear in a hodgepodge array of hockey gear, most in various states of undress. The use of historical video, which is reinforced later with cuts to animated photos of early-twentieth-century hockey teams "singing" along with the band during the chorus, situates the group's relationship to hockey as authentic. These are not just token, superficial Canadiens fans; these young men know hockey and its history, as would the true fan, for whom hockey holds deep meaning. The popular text mimics here the scholarly discourse that links hockey to history: hockey is meaningful to French Canadians because its lore has been handed down from one generation to the next.

The objectification of the male body and the sexualization of the athlete (like the rock star) are invoked both in earnest and in jest. Handsome lead singer Sylvain Séguin reveals his muscular chest, which is only partly covered by his shoulder pads; another, scrawnier band member wears drooping, baggy long johns. After inserting the videotape, they first watch and drink, but soon they begin to mimic the action on the ice and start fighting, perhaps a savvy nod to debates about the influence of television violence on North American youth. In the homoerotically charged atmosphere of half-naked, drunken young men, the sexualized male body turns into the violent male body. Recall that in the final scene of *Slap Shot,* resorting to a sort of "let's make love, not war" imagery, Ned Braden (Michael Ontkean) stops an on-ice brawl by stripping down to his jockstrap and circling the ring, thereby also recapturing his wife's desiring gaze and restoring the unity of the monogamous heterosexual couple, placed under siege by all of the film's other sex-related subplots. In the Dales Hawerchuk video, no women are present at all in the frame, although they are clearly projected into the ideal audience because of the displays of the half-nude male body. However, as if to forestall any homoerotic readings of this image, aggression replaces desire, and in the final frame, the band members return to their original positions on the couch in front of the television, still only partly dressed in hockey gear, but now bloodied and exhausted. As further reflection of the often misogynous and homophobic nature of locker room banter, the lyrics admit: "J'fais jamais de jokes avec les tapettes / Mais j'avoue j'ris des grosses femmes laides" (I don't make jokes about fags / But I admit I laugh at ugly fat women). The first-person narrator seems to admit a certain level of political correctness – he does not tell offensive gay jokes; however, his use of the derogatory "tapettes" points to his actual attitude. There is no objectification of women in the lyrics, which at first suggest that – as with *Les Boys* – hockey takes precedence over sex: "J'cherche pas l'amour / J'cherche les caresses" (I'm not looking for love / I'm looking for caresses). This notion is quickly reversed, however, once we realize he isn't looking for love, just for quick sex: "J'cherche une femme avec des belles fesses / Juste pour une nuite pis fuck le reste" (I'm looking for a woman with a nice ass / Just for a night then fuck the rest). What allows for his bravado attitude is his assuming the new identity of the hockey star: "Une belle femme qui vient d'me regarder / Depuis j'suis Dale j'me laisse aller" (A beautiful woman who just looked at me / Since I'm Dale, I let myself go for it).

The song's refrain repeats, then, the assertion that the singer has swapped identities, has become his idol: "Je ne suis plus Sylvain Séguin, moi, je suis Dale Hawerchuk!" (I'm not Sylvain Séguin any more, I'm Dale Hawerchuk!). The identification of the hockey fan with the star player is so intense that a transfer of identity occurs; in part, this is the magic and the meaning of spectator sports, or even playing sports (on the ice, young players also identify with and take on the roles of star players, as seen both in "The Hockey Sweater" and in Denis Côté's young adult series about the fictional future hockey star, Michel Lenoir; even *Lance et compte* engages this motif as a fan holds up a sign reading "We *are* Pierre Lambert"). Besides the imaginary transformation of self into hero, though, there is real emulation after identification. These young men find models for their own masculinity in those they see played out on the ice: real men play hockey and real men fight. The historical images that accompany a variation on the refrain, "Vu qu'on n'est pas tous des Séguin, on est les Dales Hawerchuk!" (Since we're not all Séguin brothers, we're the Dale Hawerchuks!), underscore their connection to the past but also refer to a shared present. Like a hockey team, the rock group has come together; even if all four are not brothers, they have united under the banner of the hockey idol's name to form a cohesive unit. At the same time, they signal the performed role of the rock star; asserting that they are all "Dale Hawerchuk," they assume the identity of the rock band, Les Dales Hawerchuk.

Bob Bissonnette: Rock Star

Singer/songwriter and former professional hockey player Bob Bissonnette thus titles his official website, advertising his concert dates and two albums: his appropriately titled début, *Recrue de l'année* (2010; Rookie of the Year), and *Les Barbes de séries* (2012; Playoff Beards). Hockey is so thoroughly integrated into the website of Bob Bissonnette that it's unclear whether he is a hockey fan who expresses his love through music or a rocker who loves hockey; for example, Paul Newman's image in a *Slap Shot* jersey directs visitors to the site's shop. His official biography clarifies things: "Ex-hockeyeur professionnel, Bob Bissonnette est auteur-compositeur-interprète depuis plus de 10 ans. D'abord chansonnier de feux camp, il est devenu chansonnier semi-professionnel il y a un peu plus de 4 ans" (Former professional hockey player, Bob Bissonnette has been an author/composer/performer for ten years. At first just singing around the campfire, he has been a semi-professional singer-songwriter for a little more than four years).[54] He also vaunts the fact that he does *not* – unlike many Quebec musical artists – benefit from any government subsidies whatsoever.

Bissonnette's career as a hockey player brought him through the Quebec Junior Major Hockey League (LHJMQ). A left winger, he was a seventh-round draft pick in 1998 for the Hull Olympics, for which he played until 2002. He spent a year at the Université du Québec à Trois Rivières before landing a slot on the AA Florida Everblades (East Coast Hockey League) in 2003. Until his retirement in 2008, he played in the mid-level pro Central Hockey League and the junior-level North American Hockey League, as well as for senior major hockey leagues in Quebec, on the West Coast, and in Côte Nord. In terms of notable statistics, his Wikipedia entry proudly declares that he ended his time in the LHJMQ with 1,260 penalty minutes, making him the tenth most penalized player in the history of that league.[55]

His music, is largely derivative, almost a pastiche of a range of rock-related stylings; his humour – sometimes tasteless – and the themes of his lyrics offer a certain puerile entertainment value. Except for the omnipresence of hockey, his approach as an entertainer is not unprecented in Quebec; in fact, it reflects a veritable subgenre of humorous music that has developed there, typified by the work of Stage Lacroix and the Trois Accords. As a hockey player turned musician, he follows in the venerable footsteps of Guy Lafleur, who recorded an album in 1979 that combined training exercises with disco music, as well as the fictional Jim Duchêne, a member of the Quebec National featured in the made-for-TV movie *Lance et compte: Le Choix* (1991).

Bissonnette's best song, both musically and lyrically, is "Mettre du tape su' ma palette" (Tapin' My Stick), which features a player's ritualistic preparations for a game, a major aspect of the sport, since hockey may well require more special equipment than any other. One of his few songs to achieve radio play,[56] its use of fiddle and the rapid delivery of its lyrics recall the neotraditional style of Mes Aïeux. Although the connection to hockey may be more tenuous in some of his songs than in others, nearly every song on Bissonnette's two albums contains some reference to hockey, be it a dense engagement with the sport found in "Hockey dans rue" (Street Hockey), "Les Barbes de séries" (Play-Off Beards), and "Max le Guerrier" (Max the Warrior, an homage to Max Talbot), or a single line, as with "Enweye donc" (Go On, Then).[57]

This last number expresses the simple desire to leave for anywhere, including "jouer une game de hockey en Sibérie" (to play a game in Siberia). While the lyrics of "Les Guimauves" (Marshmallows) – about the peaceful pleasure of roasting marshmallows around a campfire – fail to reference the sport, its video (dir. Bissonnette and Bruno Lachance) includes appearances by players and even a reference to Gary Bettman. Somewhat contrary to its title, "La Machine à scorer" (The Scoring Machine) stresses the team aspects of the game, asserting that "tous les joueurs de hockey ont un rôle à jouer / C'est de même qu'ça marche si tu veux gagner" (all hockey players have a role to play / That's the way it is when you want to win). The lyrics describe those roles, from the goalie to the goon to the equipment manager, but then admit that the most important aspect of the game is scoring. "Hanrahan (ta femme Suzanne)" (Hanrahan [Your Wife Suzanne]) pays homage to *Slap Shot*'s Charlestown Chiefs. "J'accroche mes patins" (I Hang Up My Skates) describes a player's retirement – Bissonnette's own, one presumes – which occurs without an "ovation de 20 minutes comme pour Maurice Richard" (a twenty-minute ovation like Maurice Richard). "Les Hommes Zébrés" (The Zebra Men) refers to the black-and-white stripes of officials' uniforms; surprisingly, the song's chorus admits the difficulty of their job since everyone hates them, and qualifies them as "de vrais martyrs" (real martyrs).

The idolatry of sports heroes seems to be taken to the extreme in "Max le Guerrier," which compares the Pittsburgh Penguins' number 25, Maxim Talbot, to various superheroes and comic figures, including a Vulcan (an extraterrestrial race from the *Star Trek* franchise), Gandalf (the wizard-hero from Tolkien's and now Peter Jackson's *Lord of the Rings*), Wolverine (one of Marvel Comics' *X-Men*), a Jedi (martial arts heroes from *Star Wars*), and Chuck Norris (an actor who bears comparison with these fictional heroes because of his cult status as a martial arts fighter). One song without at least a tiny hockey reference targets another sport: "Game Over" pays homage to Major League Baseball closing pitcher Éric Gagné, one of the few French Canadians in the big leagues of a sport that has a long history in the province, where it is inextricably linked with hockey as a summer sport to replace that of winter. Baseball also appears in "J'haïs Montréal" (I Hate Montreal), which begins with a reference to the inability of this "ville ben banale"'s (banal city) to keep its major league franchise, the Expos; and in "El Presidente," which recounts the legendary career of Dennis Martinez, Expos pitcher from 1986 to 1993. This sampling reveals the wide range of aspects of the game of hockey, and sport in general, that Bissonnette explores in his work. His treatment of two issues raised by the other texts examined so far in this book merits a slightly more extended analysis: nostalgia coupled with the power of the imagination, and the gendered nature of hockey discourses.

The first track on *Recrue de l'année*, "Hockey dans rue" (Street Hockey) develops the themes of nostalgia for lost youth and the power of the imagination that hockey engages, reworking the central notion of Roch Carrier's "The Hockey Sweater" as it links active play of the game with the identification with and emulation of hockey heroes. While Carrier invoked the rural boyhood of his generation, Bissonnette recalls the urban youth pastime of street hockey, linking it not to Maurice Richard but to more recent stars. The transformative power of the imagination, just as it allowed young Roch and his friends to become Maurice Richard on the ice in Carrier's beloved classic, serves a similar function in Bissonnette's song:

Quand tu joues dans rue tu peux te prendre pour qui tu veux
Stastny, Bellows ou même Mario Lemieux
Non y a vraiment aucune limite
Tu peux même te dire que c'est toi Bobby Smith

When you play in the street you can be whoever you want
Stastny, Bellows, or even Mario Lemieux
No, there's really no limit
You can even say that you're Bobby Smith.

The video (dir. Bruno Lachance), which features appearances by real-life hockey pros André Roy, Philippe Boucher, and Donald Brashear playing a game of street hockey with a group of children (and Bob Bissonnette) wearing the jerseys of stars and teams from around the NHL, reinforces the connection created between real NHL stars and hockey's engagement not only of the body but also of the human spirit. Rather than offering the usually critical discourse that the professionalization and commercialization of the sport typified by the NHL has ruined the purity and magic of pond hockey, Bissonnette inextricably connects the magic of youth with the dream of future NHL play. It is precisely because one can imagine oneself as Patrick Roy or as Joe Sakic, playing at Boston Garden, that the everyday pastime of street hockey becomes magic:

> Jouer dans rue ça te permet de voyager
> D'aller à Chicago, Philadelphie ou San Jose
> De marquer le but en prolongation
> Au vieux Garden de Boston
>
> Playing in the street lets you travel
> Go to Chicago, Philadelphia, or San Jose
> To score in overtime
> At the old Boston Garden.

The video inscribes the sport of hockey onto the urban landscape, cutting from images of play to close-ups of street signs bearing the names of famous players, such as Richer, Lafleur, Roy, Racicot, and Lemieux; it matters little whether the street name represents an intentional homage to the sport or mere coincidence, since once again, the imagination allows the citizen to attribute a hockey meaning to the sign regardless of the namer's original intent. The theme of nostalgia for childhood appears even more explicitly in the album's second track, "Pyjama à Pattes" (Feet-Pyjamas), which laments, "J'm'ennuie d'être p'tit" (I miss bein' a kid). Although it offers a looser connection to hockey (references to stars of the 1980s and to collecting O-Pee-Chee hockey cards), both songs' musical styles invoke the past as well, with the somewhat rockabilly sound of "Hockey dans rue" and the fifties rock'n'roll – including a chorus of "oo ee oo" – of "Pyjama."

As we have seen, gender roles and relations figure largely in hockey texts, and Bissonnette's oeuvre, if we can use such a lofty term, is no different. Above all, its images of hockey often echo the hyper-masculine models for Canadian male identity observed by scholars.[58] They argue that "hegemonic masculinity" is constructed on the positive bases of strength and toughness and on the negative bases of misogyny and homophobia, references to all of which can be found in Bissonnette's lyrics. For example, in "Les Barbes de séries," the growing of facial hair represents a sign of masculinity to help intimidate the opponent: "Il faut avoir l'air tough, c'est maintenant le temps des play-offs" (You've got to look tough, because now it's the play-offs). The same song borrows the hockey-as-war metaphor: "Les joueurs d'hockey sont en période de guerre" (Hockey players are in a time of war).

A more extreme example arises in Bissonnette's homage to the great Chris Chelios of the Blackhawks, the Canadiens, and later the Red Wings. Chelios was "arguably the best American ever to play the game," according to Bruce Dowbiggin, but he also had a "nasty side," serving nearly 3,000 penalty minutes for his violent play.[59] The eponymous song begins with the implied question, "Je le sais pas si t'as un gros pénis" (I don't know if you have a big penis), followed by lyrics asserting that Chelios won three Norris Trophies, among other accomplishments. This apparently implies that manliness can be measured in other ways than by penis size. Then Bissonnette praises Chelios – an unconventional hero, to say the least – by celebrating aspects of his career that reflect a certain vision of hegemonic masculinity as this is validated through hockey. The song's refrain openly claims: "Chris Chelios t'es mon héros, à Detroit, Montréal ou Chicago / Chris Chelios t'es un génie, y a personne proche de toi ni même Wayne Gretzky" (Chris Chelios you're my hero, in Detroit, Montreal, or Chicago / Chris Chelios you're a genius, nobody can touch you, not even Wayne Gretzky). It is perhaps not surprising that Bissonnette, one of the LHJMQ's most penalized players ever, valorizes a violent – but nonetheless talented, given his scoring records – player like Chelios rather than a skill player like Gretzky. Bissonnette sings an elegy to the following aspects of the controversial player's career: the violence of his play ("tu joues chien [...] / Des slashing en masse" [you play dirty / slashing up a storm]), his partying ("T'es encore dans les bars quand le soleil se lève" [You're still in the bars when dawn breaks]), his sexual escapades ("T'as fourré la femme du Président" [You fucked the President's wife]), and his youthful troubles ("Quand t'étais plus jeune t'en a fait des conneries / T'en a brassé d'la marde dans ta vie" [When you were young you did some dumbass things / You've stirred up some shit in your life]). The song concludes with a reiteration of the sport's homosocial aspects: "C'est clair que t'étais mon idole de jeunesse / Avec un gant de hockey, j'te donnerais une p'tite tape s'es fesses" (It's obvious that you were the idol of my youth / With a hockey glove, I'd give you a pat on your butt).

Precisely because of sport's homosocial aspects, any sexual charge of male-on-male admiration and contact must be defused with expressions of both homophobic rejection of homosexuality and aggressive assertion of a hegemonic heterosexuality verging on misogyny. We see these expressed in the non-hockey-themed song, "Y sont toutes folles" (They're All Crazy), in which the singer expresses his frustration with and incomprehension of women, an attitude obvious in the song's title and refrain. While hockey takes a backstage here, sports make a cameo appearance with the one-line reference to the Canadian Football League championships: "Y changent de poste de TV / Pendant la finale de la Coupe Grey" (They change the channel on TV / During the Grey Cup finals). Not only are all women crazy themselves, as demonstrated in the litany of ostensibly irrational actions the lyrics recite, but they have also undermined masculinity and threaten the singer's own sanity: "Y ont rendu toutes les hommes mous / Pis moi y vont me rendre fou" (They've made all men soft / And they're gonna drive me crazy). As is often the case, the discourse of misogyny arrives coupled with that of homophobia. This appears in the song "J'haïs Montréal" (I Hate Montreal), one of the reasons for that hatred being that the Outgames are held there; it also figures in "Y sont toutes folles," as Bob wants to reassure his listeners that "Et non je ne suis pas gay / J'aime les dounes soyez-en assuré" (No, I'm not gay / I love chicks, rest assured).

Yet another song, "L'Affamée" (The Hungry Woman), similarly thematizes women's control over men in a misogynistic fashion by describing a woman who wants sex all the time and everywhere; the lyrics are largely of a list of locations (including a locker room) where she wants to "do it." This gendered discourse, coupled with a childish fascination with the corporeal evident in many of the initiation rituals and pranks identified with the hockey locker room (and that of other sports), appears in Bissonnette's obsession with masculinity and male anatomy, already observed in relation to Chris Chelios's penis. Although it is not my aim to psychoanalyze this hockey singer/songwriter, the fear of castration that concludes "Y sont toutes folles," coupled with its paranoid anticipation of the critiques it will receive for its stereotypical misogyny, offers a nice frame to my conclusion of this section:

> Si cette toune-là passe à radio
> Je vais avoir un comité sur le dos
> Une commission d'enquête
> Pour prouver que je suis fou dans tête
> Que je suis un sexiste, un anti-féministe pis qu'on devrait me faire l'ablation du pénis.
>
> If this tune makes it to the radio
> I'm going to have a committee on my back
> An inquiry commission
> To prove that I'm crazy in the head
> That I'm a sexist, an anti-feminist and that they ought
> To cut off my penis.

Bissonnette's often tasteless humour appears with the witty reference to the "commission d'enquête," Quebec's equivalent of the congressional hearing. He savvily engages the trope of the "castrating feminist" in self-defence against the attacks he anticipates from progressive elements representing contemporary Quebec's politically correct ideology of accommodation. In doing so, however, he offers us a glaring example of how a wide range of popular culture texts function in the same way that sports films do.

Richard C. King and David J. Leonard argue that nostalgia – a key figure in Bissonnette's work, as we have seen – represents a central factor in sports films because it invokes "a fictive better time in the past when white supremacy, patriarchy, and class stratification made sense."[60] They cite Marjorie D. Kibby's argument that by making a "retrospective vision of masculinity available for popular consumption,"[61] such a discourse "eases audiences into the realities of a postfeminist world in which masculinity – and even patriarchy – must be defended and restabilized, lest the social collapses."[62] Bissonnette's music expresses a white male frustration with the current state of society, in which the white man's traditional others – blacks, women, gays – can no longer be used as objects to shore up his own subject position. In spite of efforts towards constructing hockey as a more inclusive site of participation in the Canadian and Québécois national identities, for Bissonnette – and ostensibly for his fans – hockey remains an exclusively male refuge from the contemporary realities of inclusion and accommodation.

Conclusion

This chapter would not be complete without at least a brief mention of the hockey/music synergy created for the *Les Boys* films; soundtrack CDs are an integral part of their franchisization. Quebec's best-known hard rock vocalist, Éric Lapointe, contributed the title song to the original 1997 film, but the soundtrack songs "Rocket" and "Le Boys Blues Band," performed respectively on the *Les Boys II* and *Les Boys III* – in which Lapointe played Léopold's nerdy roommate – still get airtime. In addition to the in-depth deployment of the theme of hockey in the songs of artists like Loco Locass and Mes Aïeux and its downright integration into the career and identity of music acts like Les Dales Hawerchuk and Bob Bissonnette, the hockey reference has become nearly ubiquitous as a quick and simple marker of Québécois identity in the province's French-language popular music.

To cite only a few examples of this synergy, the *chansonnier* (singer/songwriter) Vincent Vallières props a hockey stick up next to the bus stop in the video to a largely non-sport-related song about all the things we wait for during a lifetime, "Le Temps est Long" (*Le Monde tourne fort*, 2009). Like Loco Locass, Mad'MoiZèle Girafe invokes the Canadiens as a signifier of local unity in their ode to the city's diversity, "Montréal Stylé" (*Peindre la giraf*, 2009). The group's single, in "Raggamuffin" style – an updated reggae sound infused with hip hop and alternative rock – depicts the multicultural side of the metropolis, referencing the "Sainte-Flanelle" as a topic of conversation open to all. In contrast, the first-person narrator of the neotraditional band Mes Aïeux's "La Dévire" (*La Ligne orange*, 2008) expresses the anguished status of the *pure laine* Québécois through his continued dream of "la Coupe Stanley." Les Cowboys Fringants, whose founders claim on their official website that they met at a Canadiens game, pay homage to Ron Fournier, former NHL referee turned radio host, with their "Salut, mon Ron" (*Break syndical*, 2002).[63]

In the current era in which political and social theorists continually focus on globalization, asserting the advent of the "post-national," Tim Edensor argues that "the national is still a powerful constituent of identity precisely because it is grounded in the popular and the everyday."[64] In his examination of *National Identity, Popular Culture, and Everyday Life* (2002), he shifts his focus away from obvious displays of "official" nationalism, towards a range of *lieux de mémoire* and their appropriation by popular culture – sometimes in ways contrary to those offered by official or institutionalized culture. His study seeks to fill a gap; he expresses surprise that "theorists of identity have neglected the quotidian realms experienced most of the time by most people, since it is here that identity is continually reproduced in unreflexive fashion."[65] Given popular music's constant and often affectively charged presence in our lives, shouldn't it reasonably be considered as both a component of identity construction and a means of performing the identities we wish to project? Music does more than provide the background to our daily routines, as we shower, dress, and drive to work, gear up for a social outing, or calm down at the end of a busy day; for many North Americans, it also represents a meaningful expression and reflection of our feelings and ideas, the focal point for social outings (parties or nightclubbing), and even a special event in itself, such as a concert or festival.

For those of us North Americans whose mother tongue is English, choosing which language to listen to the music that functions as a backdrop to and expression of our daily lives and identities is a question not even raised. In contrast, for French-speakers living in a North America, whose popular music industry is dominated by English-language products, choosing to listen in French is itself a significant choice. French is certainly the majority language spoken in Quebec, but in terms of consumable popular culture such as movies, television, and music, English-language products, often from the United States, offer an often overwhelming alternative.

Harris Berger's argument that "in many parts of the world … native languages or regional dialects may be iconic of the colonized peoples or marginalized groups that speak them; songs set in such languages may function as a powerful affirmation of identity for their singers or listeners,"[66] thus may be applied appropriately to Quebec. When popular music artists choose to compose and perform in French, and then further deploy the time-worn yet ever renewed trope of hockey or its national icons like the Canadiens, such choices have the potential to intensify the impact of their music upon their target audience. I was born in Michigan, yet the trumpet fanfare of Loco Locass's "Hymne à

Québec" and the faint organ chords accompanied by the sound of the puck swishing across the ice that signal the opening of "Le But" jazz me every time I hear them. I can only imagine the effect on their fans at home. Quebec's filmmakers, television producers, and science fiction writers have appropriated hockey to tell deeply meaningful stories about the nation to its citizens, and so have its musicians.

Hockey Is Quebec

The roots of hockey seem to run even deeper in Québec society and culture than elsewhere in Canada, and extend into the Québécois' collective memory and imagination. One of the major reasons for this lies in the extent to which hockey has been understood symbolically in Québec as part of its national identity.

Anouk Bélanger[1]

A sense of national identity then is not a once and for all thing, but is dynamic and dialogic, found in the constellations of a huge cultural matrix of images, ideas, spaces, things, discourses and practices.

Tim Edensor[2]

I spoke no English, and they spoke no French, but we knew how to play together in a very natural way.

Maurice Richard[3]

As we have seen in the preceding pages, just as for Anglo-Canadians, for Franco-Québécois hockey represents one of the most omnipresent and meaningful markers of national identity; but for them it signifies a specific, North American francophone identity. Whether viewed nostalgically as the winter pastime of an innocent youth (Carrier's "The Hockey Sweater" or Barcelo's "Noël Lachard (I)"), as an arena to safely play out local (Nordiques vs Canadiens) or national (Canadiens vs Maple Leafs) rivalries by proxy, or as a source of French Canadian pride and models for masculinity and heroism (Maurice Richard and the Canadiens as "Nos Glorieux"), the game of hockey offers French-speaking Canadians the same functions it offers

English-speaking Canadians. Similarly, it provides them with a sense of collective unity by which they can identify themselves as different from (and superior to, as seen in *Les Boys II* and *Lance et compte*, for example) other French-speakers around the world. Although not all of the representations of hockey examined here have been positive ones, even the texts critical of the sport implicitly signal its importance and usually temper their critiques to address only certain aspects of the game. While we love "le Canadien," we can decry the violence, commercialism, and inflated salaries and egos that a major league sports dynasty generates; or if we despise the blatant capitalistic marketing of the entire National Hockey League, we can still recall with joy time spent in childhood on the ice or admire Maurice Richard for standing up and speaking out against the oppression, both real and perceived, of French Canadians.

Hockey can also show us that, while it remains a largely white, male domain, Quebec and Canada have made progress in their attempts to represent themselves as inclusive, pluralistic societies. A gay lawyer becomes the hero of his garage league team in *Les Boys*; we celebrate the advent of women's elite hockey as *Les Boys III* takes on the Canadian Olympic team; a woman can even join the coaching staff of an (albeit fictional) NHL team in *Lance et compte: La Revanche*, and its star goalie can be a black player of Haitian origin in *Lance et compte: La Nouvelle génération*. As Tim Edensor asserts of a different national symbol, the flag, hockey in Quebec represents "a mythic, polysemic symbol which is used to transmit very diverse meanings and qualities."[4] We have seen that while popular culture texts that thematize hockey largely invest it with a positive meaning, as a symbol of a national heritage of strength and endurance in a northern climate – of national excellence even, in the form of French Canadian players' success in the arena of international hockey and major league professional sports – these texts can offer social critiques as well. Some of the texts examined here identify the NHL as symptomatic not only of what is wrong with hockey, but also of what is wrong with contemporary Western or Québécois society; they target its commercialism, its praise for excessive consumption, and its narcissistic elevation of the individual over the collectivity. Edensor also argues that in this post-national era, "points of identification with the nation are increasingly manifold and contested, are situated within dense networks which provide multiple points of contact."[5] For individuals who may not consider themselves politicized or nationalists, hockey represents precisely one of those disparate points of contact with the Quebec nation as they celebrate the Montreal Canadians or Maurice Richard as its *lieux de mémoire*.

Hockey represents a locus of shared experience, and as such, it contributes a big piece of "the imagined community" of Canada; it is one of the seemingly very few cultural icons – besides the long, cold winters – held in common between Francos and Anglos in Canada, and indeed between them and indigenous peoples and recent immigrants. Canada is an imagined community built not only on snow and ice but also on skates. As Gillian Poulter and Michael Robidoux reveal in their discussions of the meaning of hockey in its early days, the sport offered French Canadians a common ground with their English-speaking concitizens.[6] The Fosty brothers make similar arguments for the players of the early black leagues that formed in Novia Scotia at the turn of the century.[7] Recently, popular culture texts reveal that other communities have also seen hockey as a "way in" to Canadian-ness. Vancouver writer Ven Begamudré's 1993 novel *Van De Graaff Days* describes a South Asian family's acculturation process, including its protagonist Krishna's determination to learn to skate "like Bobby Hull, the Golden Jet."[8] Later he watches *Hockey Night in Canada* with his son as part of a process of becoming Canadian. Similar messages appear in the recent film produced by Bollywood's Hari Om Entertainment and partly funded by Telefilm Canada, *Speedy Singhs* (2011), in which a young Canadian Sikh, Rajveer (Vinay Virmani), must prove himself to his traditional father, as well as to the white hockey players in the league. After being denied a slot on an ostensibly racist Anglo-Canadian team, Rajveer forms his own team; they make it to the championships, and, as their coach (Rob Lowe) encourages them, "show the entire community that [they] belong."

While Franco-Quebecers and South Asian immigrants may find a sense of themselves as Canadians through hockey, they nonetheless remain marginalized in English Canadians' representations of the game. As already mentioned, iconic English-language films like *Face-Off*, *Slap Shot*, and *Canada Russia '72* clearly marginalize and caricature the French Canadian players on the hockey teams they present to viewers. And while the recent hockey comedy *Goon* (2012) does cast a rising Québécois actor in a relatively central role as a minor league team's skill-playing star, Xavier Laflamme (Marc-André Grondin), this otherwise hilarious film, with its depiction of the most endearing goon you'll ever meet, offers an almost offensive stereotype of its lone French Canadian player. Obviously it is not the goal of such an over-the-top comedy – which also portrays the polite and caring goon, Doug Glatt's (Seann William Scott) best friend as an oversexed South Boston punk (Jay Baruchel) – to offer humane portraits of well-rounded individuals. Yet we might have welcomed some effort to explain Laflamme's excessive ego and womanizing as the defence mechanisms of an individual alienated by his working conditions and as rooted in the culture shock that French Canadian players face due to the reality that hockey players are an export commodity for both Canada and Quebec.

In his study of hockey in Canadian literature in English, Jason Blake proposes that "hockey is not a natural phenomenon but an imaginative, cultural activity."[9] The French-language films, television shows, songs, and literary texts examined here support that assertion. Through their appropriations and reworkings of the sport, its legends, its heroes and its myths, texts like Carrier's "The Hockey Sweater," Binamé's *The Rocket*, Saïa's *Les Boys*, and Barcelo's *Ville-Dieu* hold up a mirror, reflecting an image of Quebec. While that image may sometimes appear distorted when seen through the lenses of nostalgia, humour, and satire, it nonetheless reveals the enormous imprint left by the sport of hockey on the province's cultural and identitary landscape. But that mirror also offers a reflection of the sport itself, most often reinscribing it as the domain of muscular men, but occasionally revealing a glimpse of what the sport can signify, imagining it as an inclusive manner of cementing together the diverse elements of the nation – conceived as Quebec or conceived as Canada. I hope this analysis, written in English, of what hockey means to Franco-Quebecers, will serve a purpose similar to that of hockey itself: that of bridging the solitudes by offering a more complete understanding of one part of the Canadian mosaic. If nothing else, it certainly reveals that Franco-Quebecers largely share one thing with the Rest of Canada: a love for "Canada's Game."

Notes

Introduction

1 Beaty, "Not Playing, Working," p. 113.
2 Bélanger, "The Last Game?", p. 298.
3 Anonymous, "*Bon cop bad cop*: le plafond est défoncé."
4 A note on terminology might be useful here. Because I am examining products of French-language popular culture, when I refer to Quebecers and Québécois I generally mean francophones. While I will occasionally specify Franco-Quebecers or Franco-Québécois, repeatedly using that term would become cumbersome. Conversely, when I speak of the Rest of Canada and of Anglo-Canadians, it will appear that I am eliding the presence of francophones outside of Quebec. I am well aware that New Brunswick is the only officially bilingual province, and that Acadians live in Nova Scotia as well; there are Franco-Ontarians and French-speakers in the West. Consistently acknowledging such diversity through more specific terminology, however important and essential to a full understanding of Canadian cultural and national dynamics, would ultimately distract the reader from patterns of similarity between these texts and wider discourses about hockey, popular culture, and national and gender identity in North America.
5 See Harris, *Breaking the Ice*; Stevens, "Women's Hockey in Canada"; Theberge, *Higher Goals* and "Playing with the Boys"; and Adams, "The Game of Whose Lives?"
6 Another note on positionality and context might be timely at this point. I am an American scholar viewing both Quebec and Canada from the somewhat distanced perspective of the outsider, but I have travelled considerably throughout the nation, both as a tourist and as a scholar. In my

examinations of Quebec culture, my approach has been that Quebec is part of North America and that it is planted in many of the same economic, cultural, ideological, and political frameworks as the rest of the continent. At the same time, its French-language heritage, its historical intellectual dialogue with France (however ambivalent that dialogue has been), and its desire to preserve its difference as francophone all differentiate Quebecers' attitudes, opinions, and cultural reference points from those of the continent's anglophone majority. Having begun my career studying French literature and history, however, I can bring that training to bear on recognizing and distinguishing the French from the North American. By the same token, as an outsider, I will inevitably misinterpret or miss altogether other aspects of the *fait français*.

7 Beaty, "Not Playing, Working, p. 113."

8 Francis, *National Dreams*, p. 168.

9 Kennedy, "Confronting a Compelling Other," p. 45.

10 The Canada/Quebec divide perceived as "two solitudes" derives from the title of Hugh MacLennan's 1945 novel.

11 Saul, *Reflections of a Siamese Twin*; Taylor, "The Politics of Recognition"; Kymlicka, "The New Debate."

12 The twenty-eight-man roster included eight native Québécois (Yvan Cournoyer, Marcel Dionne, Rod Gilbert, Jocelyn Guevremont, Guy Lapointe, Gilbert Perreault, Jean Ratelle, and Serge Savard), the Franco-Ontarian J.-P. Parisé, and six Montreal Canadiens (Yvan Cournoyer, Ken Dryden, Frank and Pete Mahovlich, Serge Savard, and Guy Lapointe).

13 Here and elsewhere, unless a published translation is acknowledged in Works Cited, translations are my own.

14 See Marc Lavoie, *Désavantage numérique*; "Entry Draft"; "Stacking"; Bob Sirois, *Discrimination in the NHL*; and Longley, "Measuring Employer-Based Discrimination."

15 Robidoux, "Imagining a Canadian Identity."

16 Bélanger, "The Last Game?"

17 Lasorsa, *La Rivalité Canadien-Nordiques*, p. 2.

18 Harvey, "Whose Sweater is This?" and "Sport and Québec Nationalism."

19 Richard, *La Série du siècle*; Lasorsa, *La Rivalité Canadien-Nordiques*; Chabot, *La Grande Rivalité Canadiens-Nordiques*.

20 Baillargeon and Boissinot, eds., *La Vraie Dureté du mental;* Bauer and Barreau, eds., *La Religion du Canadien de Montréal*.

21 Melançon, *The Rocket*.

22 Laurin-Lamothe and Moreau, eds., *Le Canadien de Montréal: Une légende repensée*.

23 Jason Blake points out that the vast majority of hockey novels from English Canada have been published since the 1990s; Blake, *Canadian Hockey Literature*, p. 6.
24 Benoît Melançon's list of "Le Roman de la puck" includes works such as Eugène Cloutier's *Les Inutiles* (1956), which offer only a single chapter or even a few pages that refer to hockey. See also V.-L. Tremblay, "Masculinité et hockey dans le roman québécois."
25 Lefebvre, "Le Concept de cinéma national," p. 86; original emphasis.
26 Lefebvre, "Le Concept de cinéma national," p. 91; original emphasis.
27 Parts of the analysis of *Bon Cop, Bad Cop* were first presented in a paper delivered at the Canadian Popular Culture Association conference in Niagara Falls, Ontario, 10–12 May 2012.
28 Credit for this identification goes to the *Internet Movie Cars Database*.
29 See Hadley, "Translating the Québécois Sociolect," and Macdougall, "Facing Off," for extended discussions of language use in this film.
30 Dyer, *Stars*.
31 Canadian DVD distributors have developed the interesting practice of reversible sleeves, the French version on one side and the English on the other. In the French versions, Huard's name appears above his own image.
32 Although the conflict eventually took on the dimensions of an ethnic conflict in Lower Canada, it began as a bicultural movement demanding greater economic freedom and political autonomy for the colonies of Upper and Lower Canada. See Greer, *The Patriots and the People*.
33 See chapter 2 for a full discussion of this incident.
34 This phrase is attributed to nineteenth-century popular French writer and journalist Alphonse Karr; in Quebec, one might hear its variant, "Plus ça change, plus c'est pareil."

1 From Canadiens to Québécois

1 Whitson and Gruneau, *Artifical Ice*, p. 3.
2 Carrier, "The Hockey Sweater," p. 78.
3 Cited before the closing credits, *The Rocket* (2005).
4 Carrier, "The Hockey Sweater," pp. 80–1.
5 Carrier, "The Hockey Sweater," p. 77.
6 This and the following section previously appeared in a slightly different form in Ransom, "*Lieux de mémoire* or *lieux du dollar*?: Montreal's Forum, the Canadiens, and Popular Culture," *Quebec Studies* 51 (Spring–Summer 2011), pp. 21–39.
7 Gruneau and Whitson, *Hockey Night in Canada*, p. 2.

8 Lafrance, "Je ne suis plus pratiquant," p. 20.
9 Patoine, "On est Canayen," p. 9.
10 Gruneau and Whitson, *Hockey Night in Canada*, p. 101.
11 Robidoux, *Men at Play*, pp. 4, 5.
12 Pitter, "Racialization in Hockey"; Harris, *Breaking the Ice*. George and Darril Fosty, however, seek to correct this image in their acclaimed study *Black Ice: The Lost History of the Colored Hockey League of the Maritimes, 1895–1925.*
13 Theberge, *Higher Goals*, p. x; Stevens, "Women's Hockey in Canada"; Adams, "The Game of Whose Lives?"
14 See especially Wilson, "Selective Memory," in Whitson and Gruneau, *Artificial Ice.*
15 See Bauer and Barreau, *La Vraie Dureté du mental;* Baillairgeon and Boissinot, *La Religion du Canadien de Montréal.*
16 Lavoie's work has appeared in English, as well. See Lavoie, "The Entry Draft," and "Stacking," as well as works by Longley, "Measuring Employer-Based Discrimination," and Sirois, *Discrimination in the NHL*, on this topic.
17 Harvey, "Whose Sweater Is This?", p. 30.
18 Harvey, "Whose Sweater Is This?", p. 49.
19 Nora, ed., *Les Lieux de mémoire.*
20 Nora, "Between Memory and History," p. 7. Subsequent citations refer to this readily available English translation of the introduction to the French volumes.
21 See Jenish, *The Montreal Canadiens*, pp. 319–22, for a fuller account of centennial celebration events.
22 Nora, "Between Memory and History," p. 19.
23 Nora, "Between Memory and History," p. 18.
24 Nora, "Between Memory and History," p. 19.
25 Laurin-Lamothe and Moreau, "Le Canadien," p. 8.
26 McFarlane, *The Habs*, pp. 5–6; Legrand, "Those Old Montreal Maroons," pp. 14–17; Jenish, *The Montreal Canadiens* p. 10–13.
27 Jenish, *The Montreal Canadiens*, p. 38.
28 Sinden and Grace, *The Picture History of the Boston Bruins*, p. 8.
29 Harvey, "Whose Sweater Is This?", pp. 36–7.
30 Jenish, *The Montreal Canadiens*, pp. 37, 50.
31 While the goalie's name bears an accent, *Vézina*, the NHL trophy named in his honour does not, illustrative of how dominant anglophone discourses elide French Canadian contributions to the sport.
32 Harvey, "Whose Sweater Is This?", p. 49.
33 Lafrance, "Je ne suis plus pratiquant," pp. 25–6.

34 Harvey, "Whose Sweater Is This?", p. 49.
35 Dryden, *The Game*, pp. 24–5.
36 Melançon, "Notre père," p. 118.
37 Brunelle, "Rocket Knock-out," p. 24.
38 Cha, "La Ville est hockey," p. 3.
39 Laurin-Lamothe and Moreau, "Le Canadien de Montréal," p. 7.
40 Anonymous, "La Série Montréal–Québec."
41 Parts of the analysis of *The Rocket: The Legend of Rocket Richard* were first presented in a paper delivered at the Canadian Popular Culture Association conference in Niagara Falls, Ontario, 10–12 May 2012.
42 Laberge, "L'Affaire Richard/Campbell, " pp. 13–14.
43 Carrier, *Le Rocket*, p. 122.
44 Melançon, *The Rocket*.
45 Pellerin, *Maurice Richard: L'Idole d'un peuple*, p. 235.
46 Harvey, "Whose Sweater Is This?", pp. 38–9.
47 Melançon, *The Rocket*, p. 43.
48 Interestingly, although it was also nominated for fourteen of Quebec's equivalent prizes, the Jutra, it took home no trophies, outshined by Philippe Falardeau's *Congorama*.
49 Carrier reinforces this image, repeatedly describing Richard's work ethic, implying that his working-class origins instilled this value in the hockey star; Carrier, *Le Rocket*, pp. 157, 161, 182, *passim*. See also Laberge, "L'Affaire Richard/Campbell."
50 Roch Carrier describes it as a two-pronged attack begun with a frontal hit by Léo Labine and a knee to the head by Bill Quackenbush; Carrier, *Le Rocket*, pp. 184–5.
51 Harvey, "Whose Sweater Is This?", pp. 38–9; Bélanger, "The Last Game?", pp. 296–8.
52 A number of such sequences recur; for example, Richard's first game as a Canadien features a radio advertisement and the Montreal announcers' colourful presentation of the game live from the Forum, intercut with a random Montrealer listening to the game at home (27:00–28:00); during his first season, the film cuts to his father-in-law and brother-in-law listening to the game at home as Maurice is injured (30:35–45).
53 John Christian Sanaker, in a perceptive examination of the use of language in this film, points out that its use of English also is meant to reveal the unequal power relation between English- and French-speaking Canadians during Richard's day. Sanaker, *La Rencontre des langues*.
54 Gould, "La genèse catholique," p. 148.

55 Stalker, "Bruins Fans Flood Twitter." One wonders if the Bruins' 2013 acquisition of biracial star Jarome Iginla represents, however, an effort to counter this reputation.
56 Jenish, *The Montreal Canadiens*, pp. 143–4.
57 Pellerin, *Maurice Richard: L'Idole d'un peuple*, p. 287.
58 Carrier, *Le Rocket*, p. 207; that Carrier also erroneously substitutes the evil Bruins for the Detroit Red Wings in his subsequent account of the Riot-day game of 17 March 1955 suggests perhaps that we should take his account with a grain of salt; Carrier, *Le Rocket*, pp. 211, 212.
59 Certain franchises expressly forbade the use of French in the locker room; Boileau, Landry, and Trempe, "Les Canadiens français," p. 146.
60 Irvin apologizes, however, during the post-Riot sequences: "What the hell are you talking about, quitting. You can't quit! You're the big brute of hockey. So they got a little crazy out there. So they broke a few windows. I wanted to tell you that, uh, I always felt I needed to win. And I know that you needed to win just as bad. And that's why I pulled all the crazy stuff and I pushed you really hard. And I just wanna say that, uh, I hope there are no hard feelings because you are the greatest hockey player they'll ever see."
61 While today the term "Canuck" applies to all Canadians, as well as to Vancouver's NHL franchise, just like the term *Canadien*, it originally referred to French Canadian lumber workers (hence the Canucks' alternative logo). "Le Damned Canuck" is a poem from nationalist poet Gaston Miron's watershed collection, *L'Homme rapaillé* (1970; "The Reassembled Man"; partly translated as *The March to Love: Selected Poems of Gaston Miron*), which laments the oppression of the French Canadian in the 1950s and 1960s. See Werneburg, "Origins of 'canuck.'"
62 Pierre Vallières, a member of the terrorist nationalist group, the FLQ, drawing upon Quebec intellectuals' alignment of the 1960s fight for sovereignty with that of Third World colonies seeking independence from Europe, articulated the theory of the *White Niggers of America* (1969), which compared French Canadians' economic and cultural oppression with that of African Americans in the Jim Crow South. The pejorative term "white niggers" was actually used to refer to French Canadians at that time.
63 Benoît Melançon discusses how contemporary songs by female musical artists had long ago depicted the Rocket as an object of desire, citing Jeanne d'Arc Charlebois's "Maurice Richard" (1951) and Denise Filiatrault's "Rocket Rock and Roll" (1957); *The Rocket*, pp. 72–3.
64 Carrier, *Le Rocket*, pp. 183, 188.
65 See the discussion of Guy Corneau's *Absent Fathers, Lost Sons*, in chapter 4.

66 Bélanger, "The Last Game?", p. 297.
67 Jenish, *The Montreal Canadiens,* pp. 81, 94–5.
68 Carrier, *Le Rocket,* p. 185.
69 Carrier, *Le Rocket,* p. 122.

2 "The Nordiques Have Disappeared!"

1 "Le hockey, sport national du peuple québécois, occupe une place de choix dans l'imaginaire de nos auteurs de science-fiction [...]." Dupuis, "La Science-fiction québécoise," p. 72.
2 "De même, toute personne habitant le Québec sait bien – le hockey occupant ici un grand espace télévisé, affectif, démesuré ou autre – que Guy Lafleur fut un fantastique joueur de hockey." Bérubé, "Le Fantastique, la science-fiction," p. 138.
3 Dryden, *The Game,* p. 24.
4 Dryden, *The Game,* p. 25.
5 This and other historical background information has been paraphrased from a number of sources, including Linteau et al., *Histoire du Québec contemporain,* vol. 2; and Brown, *Histoire générale du Canada.* Another essential source for my interpretation of 1960s nationalist thought and its subsequent impact is Mills, *The Empire Within.*
6 Exact figures are 40.4 per cent YES; 59.6 per cent NO; Pinard, "The Quebec Independence Movement," p. 239.
7 Belleau, *Surprendre les voix,* p. 104.
8 Lasorsa, *La Rivalité Canadien-Nordiques,* p. 3.
9 Jack McCallum asserts that "aside from baseball players, no group of athletes is more superstitious than hockey players, particularly goalies"; "Green Cars," p. 208. See also Dryden, *The Game,* p. 203; and Womack, "Why Athletes Need Ritual."
10 Bauer, "Introduction," p. 10; see also Melançon, "Hockey spectral."
11 Ransom, "*Lieux de mémoire* or *lieux du dollar?*", pp. 29–35.
12 For a detailed description of the history and development of the science fiction movement in Quebec, see Ransom, *Science Fiction from Québec,* pp. 33–59; "History Making and Canon Fodder"; and "Parabolas of SFQ."
13 April, "Le Fantôme du Forum," p. 162.
14 April, "Le Fantôme du Forum," p. 180; original emphasis.
15 April, "Sport-fiction," p. 233.
16 April, "Sport-fiction," p. 23. Scott A.G.M. Crawford asserts that "very little, it seems has been written on the relationship of sport and science fiction"; Crawford, "Film as Art," p. 50. This assertion continues to hold true; my

bibliographic searches turned up a single volume, Mead and Frelik, *Playing the Universe: Games and Gaming in Science Fiction* (2007), and a handful of articles dated since 2000, such as Silliman, "Batter up!" and Senn, "The Sport of Violence."

17 Buma, *Refereeing Identity*, p. 22. Edo Van Belkom has published two hockey-themed stories: "Heart" (2000), belonging to the horror genre, and "Hockey's Night in Canada" (1997), an alternate history that imagines the Russian takeover of hockey in Canada after Paul Henderson's failed goal attempt at the end of the 1972 Summit Series. In addition, Paul Quarrington's *Logan in Overtime* (1990) features a crazy goalie who believes his knees have been possessed by aliens. See also Blake, *Hockey Literature in Canada*; Skinazi, "The Mystery of a Canadian Father," pp. 121–2.

18 To name only a few examples from the significant corpus of children's and young adult literature featuring both hockey and science-fictional or fantasy elements to appear in Quebec, François Gravel's prize-winning *Zamboni* (1990; trans. Sarah Cummins, *Mr. Zamboni's Dream Machine*, 1992), Francine Pelletier's *La Saison de l'exil* (1992), and Michel Foisy's *La Carte de hockey magique* (2000; *The Magic Hockey Card*) bear mention. Let us recall that even Roch Carrier's well-known "The Hockey Sweater" (1979), discussed in chapter 1, has elements of fantasy as young Roch's prayers are answered by a host of clothes eater moths arriving to destroy the abominable Maple Leafs sweater.

19 Bérubé, "Le Fantastique, la science-fiction," 148.

20 April, "Sport-Fiction," p. 237.

21 April, "Le Fantôme du Forum," p. 181; original emphasis.

22 Dennis, "Forever Proud?"

23 While April's reference was historical, he also successfully extrapolated future developments in excessive behaviours by Montreal Canadiens fans; similar riots occurred in 1986, 1993, 2008, and 2010, all in celebration of victories either in the Stanley Cup finals (1986 over the Calgary Flames; 1993 over the LA Kings) or in elimination rounds (round one over the Bruins in 2008; round two over the Penguins in 2010); Canadian Press, "Hockey Riots."

24 Jean Harvey and Alan Law, "'Resisting' the Global Media Oligopoly?"; see also Bélanger, "Sports Venues," pp. 383, 388.

25 April, "Le Fantôme du Forum, " p. 164.

26 April, "Le Fantôme du Forum, " p. 163.

27 April, "Le Fantôme du Forum, " p. 179.

28 Gruneau and Whitson, *Hockey Night in Canada*, pp. 216–17.

29 Janelle, "La Science-fiction au Québec," p. 7; Gouanvic, "A Past, A Future," p. 73; Ketterer, *Canadian Science Fiction and Fantasy*, p. 88. According to

Gouanvic, Barcelo has rejected the label of SF for his works; Gouanvic, "Rational Speculations," pp. 71–2; one of his short stories, however, "Les Semeurs de robots," twice appeared in anthologies of SFQ.

30 Vautier, *New World Myth*, pp. 205–7; p. 4.

31 Bowers, *Magic(al) Realism*, p. 1. Bowers also asserts that among the various terms applied to the concept, "magical realism" appears to have gained the most widespread use, as opposed to "magic realism." In the francophone context, as I have observed elsewhere, although *réalisme magique* has been widely adopted for use, Alejo Carpentier's original term *lo real maravilloso* was first borrowed by Haitian writer Jacques-Stephen Alexis as *réalisme merveilleux*; Ransom, "La Gamme du fantastique," pp. 152–3.

32 Bowers, *Magic(al) Realism*, p. 3.

33 See, for example, the nearly annual series of Canadian "SF" anthologies, *Tesseracts*, begun by Judith Merril and currently published by Calgary's Edge SF & F.

34 Barcelo, *Ville-Dieu*, p. 221.

35 Bélanger and Valois-Nadeau, "Entre l'étang gelé," p. 73; Francis, *National Dreams*, p. 168; Gruneau and Whitson, *Hockey Night in Canada*, p. 1. Mary Louise Adams critiques such nostalgia, arguing that it "is a powerful means of keeping us from imagining how Canada might be different; it is part of the process of marginalizing women and people of colour, of limiting the stories we can tell about ourselves"; Adams, "The Game of Whose lives?" p. 82.

36 Barcelo, *Ville-Dieu*, p. 223.

37 Barcelo, *Ville-Dieu*, p. 222.

38 Barcelo, *Ville-Dieu*, pp. 224, 221.

39 Barcelo, *Ville-Dieu*, p. 226.

40 Barcelo, *Ville-Dieu*, p. 227.

41 Adding a "z" to terms derived from the French, *anglais* or *Anglos* for English-speakers, is a common device in allegorical and SF texts; it simply reproduces orthographically the phonetic liaison that occurs between the article *les* and the following vowel.

42 Barcelo, *Ville-Dieu*, p. 231.

43 Barcelo, *Ville-Dieu*, p. 231.

44 See, among others, Bélanger and Valois-Nadeau, "Entre l'étang gelé"; Gruneau and Whitson, *Hockey Night in Canada;* and several of the essays included in Whitson and Gruneau, *Artificial Ice*; and Harvey and Law, "'Resisting' the Global Media Oligopoly?"

45 Barcelo, *Ville-Dieu*, p. 231–2.

46 Barcelo, *Ville-Dieu*, p. 232.

47 Barcelo, *Ville-Dieu*, p. 223.
48 Barcelo, *Ville-Dieu*, p. 234.
49 Robidoux, *Men At Play*, p. 95.
50 Barcelo, *Ville-Dieu*, p. 113.
51 Barcelo, *Ville-Dieu*, p. 113.
52 Barcelo, *Ville-Dieu*, p. 113.
53 Benoît Melançon's blog offers an interesting article on hockey vocabulary in Quebec, "La Langue du hockey à travers les âges," which refers to lexicons published by the abbé Étienne Blanchard dating from 1915 to 1925. It is possible that Blanchard was the real-life model for Barcelo's well-meaning curate.
54 These observations derive from reading a number of real hockey biographies and autobiographies, of Franco-Québécois and Anglo-Canadian players alike. See Béliveau (with Goyens and Turowetz), *My Life in Hockey;* Denault, *Jacques Plante;* Germain, *Guy Lafleur;* and Roy, *Le Guerrier.*
55 Barcelo, *Ville-Dieu*, p. 114. Apparently Yvan Cournoyer had improvised pucks cut "from iron bars at his father's machine shop"; Jenish, *The Montreal Canadiens*, p. 181.
56 Barcelo, *Ville-Dieu*, p. 114.
57 Barcelo, *Ville-Dieu*, pp. 114–15.
58 Barcelo, *Ville-Dieu*, pp. 115, 116.
59 See for example, Lafrance, "Je ne suis plus pratiquant."
60 Barcelo, *Ville-Dieu*, p. 124.
61 Barcelo, *Ville-Dieu*, p. 124.
62 Barcelo, *Ville-Dieu*, p. 233.
63 See Robidoux, *Men at Play;* Barreau, "La religion du Canadien," p. 94; Burstyn, *Rites of Men;* Pronger, *The Arena of Masculinity*. A more thorough account of the question of masculinity and hockey is provided in chapter 4.
64 Barcelo, *Ville-Dieu*, p. 235.
65 We should recall the publication and setting of this text in the early 1980s, when shaved heads were not the sign of masculinity – or at least the fashion statement – that they appear to be today. In any case, the shaved head appears less often in the hockey locker room than in that of other sports, notably basketball and baseball.
66 Barcelo, *Ville-Dieu*, p. 241.
67 Barcelo, *Ville-Dieu*, p. 244.
68 Jamie Dopp's paper "Hockey, Zen, and the Art of Bill Gaston" brought this novel to my attention; see also Dopp, "Win Orr Lose," pp. 81–97; and Blake, *Canadian Hockey Literature*, pp. 123–9.

69 Robidoux, *Men at Play*, p. 27.
70 Robidoux, *Men at Play*, pp. 26–7; Robidoux cites Foucault, *Discipline and Punish*, p. 138, to support his arguments.
71 Robidoux, *Men at Play*, pp. 27–8.
72 I presented some aspects of this section and that on *Les Hockeyeurs cybernétiques* in a paper, "Hockeyers cybernétiques et disparus: le sport et l'identité dans la science-fiction québécoise," at the Conseil International des Études Francophones Conference in Montréal, 27 June to 4 July 2010.
73 Indeed, Claude Janelle's prediction for this obscure novel in a review contemporary to its original release has nearly come true: "*Les Nordiques sont disparus* est ce genre de récit qui dans cinquante ans, s'il n'a pas complètement sombré dans l'oubli, fera sourire les lecteurs au même titre que nous sourions avec condescendance aujourd'hui en lisant des romans québécois de SF écrits dans les années trente" (*The Nordiques Have Disappeared* is the type of story that in fifty years, if it hasn't completely foundered into obscurity, will make its readers smile just like we smile today reading Quebec SF novels from the 1930s). Janelle nonetheless agrees with me that "Ce qui est intéressant, par contre, c'est la volonté bien arrêtée de l'écrivain de privilégier la couleur locale et d'utiliser plusieurs référents culturels comme la passion du hockey chez les Québécois, [et] le statut politique du Québec" (What is interesting, on the other hand, is the author's well-defined desire to privilege local colour and to use several cultural references like the Québécois's passion for hockey [and] the political status of Quebec); Janelle, "Le Sport est-il littéraire?," p. 13.
74 April, "Sport-fiction," p. 235.
75 Sirois, *Discrimination in the NHL*, p. 87.
76 Brunt, "Quebec Ready for Nordiques Return."
77 Poulter, *Becoming Native*, p. 2; Lucas, *Lord Durham's Report*.
78 Well after the publication of Tremblay's novel, the discourse saw a resurgence in the controversy surrounding Lise Payette's documentary *Disparaître* (1990), whose title, To Disappear/Disappearing, reveals its premise "that the French Canadian nation was losing ground in Canada (demographically, socially, and politically) to the anglophone majority, due to Quebec's low birthrate and insufficient measures to ensure that immigrants to Quebec would learn French"; Lamoureux, "The Paradoxes of Quebec Feminism," p. 316.
79 Chabot, *La Grande Rivalité*, pp. 87–8.
80 Tremblay, *Les Nordiques sont disparus*, p. 218.

81 From the publication of François-Xavier's Garneau's *Histoire du Canada* (1845–8) as a direct riposte to Lord Durham's comment on a "nation without history" to Lionel Groulx's assertion of *Notre Maître, le Passé* (Our Master, The Past; 1937–44), to present-day calls for a revised, more nuanced vision of Quebec's history, such as that of Jocelyn Létourneau in *A History for the Future*, history remains at the core of Quebec's intellectual and identitary discourses.
82 See, for example, Élisabeth Vonarburg's alternate history novel, *Reluctant Voyagers* (1994).
83 See Ransom, "L'Uchronie québécoise"; "Un utopiste québécois"; and "Warping Time"; as well as Serruys, "Xénototalité" for general discussions of alternate history in SFQ, as well as Hellekson, *The Alternate History;* and Henriet, *L'Histoire revisitée,* for discussions of this particular subgenre of science fiction.
84 Tremblay, *Les Nordiques sont disparus*, p. 57.
85 Tremblay, *Les Nordiques sont disparus*, p. 144.
86 Tremblay, *Les Nordiques sont disparus*, p. 144-45.
87 Tremblay, *Les Nordiques sont disparus*, p. 196.
88 Tremblay, *Les Nordiques sont disparus*, p. 218.
89 Chabot, *La Grande Rivalité*, For a lengthier discussion of the rivalry, see chapter 3.
90 Tremblay, *Les Nordiques sont disparus*, p. 20.
91 Tremblay, *Les Nordiques sont disparus*, p. 131.
92 As evidence, Tremblay reproduces their correspondence in the novel's preface; Tremblay, *Les Nordiques sont disparus*, pp. 4–6.
93 Bourgeois, "Les *Nordiques* et le nouveau Colisée," p. 217.
94 Bourgeois, "Les *Nordiques* et le nouveau Colisée," pp. 218–19.
95 Attendance figures show averages over 14,000, which would be close to capacity in the small arena; Markosun, "NHL Average Attendance since 1989-90."
96 Tremblay, *Les Nordiques sont disparus*, p. 48.
97 Tremblay, *Les Nordiques sont disparus*, pp. 53, 54.
98 Filmmaker Pierre Falardeau offers an intense but also controversial depiction of the actual kidnapping and hostage situation in *Octobre* (1994); for contemporary accounts, see Pelletier, *La Crise d'octobre,* and Provencher, *La Grande Peur d'octobre '70*; and for distanced historical analysis, see Mills, *The Empire Within*.
99 Brodeur, "Un acteur autonome," pp. 287–97; Dagenais, "Est-il responsable?", pp. 307–15.
100 Tremblay, *Les Nordiques sont disparus*, p. 53.

101 Tremblay, *Les Nordiques sont disparus*, p. 60.
102 Tremblay, *Les Nordiques sont disparus*, p. 83.
103 The novel won not only the Grand Prix de la science-fiction et du fantastique québécois and the Prix Boréal in Quebec, but also a Canada Council Prize for Juvenile Literature (*Shooting*, back cover), and it has seen several new editions.
104 The Japanese coach Tanaka harangues his players in the locker room: "Winning means working as one man, functioning like one healthy, highly trained and disciplined body. That is what I am asking of you, gentlemen: the discipline to win" (36). Meanwhile, players indulge in the mandatory grousing about the excessive workouts: "Hey guys, is that some sadistic bastard or what? This is killing me!" (37); "What's the point of working out in a gym when we're hockey players? Hockey's played on ice isn't it?" (37–8). One admiring player from Japan explains the method behind Tanaka's so-called madness to his new teammates: "In my country, […] Tanaka has moulded these men into a single unit. And it works. He doesn't believe in stars. That's why he treats us this way. He doesn't give a damn whether or not we're considered the world's best players." (38) This scene sounds like dialogue right out of recent films depicting the hockey of this period, such as *Miracle* and *Canada/Russia '72*, although *Slap Shot* and *Rollerball* – elements of which do appear in Côté's vision of the future of sport – are the novel's near contemporaries.
105 Côté, writing not long after the height of the WHA era, during the flamboyant 1970s (see Willes, *The Rebel League*) extrapolates a team of Dennis Rodman-like figures; *Shooting for the Stars*, p. 44.
106 Westfahl, *Hugo Gernsback*, p. 47.
107 For example, Kingsley Amis – one of the first mainstream literary writers to take science fiction seriously – offers this definition in a pioneering study: "science fiction presents with verisimilitude the human effects of spectacular changes in our environment, changes either deliberately willed or involuntarily suffered"; *New Maps of Hell*, p. 26. Similarly, Reginald Bretnor defines the genre as "fiction based on rational speculation regarding the human experience of science and its resultant technologies"; "Science Fiction in the Age of Space," p. 150. More recently, Roger Luckhurst has confirmed in his cultural history of SF that "an SF future is one that is meant to extrapolate rationally or scientifically from tendencies within the 'empirical environment'"; *Science Fiction*, p. 7.
108 In contrast, Francine Pelletier's young adult novel *La Saison de l'exil* (1992) describes human efforts to play hockey in the conditions prevalent on an extraterrestrial colony planet with lower gravity (and thus less muscle

strength), extremely cold temperatures, and a harmful atmosphere. The sport is thus played in fully insulated and self-contained space suits.

109 Ransom, "Hockey of the Future."

110 Côté, *Shooting for the Stars*, p. 9.

111 Côté, *Shooting for the Stars*, p. 18.

112 Côté, *Shooting for the Stars*, p. 22.

113 Melançon, *The Rocket*, pp. 43–9.

114 Côté, *Shooting for the Stars*, p. 25.

115 Côté, *Shooting for the Stars*, pp. 28, 45.

116 As long ago as 1960, Kingsley Amis articulated the notion that "few things reveal so sharply as science fiction the wishes, hopes, fears, inner stresses and tensions of an era, or define its limitations with such exactness"; Amis, *New Maps of Hell*, p. 64. More recently, Carl Freedman elaborated an entire theory of SF as a critical discourse through the use of Marxist critical theory; Freedman, *Critical Theory and Science Fiction*.

117 Côté, *Shooting for the Stars*, p. 26.

118 Côté, *Shooting for the Stars*, pp. 42–3.

119 Côté, *Shooting for the Stars*, p. 43. Ransom, "Hockey of the Future," pp. 73–4, explicitly links media depictions of the Soviets during the Summit Series to that of robots.

120 Côté, *Shooting for the Stars*, p. 50.

121 Côté, *Shooting for the Stars*, p. 34.

122 Côté, *Shooting for the Stars*, p. 102; original emphasis.

123 Ironically, the lack of a name above the number can reflect a team's attainment of the most elite status, in that real fans don't need a name on the jersey to know the player's individual identity. We see this in the nearly unique example of the New York Yankees sporting only the players' numbers, not their names on their uniforms.

124 Robidoux, *Men at Play*, pp. 127–8.

125 Côté, *Shooting for the Stars*, pp. 54–5.

126 Côté, *Shooting for the Stars*, p. 55.

127 Robidoux, *Men at Play*, p. 26.

128 Côté, *Shooting for the Stars*, p. 28.

129 While this is not the place to argue the validity of Vallières's discourse – one also found among more conservative nationalists, such as André d'Allemagne in *Le Colonialisme au Québec* (1966) – the perpetual failure to understand the *real*, statistically supported economic oppression of the French-Canadian majority in Quebec as late as the 1970s remains a barrier to understanding between the solitudes. Sean Mills documents

the situation: "In 1961, a 35% difference in average income separated anglophones from francophones, and statistics which correlated income with ethnicity found that francophones ranked twelfth of fourteen ethnic groups in the province. 56% of the Montreal region's best-paid workers were anglophones, although they made up only 24% of the labour force. [...] Although francophones comprised the vast majority of Quebec's population, they controlled only 20% of its economy. And the province – which represented 27% of Canada's population – contained 40% of the country's unemployed workers"; Mills, *The Empire Within*, p. 21. Brian McKenna and Susan Purcell describe such conditions during Jean Drapeau's tenure as mayor of Montreal as still current in 1970, a decade after the Quiet Revolution; McKenna and Purcell, *Drapeau*, pp. 222–3.

130 Côté, *Shooting for the Stars*, p. 79; original emphasis.
131 Côté, *Shooting for the Stars*, p. 117.
132 Côté, *Shooting for the Stars*, pp. 115, 116–17.
133 Ransom, "Hockey of the Future."
134 Côté, *Le Retour des Inactifs*, p. 157.
135 Lisée, *The Trickster*, pp. 7–14.
136 Pinard, "The Quebec Independence Movement," p. 256.
137 For more detailed discussion of texts from this era, see Ransom, "(Un) common Ground"; and Beaulé, '"Il n'y a que des cauchemars'" and "Regards sur le Québec."
138 Bouchard, *Les 42,210 Univers de la science-fiction*; "The Female Utopia in Canada," "Féminisme, utopie, philosophie," "L'Inversion des rôles masculins et féminins," and "Les utopies féministes, le fantastique et la science-fiction."
139 Bouchard, "Au jeu," p. 59.
140 Bouchard, "Au jeu," p. 56.
141 Bouchard, "Au jeu," p. 56.
142 See such laments as Kidd and Macfarlane's *The Death of Hockey* and some chapters of Dryden and McGregor, *Home Game*, as well as Jodoin, "Les Salaires au hockey."
143 Lasorsa, *La Rivalité*, p. 105.
144 Lindros, with Starkman, *Fire on Ice*, pp. 190–1.
145 Lindros, *Fire on Ice*, pp. 194–5.
146 Lindros, *Fire on Ice*, pp. 163–7.
147 Lindros, *Fire on Ice*, pp. 169–70.
148 Bouchard, "Au jeu," 58–9.
149 Richard, *La Série du siècle*, p. 45.
150 Bouchard, "Au jeu," p. 58–9.

151 See among others, Gaboury, *Le Nationalisme de Lionel Groulx*; Bouchard, *Les Deux Chanoines*; and Gauvreau, "From Rechristianization to Contestation," for an account of the beginnings of clerico-nationalism's demise.
152 See Somay, "Towards an Open-Ended Utopia"; Suvin, "The SF Novel"; Moylan, *Demand the Impossible*; and Csicsery-Ronay, Jr, "Marxist Theory and Science Fiction," p. 117.
153 Bouchard, "Au jeu," p. 67.
154 Bouchard, "Au jeu," p. 67.
155 Bouchard, "Au jeu," p. 68.
156 April, "Sport-fiction," p. 238.
157 Indeed, Jean-François Doré constructs a systematic correlation between Greek mythology, its heroes and its functions, and "notre sport national: le hockey"; Doré, "Mythologie," p. 95.
158 Saint-Éloi, "Haïtiens," p. 254.
159 Dupuis, "La Science-fiction," p. 72.
160 Vautier, *New World Myth*, p. 4.
161 Vautier, *New World Myth*, p. 207-8.
162 Incidentally, April also wrote a short story that deals with the Olympic Stadium in a science-fictional manner; I examine his "Le Vol de la ville" along with a Mes Aïeux song about the *Stade* elsewhere; Ransom, "Constructions of the Future."
163 April, "Sport-fiction," p. 237.
164 Bélil, "Barcelo et Beauchemin," p. 55.
165 Barcelo, *I Hate Hockey*, pp. 7, 100.
166 Barcelo, *I Hate Hockey*, pp. 7, 8, 12, 14.
167 Barcelo, *I Hate Hockey*, p. 9.
168 Barcelo, *I Hate Hockey*, p. 9.
169 Barcelo, *I Hate Hockey*, p. 9.
170 Barcelo, *I Hate Hockey*, p. 10.
171 Barcelo, *I Hate Hockey*, p. 10.
172 Barcelo, *I Hate Hockey*, p. 10.
173 Barcelo, *I Hate Hockey*, p. 8.
174 Barcelo, *I Hate Hockey*, p. 20.
175 Barcelo, *I Hate Hockey*, p. 26.
176 Barcelo, *I Hate Hockey*, p. 29.
177 Barcelo, *I Hate Hockey*, p. 29.
178 Barcelo, *I Hate Hockey*, p. 38.
179 Barcelo, *I Hate Hockey*, p. 40.
180 Barcelo, *I Hate Hockey*, p. 46.
181 Barcelo, *I Hate Hockey*, p. 100.

3 Plus ça change

1 "Avec Lance et compte, nous réalisons ce que le CRTC dit souhaiter: diffuser une production pancanadienne adoptée par les téléspectateurs d'un océan à l'autre"; Héroux and Pagé, *Lance et compte*, p. 154.

2 "En introduisant la figure du gagnant, *Lance et compte* transforme radicalement l'imaginaire téléromanesque. La réussite personnelle devient la nouvelle panacée et Pierre Lambert est un winner qui cristallise les aspirations de milliers de téléspectateurs"; Désaulniers, *De la famille Plouffe*, p. 86.

3 1,993,000; Héroux et Pagé, *Lance et compte*, p. 110.

4 Héroux et Pagé, *Lance et compte*, pp. 117–18.

5 Héroux et Pagé, *Lance et compte*, p. 61.

6 Already in 1954, Theodor W. Adorno had begun to reflect on the possibility of a cultural critique of television. While I do not share his interest in examining this particular cultural industry's psychological impact on viewers and society outlined in his "How to Look at Television," I work from the general assumption that "the socio-psychological implications and mechanisms of television [...] often operate under the guise of false realism"; p. 158. As we shall see in this chapter, such is the case with a mainstream television series produced for a mass audience; through its very pretentions to realism, *Lance et compte* offers a seductive fantasy that pacifies viewers, occupying their free time in a manner that ultimately reinforces the ideological system of capitalism. Precisely because of its mass audience and commercial nature, the television series reflects the dominant ideology. In contrast, we more frequently see the possibility of resistance in small market texts produced for modest (or no) financial gain, such as many of the science fiction stories and musical texts examined here.

7 In addition, the producers hired a hockey consultant. For the first series, hockey journalist and amateur coach Pierre Ladouceur choreographed play and watched archival footage to reproduce actual game segments; Héroux et Pagé, *Lance et compte*, p. 92.

8 Interview on the DVD accompanying Héroux et Pagé, *Lance et compte.*

9 Indeed, Raboy argues that "the raison d'être of public broadcasting in Canada was to promote and support the Canadian difference vis-à-vis the United States," "Public Television," p. 65.

10 Raboy, "Public Television," pp. 75–6, 83; Skinner, "Television in Canada," pp. 7–8.

11 Héroux and Pagé, *Lance et compte*, pp. 21–2.

12 Héroux and Pagé, *Lance et compte*, pp. 12–15.

13 See Arpin, Preface, p. 3; Désaulniers, *De la famille Plouffe*, p. 7.
14 Héroux and Pagé, *Lance et compte*, p. 11.
15 Héroux and Pagé, *Lance et compte*, p. 7.
16 See for example, Savoie, *Thatcher, Reagan, Mulroney*.
17 For Bourassa's support of free trade ideology, see for example Chodos, Murphy, and Hamovitch, *Selling Out*, pp. 28–9.
18 Héroux et Pagé, *Lance et compte*, pp. 153–6, 189.
19 Héroux et Pagé, *Lance et compte*, pp. 109–10, 157ff.
20 Héroux et Pagé, *Lance et compte*, p. 108.
21 Héroux et Pagé, *Lance et compte*, p. 19.
22 Désaulniers, *De la famille Plouffe*, p. 87.
23 Héroux et Pagé, *Lance et compte*, pp. 30, 25, 36.
24 Héroux et Pagé, *Lance et compte*, pp. 17–18.
25 Héroux et Pagé, *Lance et compte*, pp. 45–9.
26 Héroux et Pagé, *Lance et compte*, pp. 52–3, 56.
27 Héroux et Pagé, *Lance et compte*, p. 59.
28 Héroux et Pagé, *Lance et compte*, pp. 68, 155–6.
29 Héroux et Pagé, *Lance et compte*, p. 92.
30 Héroux et Pagé, *Lance et compte*, pp. 91–3.
31 Regarding parenthetical citations in this chapter, see Works Cited for the abbreviations corresponding to each season or television movie in the Lance et compte franchise.
32 Bryshun and Young, "Sport Related Hazing," p. 278.
33 According to Sirois's analysis of draft statistics, "the Montreal Canadiens top the league in the average number of French-speaking Quebec hockey players drafted, with 2.63 players per year (a total of 105)"; *Discrimination in the NHL*, p. 77. In addition, "the Nordiques are second for the average number of French-speaking Quebec hockey players drafted, with 2.38 players per year (a total 38)"; p. 87.
34 This figure is from 1987 on Werner Antweiler's University of British Columbia posting at: http://fx.sauder.ubc.ca/etc/CADpages.pdf.
35 Indeed, Pierre refers to them as "Des losers," complaining about his time there. (LCI, ep. 9)
36 My gratitude to the independent reader who pointed this pertinent citation out to me.
37 See Saudohar, "The Hockey Lockout."
38 Ransom, "He Shoots! He Scores!"
39 Richard, *La Série du siècle*, p. 163.
40 Genest, "L'Internationalisation du hockey sur glace," pp. 177, 182.

41 Although the first black NHLer was Willie O'Ree of the Bruins, as long ago as 1958, major league hockey has not reached the level of full integration seen in major league baseball since Jackie Robinson broke the colour line in that sport. In addition to the scholarly examination of the black presence in hockey by Cecil Harris, *Breaking the Ice* (2003) and the Fosty brothers' *Black Ice* (2008), Philip van der Vossen's article "The All-Black Hockey Team" describes the growing attempts at bringing diversity not only to NHL franchises but to the hockey audience as well.
42 Héroux et Pagé, *Lance et compte*, p. 112.
43 Héroux et Pagé, *Lance et compte*, pp. 112–13.
44 Kennedy was allegedly a victim of coach Graham James, also accused of abuse by Theo Fleury in his autobiography *Playing with Fire*. James was sentenced for the abuse of Kennedy and Greg Gilhooly in February 2012; Associated Press, "Former Hockey Coach."
45 Chabot, *La Grande Rivalité*, p. 18.
46 Lasorsa, *La Rivalité Canadien-Nordiques*, p. 32.
47 Héroux et Pagé, *Lance et compte*, p. 51; on the two cities' rivalry, see also Chabot, *La Grande Rivalité*, pp. 26ff, 44–5, 127; and Lasorsa, *La Rivalité Canadien-Nordiques*, pp. 4, 16, 34, 40.
48 Lasorsa, *La Rivalité Canadien-Nordiques*, p. 3.
49 Héroux et Pagé, *Lance et compte*, p. 101.
50 Héroux et Pagé, *Lance et compte*, p. 97.
51 Héroux et Pagé, *Lance et compte*, p. 79.
52 Héroux et Pagé, *Lance et compte*, p. 93.
53 Héroux et Pagé, *Lance et compte*, p. 97.
54 Chabot, *La Grande Rivalité*, p. 154.
55 Lasorsa, *La Rivalité Canadien-Nordiques*, p. 30.
56 Lasorsa, *La Rivalité Canadien-Nordiques*.
57 Gordie Howe, whose retired #9 jersey hangs over the Detroit Red Wings' home ice, came out of retirement in 1973 and signed his sons Mark and Marty to play with the Houston Aeros and the New England Whalers of the WHA; brothers Bobby and Dennis Hull, linchpins of the 1960s Chicago Blackhawks and later of the Winnipeg Jets in the WHA, were followed into the NHL by their nephew and son respectively, Brett.
58 Désaulniers, *De la famille Plouffe*, p. 86.
59 Lasorsa, *La Rivalité Canadien-Nordiques*, p. 19.
60 Désaulniers, *De la famille Plouffe*, p. 18.
61 Lasorsa, *La Rivalité Canadien-Nordiques*, p. 3.
62 Demers, Preface, p. 10.

63 Chabot, *La Grande Rivalité*, p. 19; Lasorsa, *La Rivalité Canadien-Nordiques*, p. 22.
64 Lasorsa, *La Rivalité Canadien-Nordiques*, pp. 27, 32.
65 Demers, Preface, p. 10.
66 Aubut apparently convinced the PQ government that the blue-and-white, fleurdelisé jerseys of the Nordiques represented advertising for the province and obtained funds allocated for this purpose; Chabot, *La Grande Rivalité*, p. 85.
67 Lasorsa, *La Rivalité Canadien-Nordiques*, pp. 4, 30.
68 Lasorsa, *La Rivalité Canadien-Nordiques*, p. 23.
69 Chabot, *La Grande Rivalité*, p. 85.
70 Chabot, *La Grande Rivalité*, p. 32.
71 Lasorsa, *La Rivalité Canadien-Nordiques*, pp. 17, 25.
72 Chabot, *La Grande Rivalité*, p. 32.
73 Lasorsa, *La Rivalité Canadien-Nordiques*, p. 57.
74 Chabot, *La Grande Rivalité*, p. 23.
75 Guay, "Problèmes de l'intégration," pp. 22–3; Janson, "La Lente Évolution," p. 73.
76 Edensor, *National Identity*, pp. 25–8.
77 See for example Maguire, "Blade Runners," p. 153; Dowbiggin, *Of Ice and Men*, pp. 5, 91, 125.
78 V.-L. Tremblay cites others making this assertion, although he doesn't appear to subscribe to it himself; "Masculinité et hockey," p. 112.
79 Linteau et al., *Histoire du Québec Contemporain*, II:623.
80 See Savoie, *Thatcher, Reagan, Mulroney*; Bercuson, Granatstein, and Young, *Sacred Trust?*
81 Savoie, *Thatcher, Reagan, Mulroney*, pp. 177–8, 103, 181, 166, 158.
82 This was, however, Bourassa's second mandate; as seen in chapter 2, he was also provincial premier from 1970 to 1976.
83 L. Gagnon, "Le 'style' social-démocrate," p. 18; Fortin, "L'économie du Québec," pp. 40–1.
84 Linteau et al., *Histoire du Québec Contemporain*, II:623–33.
85 Linteau et al., *Histoire du Québec Contemporain*, II:637–88.
86 Héroux et Pagé, *Lance et compte*, p. 150.
87 Lamoureux, "The Paradoxes of Quebec Feminism," pp. 311–20.
88 One glaring example appears in a handbook that the Government of Quebec created for women's titles and positions in government. See Office, Au Féminin; Larivière, "Diversité des règles"; van Compernolle, "What Do Women Want?"
89 Anonymous, "Prendre le nom de son mari."

90 Lamoureux, "The Paradoxes of Quebec Feminism," p. 308.
91 Lamoureux, "The Paradoxes of Quebec Feminism," p. 308
92 Ransom, "He Shoots! He Scores!"
93 In an overview to an extensive two-volume comparative study of immigration and refugee policy in Canada and Australia, Inglis, Birch, and Sherington attribute Canada's delayed efforts at dealing with diversity to "the more central issue of the relationship between the founding 'charter' groups of colonial French-Canadians and English-Canadians"; p. 4. In spite of certain historical periods in which Canadian policy sought to limit non-European immigration, in the late 1980s, Canada "implemented its expansionary Five Year Immigration Plan which has resulted in a steady increase to an annual intake intended to reach 250,000 by 1993"; p. 7. See also *Canadian Demographics at a Glance* for a reflection of this image of Canada as immigrant-friendly and diverse; Minister of Industry, pp. 31–2.
94 Iacovino and Sévigny, "Between Unity and Diversity." For an excellent summary of the changing conception of nationalism in Quebec from an ethnic to a civic form, see Cunningham, "Nations and Nationalism"; as well as Arel, "Political Stability," pp. 69–77; and Karmis and Gagnon, "Federalism, Federation, and Collective Identities."
95 Héroux et Pagé, *Lance et compte*, p. 36.
96 As early as the 1940s, Haitians began to arrive in Quebec, with their numbers rising so that the most intense pattern occurred during a decade of Quebec's affirmation of its French culture; Max Dorsinville argues that "Haitians are the first immigrant group to be attracted to Canada primarily on the strength of the Québécois influence"; Preface, n.p.
97 Paul Dejean's landmark study of Haitian immigration to Quebec unfortunately ends in 1980; however, he clearly documents that up until the late 1960s, because French culture was an elite culture in Haiti, Quebec attracted largely elites. He asserts that "up to 1971, a majority of Haitian immigrants had a high level of formal education," and that a brain drain of professionals from Haiti – largely under the oppressive Duvalier regimes – apparently occurred, with the profession of physician strongly represented; Dejan, *Haitians in Quebec*, p. 7–19; 19; 55–6.
98 Chito Childs, "Prime-Time Color Line," pp. 34–6, 41.
99 Chito Childs, "Prime-Time Color Line," p. 39.
100 Héroux et Pagé, *Lance et compte*, p. 36.
101 For example, at the end of *LCI*, Pierre Lambert and Denis Mercure listen to the NHL draft on the car radio as they deliver potato chips, their day job.
102 Babynamefacts.com. "The Top Baby Names in Québec for 2010" lists William as the top boys' name.

103 Although Lamoureux asserts that feminism is alive and well in Quebec today, Miléna Santoro writes in a 2002 study of feminism in Quebec and French women's novels that the backlash affecting the United States also applies there; *Mothers of Invention*, p. 3. Given the enormous level of cultural exchange between the United States and all of Canada, including films and television dubbed into French, as well as untranslated popular music, it remains hard to believe that the province's culture has not been impacted by what Susan Faludi in 1991 termed an anti-feminist backlash; see her *Backlash: The Undeclared War against American Women*. The Reagan–Bush era, including the presidential terms of George W. Bush, are hotly critiqued for their anti-woman policies in works like Laura Flanders' edited volume, *The W Effect: Bush's War on Women* (2002), and Kellie Bean's *Post-Backlash Feminism: Women and the Media Since Reagan-Bush* (2008). This period corresponds precisely to that of the first *Lance et compte* series and telefilms and of the development phases of the reprise series in the early years of the new millennium.

104 Manon Tremblay, *Quebec Women and Legislative Representation*, p. 1. Quebec does better than Canada as a whole, in terms of percentages. In 2010, 22 per cent of the federal Parliament's members were women; around the same time, Jean Charest told the *Globe and Mail* in an interview that "at this point, in the Assembly in Quebec, close to 30 per cent of the elected members are women. We are at 29.8 per cent. That's close to the record we had in 2003, which was 40 women. We now have 37 out of 125"; Galloway, "No Old Boy's Club Here."

105 In the United States, Susan Gunelius reports a 10:1 ratio in favour of men over women in lead executive positions; "More Men in Executive Positions." In Quebec, the figures appear even lower; Marie-Claude Morin reports that "sur les 466 plus hauts dirigeants des 100 plus grandes entreprises québécoises cotées en Bourse, seulement 36 sont des femmes, soit 7,73% "; "Les femmes sont rares."

106 Bauch, "Canada Survives."

107 See for example, Ancelovici and Dupuis-Deri, *L'Archipel identitaire*; Balthazar, "The Dynamics of Multi-Ethnicity"; Dumont, *Raisons communes*; and Elbaz, Fortin, and Laforest, *Les Frontières de l'identité*. See also Cunningham, "Nations and Nationalism," for a summary of the issues in English.

108 Bouchard and Taylor, *Building the Future*.

109 See my discussion of this fascinating character in Ransom, "He Shoots! He Scores!"

4 Real Men Play Hockey

1 Historian and professor of Quebec Studies at Queen's University (Ontario), Caroline-Isabelle Caron informs me of the film *Slap Shot* that in Quebec, "anyone who likes hockey has seen it and knows it by heart" (my translation); e-mail to the author 24 May 2010.
2 Waugh, "The Boys and the Beast," p. 192.
3 Trujillo, "Hegemonic Masculinity," p. 15; see also, Connell, *Gender and Power*, pp. 183–6.
4 Parpart, "The Nation and the Nude," pp. 172, 173.
5 Parpart, "The Nation and the Nude," p. 174.
6 A much abridged version of these comments on the first *Les Boys* film was presented in a conference paper given at the Association for Canadian Studies in the United States Conference held in Ottawa in November 2011. I would like to thank those attending for their insightful feedback during the early stages of this project.
7 McClean, "So Here's the Deal," p. 175.
8 Pierre Falardeau's *Elvis Gratton* films ride a strange line here between the independent film and the commercial franchise. As Vincent Desroches reveals in an unpublished paper given at the Association for Canadian Studies in the United States conference in Ottawa in 2011, it began as a highly acerbic social commentary and ended with a popular congratulation of a certain died-in-the-wool, populist Québécois identity.
9 Arcand long reigned as contemporary Quebec's most internationally acclaimed filmmaker, beginning with *The Decline of the American Empire* (1983) and its sequel *The Barbarian Invasions* (2003), which won the Academy Award for Best Foreign Language Film. Villeneuve, whose *Incendies* (2010) received an Oscar nomination that year, and a number of other young directors have recently come to the fore.
10 I'm referring here to highly successful films at the box office like *Bon Cop, Bad Cop* (2006), discussed in the introduction, and *De Père en flic* (2009), just to cite two examples of action comedies. In other mainstream popular cinematic genres, we see *Piché: entre ciel et terre* (2010), which examined the life of controversial pilot Robert Piché; Québec's nascent horror/thriller film genre has also included some surprise successes, such as *Les Sept Jours du Talion* (2010) and *Sur le seuil* (2005).
11 According to Heather Macdougall, "released in the summer of 2006 and made history by being the first fully bilingual Canadian feature film given mainstream release. It also, somewhat unexpectedly, made history by breaking box-office records; with over $12 million in ticket sales, it was

the highest-grossing Canadian film ever in terms of domestic theatrical revenue"; Macdougall, "Facing Off," para. 2.

12 See Burstyn, *The Rites of Men*; Messner, *Power at Play*; Pronger, *The Arena of Masculinity*; Whitson, "Sport in the Social Construction of Masculinity."

13 Lawrence Scanlan sees this simile as a national trait: "the peculiarly Canadian hockey mindset that views hockey as war"; *Grace Under Fire*, 29.

14 Jason Blake asserts in his study of *Canadian Hockey Literature* (2010) that "nostalgia is probably the strongest tendency in hockey"; p. 43. Michael Peterman, in a review of several recent books about hockey, takes pause himself to recall the good old days of his west Toronto boyhood games of shinny; "Hockey Dreams," p. 142. My thanks to Jane Moss for bringing that piece to my attention.

15 See Bélanger, "The Last Game?"; Blake, *Canadian Hockey Literature*, pp. 81–90; Robidoux, *Men At Play*; Whitson, "Sport in the Social Construction of Masculinity."

16 Connell, *Gender and Power*. In *The Rites of Men*, Varda Burstyn coins the term "hypermasculinity"; p. 4. She also cites Gad Horowitz's term, "surplus masculinism"; p. 23.

17 Trujillo, "Hegemonic Masculinity," p. 15.

18 Both of whom appear later in the *Lance et Compte* reprise series, with Roy appearing as Pierre Lambert's love interest, Michèle Béliveau, in *La Nouvelle Génération* and *La Reconquête* and Charette appearing as the annoying and sensationalist television journalist and *bête noire* to fan favourite Lucien Boivin aka Lulu (Denis Bouchard) in *Le Grand Duel*.

19 Summerfield and Downward, *New Perspectives*, p. 1.

20 Stangl, "White *Sauvage-ry*," p. 71.

21 The eternal cross-fertilization, borrowing, and intertextual referencing between the *Les Boys* franchise and that of *Lance et compte* appears in the repetition of plotlines, as well as in the recasting of actors already noted. Marc Gagnon in *Lance et compte: Le Grand Duel* also discovers the existence of a daughter in whose life he wants to participate.

22 Summerfield and Downward, *New Perspectives*, p. 1.

23 Bélanger, "The Last Game?"

24 Corneau, *Absent Fathers*, p. 2.

25 Corneau, *Absent Fathers*, p. 3.

26 For example, Corneau's "Bob the Hero," an actor who wears masks and who does everything to please his mother, also a popular high achiever, but who eventually comes to live these roles and thus loses any authentic personality, resembles Ti-Guy (Corneau, *Absent Fathers*, pp. 42–50). "Peter the Seducer," a Don Juan type who seeks the perfect woman by collecting

a part from each conquest, may be Bob (pp. 59–63), while Julian bears the hallmarks of "Eric the Eternal Adolescent," who refuses to buy into anything or accept responsibility, who is typically a partier and a non-conformist with the need to be "cool," and who may also be an artistic, creative type (pp. 53–9).

27 Corneau, *Absent Fathers*, p. 14.

28 Michael A. Messner cites Ray Raphael's arguments of this nature, but does not see them as a fully adequate explanation of the function of sport in society today; *Power at Play*, p. 7.

29 Corneau, *Absent Fathers*, p. 118.

30 Bélanger, "The Last Game?", p. 299.

31 McClean, "So Here's the Deal," pp. 171–2.

32 Castle, *Reading the Modernist Bildungsroman*, pp. 4, 8.

33 Pomerance and Gateward, *Where the Boys Are*, p. 5.

34 See Ransom, "Deterritorialization," for further discussion of this film.

35 Daniels, "You Throw Like a Girl," pp. 123–4.

36 Pronger, *The Arena of Masculinity*, pp. 2, 3, 19. See also Sabo, "The Politics of Homophobia in Sport," pp. 101–2.

37 Bélanger, "The Last Game?", p. 299.

38 Waugh, "Boys and The Beast," p. 194.

39 Pronger explains in a note that "'Screamers' refers to 'screaming queens,' which is an expression for gay men who make a point of their gayness by behaving in blatantly effeminate ways – it often entails a lot of shrieking"; *The Arena of Masculinity*, p. 36.

40 See McSorley, Foreword, x.

41 Waugh, "Boys and The Beast," p. 195.

42 Saunders, *Imps of the Perverse*, p. 2.

43 Theberge, "Playing with the Boys," p. 37.

44 Messner, *Power at Play*, p. 16.

45 However, Susan Burris problematizes the success of that women's professional league relative to its men's counterpart; Burris, "She Got Game," p. 85.

46 Quoted in Pronger, *The Arena of Masculinity*, p. 22.

47 Stevens, "Women's Hockey in Canada."

48 Adams, "The Game of Whose Lives?," p. 71.

49 Theberge, "Playing with the Boys," p. 38.

50 The end credits mention Coach Danièle Sauvageau, Marie-Claude Allard, Virginie Bilodeau, Cathy Chartrand, Isabelle Chartrand, Annie Desrosiers, Nancy Drolet, Danielle Goyette, Gina Kingsbury, Mai-Lan Lé, Kathleen O'Reilly, Caroline Ouellette, France St-Louis, and Kim St-Pierre.

51 Daniels, "Gender Slurs," pp. 222–3, 226–7.
52 Messner, *Power at Play*, p. 17. Birrell and McDonald, among many others, reiterate this notion; *Reading Sport*, p. 6.
53 Baker, *Contesting Identities*, pp. 2, 11, 49.
54 Jung, *Four Archetypes*, pp. 133–52.
55 G. Jones, "Tricksters and Shamans," p. 110.
56 Hynes and Doty, *Mythical Trickster Figures*, p. 4.
57 Hynes, "Mapping the Characteristics of Mythic Tricksters," p. 34; citation modified to present in list form.
58 For discussions of hockey as religion see the essays collected in Bauer and Barreau, *La Religion du Canadien;* and Faulkner, "A Puckish Reflection."
59 Lavoie, "Stacking," p. 22.
60 Lavoie, *Désavantage numérique*; see also Sirois, *Discrimination in the NHL*.
61 Daniel Poliquin in *Le Roman colonial* (2000) makes a particularly convincing condemnation of this position.
62 Waugh, "Boys and The Beast," p. 188.
63 Numerous news articles as well as the assertions on the DVD boxes themselves attest to the box office records set by the franchise. See, for example, the continued popularity of *Les Boys III* in Anonymous, "'Les Boys'" Scores Box Office Record."
64 Beaty, "Not Playing, Working," p. 116.
65 For example, Jean Harvey expresses the concern that through hockey, "Québecers have found new avenues for the national confirmation through politics and the economy"; "Whose Sweater Is This?," p. 49.
66 The term "cinema of recognition" invokes the concept of recognition from two different sources. On the one hand, it acknowledges the basic meaning of the term, in that, while watching such films, the audience recognizes itself on the screen. Such a cinema presents to its viewers clearly recognizable tropes of a certain group identity, feeding in turn the "imagined community," as Benedict Anderson has described the nation's self-image and constructed identity. This construction of a sense of "us" and "we" appears literally and repeatedly in Québécois cultural discourses, described as a literature, a cinema, a music "de chez nous," of our own, from our place. On the other hand, the term draws on Gilles Deleuze's complexification of the concept of recognition, as described by Felicity J. Colman: "Recognition occurs through complex processes, and is not just a matter of viewing an image on a screen. Rather, that image must contain the processes of thought within it to be affective, actionary, perceivable"; Colman, "Cinema," p. 151.

67 Quebec has evolved an entire system completely distinct from that of France via the transformation of the articles of the Catholic liturgy into swear words. Indeed, in Quebec swearing is called *sacrer*, from the root for sacred; specific terms invoke the host (*ostie*), the chalice (*câliss*), the wafer box (*ciboire*), the tabernacle (*tabernacle*), and so on.

68 Savard, Preface, p. 13.

69 Historical accounts, although sometimes laced with nostalgia, consistently describe the hockey of the past as much more violent than today's. Scanlan asserts that "early hockey was very much like war"; *Grace under Fire*, p. 30.

70 Writing about hockey, both fiction and non-fiction, consistently contrasts the "skill" of European players with the Canadian emphasis on, ostensibly strategic, bodychecking. Legendary Montreal Canadiens goalie turned member of parliament Ken Dryden offers a poetic description: "Delivered mid-ice with shoulder or hip, a body-check is the universal symbol of Canadian hockey. Hard, clean, elemental, a punishing man-to-man contest, as it fades from our game it is more and more symbolic of glories themselves past"; Dryden, *The Game*, p. 222. On European skill, see, for example, Robidoux, *Men at Play*, p. 147; Kidd and Macfarlane, *The Death of Hockey*, p. 75; and Willes, *The Rebel League*, p. 6. On bodychecking as definitive of Canadian-style hockey, see, for example, Cherry and Strachan, *Don Cherry's Hockey Stories*, pp. 75–6, 84, 78–80; and Robidoux and Trudel, "Hockey in Canada." Beaty also raises Cherry's views on hockey; "Not Playing, Working," pp. 119–20.

71 For contemporary accounts of the Summit Series, see Dryden and MacGregor, *Home Game*, pp. 192–235; and Ludwig, *The Great Hockey Thaw* (alt. title *Hockey Night in Moscow*). The docudrama *Canada/Russia '72* (2006, dir. T.W. Peacocke) does a nice job of reconstructing the media atmosphere, the players' attitudes, and the series itself and reactions in Canada as play progressed.

72 For example, Alan Eagleson, then president of the NHL Players' Association, predicted before the series that "anything less than an unblemished sweep of the Russians would bring shame down on the heads of the players and the national pride"; quoted in Ludwig, *The Great Hockey Thaw*, p. 37. Simon Richard documents the heavy-handed predictions by Quebec journalists of an overwhelming victory; *La Série du siècle*, pp. 81–2.

73 Archives Radio-Canada, "Nous sommes venus pour apprendre"; Chabot, *La Grande Rivalité*, p. 89.

74 Kennedy, "Confronting a Compelling Other," p. 47.

75 Kennedy, "Confronting a Compelling Other," p. 45.

76 See page 194, note 12.

77 McDonell, *For the Love of Hockey*, p. 46. See also Ratelle's comments; pp. 142–3.
78 Ludwig, *The Great Hockey Thaw*, pp. 49, 29.
79 Richard, *La Série du siècle*, p. 98.
80 Quoted in Richard, *La Série du siècle*, pp. 95–6.
81 Mills, *The Empire Within*, pp. 21–2.
82 Orr, *Puck Is a Four Letter Word*, p. 4.
83 Sirois, *Discrimination in the NHL*, p. 23.
84 Sirois, *Discrimination in the NHL*, p. 295.
85 *Les Boys, La Série* includes several unnamed extra players to fill out the roster in the rare instances of ice time. One of these appears to have some Asian or First Nations heritage.
86 King and Leonard, "Screening," p. 4.
87 McClean, "So Here's the Deal," p. 173.
88 McClean, "So Here's the Deal," p. 171.
89 Nathan, '"I'm Against It,'" p. 40.
90 Fleury, *Playing with Fire*, pp. 28–36. This issue is also discussed in the coda to chapter 2, in relation to François Barcelo's *I Hate Hockey*.
91 Incidentally, Fleury's family name reflects his Métis—French-Canadian and Cree—heritage, although his family is now anglophone. Fleury, *Playing with Fire*, p. 6.
92 In *Stars* (1979), Richard Dyer posits that casting of known actors influences viewers' reception and interpretation of film texts; and that the "star" carries a textual significance that brings baggage from the actors' prior roles and his public–private life as portrayed in the media to any new portrayal. Space constraints prevents any extended discussion of the role of "star" theory in the casting of the *Les Boys* franchise texts, but it is undeniably present. As François Paré pointed out at the ACSUS session where the first seeds of this chapter were presented publicly (see note 6), the fact that one of Quebec's most beloved mature actors, Rémy Girard, is cast as Stan is significant in building audience sympathy and identification with Stan. Since *Les Boys*, Pierre Lebeau has brought Méo's villain qualities to historical roles like that of the lecherous miser in *Séraphin: Un homme et son péché* (2002). Marc Messier was probably cast as Bob in part because of his connection to the highly successful franchise, *Lance et Compte*.
93 Baker, *Contesting Identities*, pp. 1–2.

5 Rock and Roll, Skate and Slide

1 Gainey, Introduction, p. x.
2 Grenier, "Cultural Exemptionism," p. 308.

3 Obviously, a number of Anglo-Canadian artists have thematized or at least referenced hockey in their work, including a number of acts that would not intuitively be connected to hockey; the following list does not aim to be inclusive, but rather illustrative of the range of references I have unearthed. Neil Young, whose father was a sports journalist, is a hockey fan and Leonard Cohen was "an unlikely member of the [Westmont High] school hockey team" (Nadel, *Various Positions*, p. 20). Gordon Lightfoot's "Did She Mention My Name" has a hockey reference. Goldfinger's "Wayne Gretzky" (2002) describes the "Great One" as "the only man I'd have sex with." A number of contemporary alternative rock acts reference the sport as well: Arcade Fire – who, to their credit (and profit?), have become increasingly bilingual in their musical releases – has a hockey song, "Neighborhood #5"; the Barenaked Ladies wrote a song for *Score: A Hockey Musical* (2010); and Facebook features a photograph of the New Photographers on the ice, ready to play. More tenuous connections appear for acts like Feist and Broken Social Scene, the latter linked to hockey by exclusion in a Web post: "Everybody in Canada is either in the hockey team or Broken Social Scene."

4 DesRoches, "Nine Glorious Epochs," p. 101.

5 Wind, "Les Canadiens sont là," p. 82.

6 Melançon, *The Rocket*, pp. 72–3.

7 Yelle, "Les Études en communication médiatique," p. 2.

8 Chamberland, "Rap in Canada," p. 307.

9 Grenier, "Cultural Exemptionism," p. 308.

10 See, for example, Chamberland, "The Cultural Paradox of Rap Made in Quebec."

11 Grenier, "Cultural Exemptionism," p. 312; Grenier and Morrison, "Le Terrain socio-musical," pp. 78–83, 88.

12 E. Morin, "Salut les copains," p. 11. Many thanks to Luc Bellemare for tracking down sociologist Edgar Morin's early critique of *yé-yé*, which provides the origin of the term and helps clarify a question of chronology. Although the Beatles' "She Loves You," may have been the best-known song to feature the phrase "Yeah, yeah, yeah," in its chorus, Morin's articles in *Le Monde* on the development of a youth culture in France centred on this newly identified musical form, *yé-yé*, antedates its August 1963 release by a month. Bellemare, e-mail to the author, 3 April 2013.

13 Hawkins, *Chanson*, pp. 4, 24, 31–2, 54.

14 Prévost-Thomas, "Céline, Isabelle," p. 170.

15 Grenier and Morrison, "Le Terrain socio-musical," pp. 88–9. See Ransom, "Language Choice and Code Switching," for a discussion of language in contemporary Quebec popular music.

16 Wright, *Virtual Sovereignty*, pp. 60–1. See Wright, p. 83, for specific criteria for a work to qualify as "Cancon."
17 Wright, *Virtual Sovereignty*, p. 19.
18 Grenier, "Cultural Exemptionism," p. 315.
19 Wright, *Virtual Sovereignty*, pp. 83–4; Grenier, "Cultural Exemptionism," p. 314.
20 To offer a personal example, the CanCon requirements mean that XM/Sirius satellite radio must offer French-language music programming; living in Michigan, well outside the broadcast range of any Quebec-based radio station, I nonetheless have access to emerging music from the province via two XM channels. In addition to Radio-Canada's Bande-à-part, streaming over the Internet, YouTube offers listeners around the globe the ability to listen to alternative musics *and* to identify more, similar music through its format.
21 Messier, "André Fortin: Un mythe en devenir?"
22 Francis, *National Dreams*, p. 167; the North as a marker of Canadian and Québécois identities is a frequently identified theme, not only by Daniel, but also by Margaret Atwood, *Survival* (p. 33), and by Jack Warwick in *L'Appel du nord*.
23 The analyses of Loco Locass's "Le but" and Mes Aïeux's "Le Fantôme du Forum" first appeared in *Quebec Studies* 51 (Spring/Summer 2011): 25-31.
24 For more on French rap, see the essays in Durand, *Black, Blanc, Beur*.
25 C.M. Jones, "Un Interview avec Loco Locass," p. 37.
26 C.M. Jones, "Un Interview avec Loco Locass," p. 28.
27 M.-C. Tremblay, *Loco Locass*, pp. 16–17.
28 M.-C. Tremblay, *Loco Locass*, pp. 18–22.
29 M.-C. Tremblay, *Loco Locass*, pp. 22–6.
30 C.M. Jones, "Un Interview avec Loco Locass," pp. 33, 34.
31 M. Trudel, *The Beginnings of New France*, p. 28; for a more extensive discussion of both "La Paix des Braves" and "Hymne à Québec" see Ransom, "Quebec History X."
32 The show first ran on TVA from 24 January to 28 March 2010. Guy Carbonneau coached for Montreal, while Michel Bergeron – former coach for the Nordiques, of course – headed up the capital's team. Some of the Québec matches were played in the Nordiques' former home, the Colisée Pepsi; in Montreal several were played in the Verdun arena. Season Two, January–February 2011, featured Patrice Brisebois coaching for Montreal and Bob Hartley for Quebec. Anonymous, "La Série Montréal-Québec."
33 Nora, "Between Memory and History," p. 7.

34 Gruneau and Whitson, *Hockey Night in Canada*, p. 132.
35 Wilson, "Selective Memory," pp. 55–6.
36 Nora, "Between Memory and History," p. 8.
37 Simard, "Hockey et politique," p. 39.
38 Bauer, "Le Canadien de Montréal, " p. 51.
39 Cha, "'La Ville est hockey,'" p. 3.
40 Cha, "'La Ville est hockey,'" p. 3.
41 Born in Ontario, Blake's mother was French Canadian, and he was fluent in French. Maurice Richard's biographer Jean-Marie Pellerin cites contemporary news accounts referring to Blake as a "Canadien Français"; Pellerin, *Maurice Richard*, pp. 40–1. Pellerin also refers to goaltender Gerry McNeil as such (p. 135). André-A. Lafrance describes McNeil as his favourite player as a child, but also as an anglophone: "Certes, c'était un 'Anglais'. Mais chez nous, nous n'étions pas 'racistes'" (Sure, he was an Englishman. But at our place, we weren't "racist"); Lafrance, "Je ne suis plus pratiquant," p. 21.
42 Hunt, *The Men in the Nets*, p. 30.
43 Bauer, "Introduction," p. 8. The reference here is to the city's nickname, "the city of a thousand bell towers," because of its numerous churches.
44 Bélanger, "Sports Venues. "
45 Dennis, "Forever Proud?", pp. 168–70.
46 Dennis, "Forever Proud?", p. 160.
47 Gunderson, "Memory, Modernity, and the City."
48 Elsewhere, I examine that song, "Le Stade (conte complet)," with another Jean-Pierre April story, "Le Vol de la ville"; Ransom, "Constructions of the Future." In spite of two texts with two similar themes, Archambault's label, Disques Victoire, kindly responded to my inquiry about any possible influence by April's work on Mes Aïeux, stating there was none (personal correspondence, 23 June 2009).
49 McFarlane, *The Habs*, p. 48.
50 Hockey historian Andrew C. Holman offers interesting insight on identity and the pronunciation of Morenz's name. Today, the stress is placed on the second syllable. Holman's grandfather knew the Morenz family, which pronounced its name with the stress on the first syllable. Morenz was adopted by French Canadians as a hero, in a sort of reverse assimilation, and his legacy through contact with them has changed the pronunciation of his name; e-mail to the author, 6 August 2009.
51 Cha, "'La Ville est hockey,'" p. 15.
52 Roy, *Le Guerrier*, p. 200.
53 See for example Stein, *Plower Plays*, pp. 154–67.

54 "Biographie," *Bob Bissonette.com.*
55 http://fr.wikipedia.org/wiki/Bob_Bissonnette.
56 I have heard it and "Taureau Mécanique" on Sirius XM satellite's French-language channel.
57 The expression is spelled by Bissonnette as "enweye" and can also be spelled "enweille," derived from "envoye."
58 See Robidoux, *Men at Play* and "Imagining a Canadian Identity"; Robidoux and Trudel, "Hockey in Canada"; Gruneau and Whitson, *Hockey Night in Canada;* and Whitson and Gruneau, *Artificial Ice.*
59 Dowbiggin, *Of Ice and Men*, pp. 92, 94.
60 King and Leonard, "Screening the Social," p. 4.
61 Kibby, "Nostalgia for the Masculine," p. 16.
62 King and Leonard, "Screening the Social." p. 4.
63 I would like to thank University of Toronto Press's independent readers for a number of suggestions of additional references that I have used in this and other chapters, including the clarification that this song is about Ron Fournier.
64 Edensor, *National Identity,* p. vi.
65 Edensor, *National Identity,* p. 17.
66 Berger, "Introduction: The Politics of Language Choice," p. xiv.

Conclusion

1 Bélanger, "The Last Game?", pp. 293–4.
2 Edensor, *National Identity,* p. 17.
3 McDonell, *For the Love of Hockey,* p. 146.
4 Edensor, *National Identity,* p. 26.
5 Edensor, *National Identity,* p. 30.
6 Poulter, *Becoming Native in a Foreign Land;* Robidoux, "Imagining a Canadian Identity."
7 Fosty and Fosty, *Black Ice.*
8 Begamudré, *Van De Graaff Days,* p. 230.
9 Blake, *Canadian Hockey Literature,* p. 5.

Works Cited

Primary Sources

Film and Videography

Les 7 Jours du Talion. Dir. Podz [Daniel Grou]. Perf. Claude Legault, Rémy Girard. GoFilms, 2010.

The Barbarian Invasions. Dir. Denys Arcand. Perf. Rémy Girard, Pierre Curzi, Louise Portal. Alliance Atlantis Vivafilm, 2003.

Bon Cop, Bad Cop. Dir. Érik Canuel. Perf. Patrick Huard, Colm Feore. DVD. Alliance Atlantis Vivafilm, 2006.

Les Boys. Dir. Louis Saïa. Perf. Rémy Girard, Patrick Huard, Yvan Ponton. DVD. Christal Films, 1997.

Les Boys II. Dir. Louis Saïa. Perf. Rémy Girard, Patrick Huard, Yvan Ponton. DVD. Christal Films, 1998.

Les Boys III. Dir. Louis Saïa. Perf. Rémy Girard, Patrick Huard, Yvan Ponton. DVD. Christal Films, 2001.

Les Boys IV. Dir. Georges Mihalka. Perf. Rémy Girard, Yvan Ponton. DVD. Christal Films, 2005.

Les Boys, la série. Dir. Louis Saïa. Writ. Francis Avard. DVD. Mélenny, 2007–2012.

Cadavres. Dir. Érik Canuel. Perf. Patrick Huard, Julie Le Breton. DVD. Zoofilms, 2009.

Canada/Russia '72. Dir. T.W. Peacocke. Perf. Booth Savage. DVD. Trailer Park Productions, 2004.

The Chiefs. Dir. Jason Gileno. DVD. East Hill Productions, 2004.

Comment ma mère accoucha de moi durant sa ménopause. Dir. Sébastien Rose. Perf. Micheline Lanctôt, Sylvie Moreau, Patrick Huard. DVD. Max Films, 2003.

Dans une galaxie près de chez vous. Dir. Pierre Théorêt. Perf. Guy Jodoin. Canal Famille/Vrak TV, 1999–2001.

The Decline of the American Empire. Dir. Denys Arcand. Perf. Pierre Curzi, Rémy Girard. M & M Films/National Film Board, 1986.

De père en flic. Dir. Émile Gaudrault. Perf. Michel Côté, Louis-José Houde. Cinémaginaire, 2009.

Elvis Gratton. Dir. Pierre Falardeau. ACPV, 1981.

Face-Off. Dir. George McCowan. Perf. Art Hindle. Agincourt, 1971.

The Fan. Dir. Tony Scott. Perf. Robert Deniro. TriStar Pictures, 1996.

Friday the 13th. Dir. Sean S. Cunningham. Perf. Kevin Bacon. Paramount, 1980.

The Hockey Sweater. Dir. Sheldon Cohen. Perf. Roch Carrier. National Film Board, 1980.

Horse Feathers. Dir. Norman Z. McLeod. Perf. Groucho Marx. Paramount, 1932.

Incendies. Dir. Denis Villeneuve. Perf. Rémy Girard, Lubna Azabal. micro_scope, 2010.

Junior. Dir. Isabelle Lavigne, Stéphane Thibault. National Film Board, 2007.

Lance et Compte. Dir. Jean-Claude Lord. Perf. Carl Marotte, Marc Messier, Yvan Ponton. DVD. Communications Claude Héroux, 1986. [*LCI*]

Lance et Compte II. Dir. Richard Martin. Perf. Carl Marotte, Marc Messier, Yvan Ponton. DVD. Communications Claude Héroux, 1988. [*LCII*]

Lance et Compte III. Dir. Richard Martin. Perf. Carl Marotte, Marc Messier, Yvan Ponton. DVD. Communications Claude Héroux, 1989. [*LCIII*]

Lance et Compte: Tous Pour Un. Dir. Richard Martin. Perf. Marc Messier, Marina Orsini, Roy Dupuis. DVD. Communications Claude Héroux, 1991. [*Tous*]

Lance et Compte: Le Crime de Lulu. Dir. Richard Martin. Perf. Denis Bouchard, Marc Messier. DVD. Communications Claude Héroux, 1991. [*Crime*]

Lance et Compte: Envers et contre tous. Dir. Richard Martin. Perf. Sylvie Bourque, Pierre Gendron. DVD. Communications Claude Héroux, 1991. [*Envers*]

Lance et Compte: Le Moment de vérité. Dir. Richard Martin. Perf. Yvan Ponton, Marina Orsini. DVD. Communications Claude Héroux, 1991. [*Moment*]

Lance et Compte: Le Choix. Dir. Richard Martin. Perf. Patrice Bissonnette, Marc Messier, Denis Bouchard. DVD. Communications Claude Héroux, 1991. [*Choix*]

Lance et Compte: Le Retour du Chat. Dir. Richard Martin. Perf. Carl Marotte, Isabelle Miquelon, Marc Messier. DVD. Communications Claude Héroux, 1991. [*Retour*]

Lance et Compte: La Nouvelle Génération. Dir. Jean-Claude Lord. Perf. Carl Marotte, Marc Messier, Yvan Ponton, Louis-Philippe Dandenault. DVD. Communications Claude Héroux, 2002. [*LCNG*]

Lance et Compte: La Reconquête. Dir. Jean-Claude Lord. Perf. Marc Messier, Carl Marotte, Maxim Roy. DVD. Communications Claude Héroux, 2004. [*LCRec*]

Lance et Compte: La Revanche. Dir. Jean-Claude Lord. Perf. Patrick Hivon, Julie du Page, Karim Toupin-Chaïeb. DVD. Communications Claude Héroux, 2006. [*LCRev*]

Lance et Compte: Le Grand Duel. Dir. Jean-Claude Lord. Perf. Marc Messier, Carl Marotte, Jason Roy-Léveillée, Marina Orsini. DVD. Communications Claude Héroux, 2008. [*LCGD*]

Lance et Compte: Le Film. Dir. Frédéric D'Amours. Perf. Marc Messier, Carl Marotte, Julie McClemens, Marina Orsini. Gaëa Films, 2010.

Lethal Weapon. Dir. Richard Donner. Perf. Mel Gibson, Danny Glover. Warner Bros., 1987.

Lethal Weapon II. Dir. Richard Donner. Perf. Mel Gibson, Danny Glover. Warner Bros., 1989.

Lethal Weapon III. Dir. Richard Donner. Perf. Mel Gibson, Danny Glover. Warner Bros., 1992.

Lethal Weapon IV. Dir. Richard Donner. Perf. Mel Gibson, Danny Glover. Warner Bros., 1998.

Miracle. Dir. Gavin O'Connor. Perf. Kurt Russell, Patricia Clarkson. Disney, 2004.

Mirador. "Nourir la bête." Dir. Louis Choquette. Perf. David La Haye, Patrick Labbé. Encor Télévisions, 2010.

Octobre. Dir. Pierre Falardeau. Perf. Luc Picard, Pierre Rivard, Denis Trudel. National Film Board, 1994.

Piché: entre ciel et terre. Dir. Sylvain Archambault. Perf. Michel Côté. TVA, 2010.

Pour toujours, les Canadiens. Dir. Sylvain Archambault. Perf. Céline Bonnier. Cité-Amérique, 2009.

The Rocket: The Legend of Maurice Richard. Dir. Charles Binamé. Perf. Roy Dupuis, Julie Le Breton. Palm Films, 2005.

Rollerball. Dir. Norman Jewison. Perf. James Caan, John Houseman. MGM, 1975.

Score: A Hockey Musical. Dir. Michael Mcgowan. Mongrel Media, 2010.

Séraphin: Un homme et son péché. Dir. Charles Binamé. Perf. Roy Dupuis, Pierre Lebeau. DVD. Alliance Atlantis Vivafilm, 2002.

Silence of the Lambs. Dir. Jonathan Demme. Perf. Jodie Foster, Anthony Hopkins. Orion, 1991.

Slap Shot. Dir. George Roy Hill. Perf. Paul Newman, Michael Ontkean. DVD. Universal, 1977.

Speedy Singhs (aka *Breakaway*). Dir. Robert Lieberman. Perf. Vinay Virmani, Rob Lowe. DVD. CBC, 2011.

Sur le seuil. Dir. Éric Tessier. Perf. Patrick Huard, Michel Côté. DVD. GoFilms, 2003.

Through the Mist/Dédé: À Travers les brumes. Dir. Jean-Philippe Duval. Perf. Sébastien Fréchette. DVD. Max Films, 2009.

Un crabe dans la tête / Soft Shell Man. Dir. André Turpin. Perf. David La Haye, Isabelle Blais. DVD. Christal Films, 2001.

La Vie avec mon père. Dir. Sébastien Rose. Perf. Paul Ahmarahni, David La Haye. DVD. Max Films, 2005.

Discography

Bob Bissonnette. *Les Barbes de série*. Les Entreprises Bob Bissonnette. 2012.

–. *Recrue de l'année*. Les Entreprises Bob Bissonnette. 2010.

Les Colocs. *Les Colocs*. Québec. 1993.

–. *Dehors novembre*. Sélect. 1998.

–. *Il me parle du bonheur*. Solodarno. 2009.

Les Cowboys Fringants. *Break Syndical*. La Tribu. 2002.

Les Dales Hawerchuk. *Les Dales Hawerchuk*. C4. 2005.

–. *Les Dales Hawerchuk 2*. C4. 2008.

–. *Les Dales Hawerchuk: Le Tour du chapeau*. C4. 2011.

Guy Lafleur. *Lafleur!* Unison Sports. 1979.

Loco Locass. *Amour oral*. Audiogram. 2004.

–. *Manifestif*. Audiogram. 2000.

–. *Vive Québec, le Québec est mort*. Audiogram. 2012.

Mad'moiZèle Girafe. *Peindre la girafe*. High Life. 2009.

Mes Aïeux. *La Ligne orange*. Disques Victoire. 2008.

Tragically Hip. *World Container*. Universal. 2006.

Vincent Vallières. *Le Monde tourne fort*. Spectra. 2009.

Literature

April, Jean-Pierre. "Le Fantôme du Forum." 1981. In *Chocs baroques*, edited by Michel Lord. Montreal: Fides, 1991. 161–84.

Barcelo, François. *Agénor, Agénor, Agénor et Agénor*. Montréal: Quinze, 1980.

–. *Cadavres*. Paris: Gallimard, 1998.

–. *I Hate Hockey*. Translated by Peter McCambridge. Montreal: Baraka Books, 2012. Translation of *J'haïs le hockey*. Montreal: Coups de Tête, 2011.

–. "Les Semeurs de robots." In *Espaces imaginaires 1*, edited by Jean-Marc Gouanvic and Stéphane Nicot. Montreal: Les Imaginoïdes, 1983. 45–52.

–. *La Tribu*. Montreal: Libre Expression, 1981.

–. *Ville-Dieu*. Montreal: Libre Expression, 1982.

Begamudré, Ven. *Van de Graaff Days*. Lantzville: Oolichan, 1993.

Bouchard, Guy. "Au jeu." *imagine …* 60 (1992): 55–68.

–. *Les Gelules utopiques*. Montreal: Éditions Logiques, 1988.

Carrier, Roch. "The Hockey Sweater." Translated by Sheila Fischman. In *The Hockey Sweater and Other Stories*. Toronto: Anansi, 1979. 77–81. Translation of *Le Chandail de hockey*. 1979. Illustrated by Sheldon Cohen. 1984. Toronto: Tundra, 1999.

–. *Il est par là, le soleil*. Montreal: Stanké, 1988.

Cloutier, Eugène. *Les Inutiles*. Ottawa: Le Cercle du Livre de France, 1956.

Côté, Denis. *Shooting for the Stars*. Translated by Jane Brierely. Windsor: Black Moss, 1990. Translation of *Hockeyeurs cybernétiques*. Montréal: Éditions Paulines, 1983.

–. *L'Idole des Inactifs*. Montreal: La Courte Échelle, 1989.

–. *La Révolte des Inactifs*. Montreal: La Courte Échelle, 1990.

–. *Le Retour des Inactifs*. Montreal: La Courte Échelle, 1990.

Foisy, Michel. *La Carte de hockey magique*. Sainte-Thérèse: M. Foisy, 2000.

Gaston, Bill. *The Good Body*. Dunvegan: Cormorant, 2000.

Gravel, François. *Zamboni*. Montreal: Boréal, 1990. Translated by Sarah Cummins. *Mr. Zamboni's Dream Machine*. Toronto: James Lorimer, 1992.

MacLennan, Hugh. *Two Solitudes*. 1945. Toronto: McClelland and Stewart, 2003.

Miron, Gaston. "Le Damned Canuck." In *L'Homme rapaillé*. Paris: Maspéro, 1981. 52–3.

Orr, Frank. *Puck Is a Four Letter Word*. New York: William Morrow, 1983.

Pelletier, Francine. *La Saison de l'exil*. Montreal: Éditions Paulines, 1993.

Poulin, Jacques. *Le Coeur de la baleine bleue*. Montreal: Éditions du Jour, 1979.

Quarrington, Paul. *Logan in Overtime*. Toronto: Doubleday Canada, 1990.

Salutin, Rick, with Ken Dryden. *Les Canadiens*. Vancouver: Talonbooks, 1977.

Tremblay, Gilles. *Les Nordiques sont disparus*. Boucherville: Proteau, 1983.

Van Belkom, Edo. "Heart." In *Northern Horror*, edited by Edo Van Belkom. Kingston: Quarry, 2000. 154–60.

–. "Hockey's Night in Canada." In *Arrowdreams*, edited by Mark Shainblum and John Dupuis. Winnipeg: Nuage, 1997. 11–18.

Vonarburg, Élisabeth. *Reluctant Voyagers*. Translated by Jane Brierley. New York: Bantam, 1995. Edmonton: Tesseract, 1996.

Secondary Sources

Adams, Mary Louise. "The Game of Whose Lives?: Gender, Race, and Entitlement in Canada's 'National' Game." In Whitson and Gruneau, 85–99.

Adorno, Theodor W. "How to Look at Television." 1954. In *The Culture Industry: Selected Essays on Mass Culture*, edited by J.M. Bernstein. London: Routledge, 1991. 158–77.

Amis, Kingsley. *New Maps of Hell: A Survey of Science Fiction*. New York: Harcourt, Brace, and World, 1960.

Ancelovici, Marcos, and Francis Dupuis-Déri, eds. *L'Archipel identitaire*. Montréal: Boréal, 1997.

Anderson, Benedict. *Imagined Communities*. Rev. ed. London: Verso, 1991.

Anonymous. "*Bon cop bad cop:* le plafond est défoncé." *Box-office-Canada*. Radio-Canada. 31 October 2006. http://www.radio-canada.ca/arts-spectacles/cinema/2006/10/10/002-bon_cop_record.asp.

–. "'Les Boys' Scores Box Office Record in Quebec." *CBC News*. 9 December 2001. http://www.cbc.ca/news/canada/les-boys-scores-box-office-record-in-quebec-1.278610.

–. "Prendre le nom de son mari est illégal." *Agora Vox*. 16 August 2007. http://www.agoravox.fr/actualites/international/article/prendre-le-nom-de-son-mari-est-27856.

–. "La Série Montréal–Québec." *TVA*. http://tva.canoe.ca/emissions/laseriemontrealquebec.

April, Jean-Pierre. "Sport-Fiction: le hockey et la science-fiction québécoise." In Augustin and Sorbets, 231–43.

Archives Radio-Canada. "Nous sommes venus pour apprendre." 2008. http://archives.radio-canada.ca/sports/hockey/clips/1523/.

Arel, Dominique. "Political Stability in Multinational Democracies: Comparing Language Dynamics in Brussels, Montreal, and Barcelona." In Gagnon and Tully, 65–89.

Arpin, Roland. Preface. In Désaulniers, 3.

Associated Press. "Former Hockey Coach Graham James to Be Sentenced for Sexually Assaulting Players." *Yahoo News*. 22 February 2012. http://news.yahoo.com/former-hockey-coach-graham-james-sentenced-sexually-assaulting-090817446--spt.html.

Atwood, Margaret. *Survival: A Thematic Guide to Canadian Literature*. Toronto: Anansi, 1972.

Augustin, Jean-Pierre, and Claude Sorbets, eds. *La Culture du sport au Québec*. Talence: La Maison des Sciences de l'Homme d'Aquitaine, 1996.

Babynamefacts.com. 'The Top Baby Names in Quebec for 2010.' 2012. http://www.babynamefacts.com/popularnames/countries.php?country=QBC.

Baillargeon, Normand, and Christian Boissinot, eds. *La Vraie Dureté du mental: Hockey et Philosophie*. Quebec: Presse de l'Université Laval, 2009.

Baker, Aaron. *Contesting Identities: Sports in American Film*. Champaign: University of Illinois Press, 2003.

Balthazar, Louis. "The Dynamics of Multi-Ethnicity in French-Speaking Quebec: Towards a New Citizenship." *Nationalism and Ethnic Politics* 1, no. 3 (1995): 82–95.

Barreau, Jean-Marc. "La religion du Canadien: un leadership en question." In Bauer and Barreau, 81–110.

Bauch, Hubert. "Canada Survives: Money and Ethnics Defeated Us, Parizeau Says." *The Gazette* (Montreal), 31 October 1995, A1.

Bauer, Olivier. Introduction. In Bauer and Barreau, 7–18.

–. "Le Canadien de Montréal est-il une religion?" In Bauer and Barreau, 29–80.

Bauer, Olivier, and Jean-Marc Barreau, eds. *La Religion du Canadien de Montréal*. Montréal: Fides, 2009.

Bean, Kellie. *Post-Backlash Feminism: Women and the Media Since Reagan-Bush*. Jefferson: McFarland, 2007.

Beaty, Bart. "Not Playing, Working: Class, Masculinity, and Nation in the Canadian Hockey Film." In *Working On Screen: Representations of the Working Class in Canadian Cinema*, edited by Malek Khouri and Darrell Varga, 113–33. Toronto: University of Toronto Press, 2006.

Beaulé, Sophie. "'Il n'y a que des cauchemars et des angoisses, des délires ... :' Lecture de la nouvelle fantastique et de science-fiction québécoise depuis 1980." *University of Toronto Quarterly: A Canadian Journal of the Humanities* 69, no. 4 (2000): 871–90.

–. "Regards sur le Québec dans un numéro spécial de la revue *Solaris*." In *La Francophonie panaméricaine: état des lieux et enjeux*, edited by André Fauchon, 103–21. Winnipeg: Presses Universitaires de Saint-Boniface, 2000.

Bélanger, Anouk. "The Last Game?: Hockey and the Experience of Masculinity in Québec." In White and Young, 293–309.

–. "Sports Venues and the Spectacularization of Urban Spaces in North America: The Case of the Molson Centre in Montreal." *International Review for the Sociology of Sport* 35 (2000): 378–97.

Bélanger, Anouk, and Fannie Valois-Nadeau. "Entre l'étang gelé et le Centre Bell ou comment retricoter le mythe de la Sainte-Flanelle." In Baillargeon and Boissinot, 73–93.

Bélil, Michel. "Barcelo et Beauchemin: romanciers de la littérature générale." *imagine ...* 12 (Spring 1982): 55–6.

Béliveau, Jean, with Chris Goyens and Allan Turowetz. *My Life in Hockey*. Rev. ed. Vancouver: Greystone, 2005.

Belleau, André. *Surprendre les voix*. Montreal: Boréal, 1986.

Bercuson, David, J.L. Granatstein, and W.R. Young. *Sacred Trust? Brian Mulroney and the Conservative Party in Power*. Toronto: Doubleday Canada, 1986.

Berger, Harris M. "Introduction: The Politics of Language Choice and Dialect in Popular Music." In *Global Pop, Local Language*, edited by Harris M. Berger and Michael Thomas Carroll. Jackson: University Press of Mississippi, 2003. ix–xxvi.

Bérubé, Renald. "Le Fantastique, la science-fiction: l'inquiétante étrangeté dans 'La Légende de l'homme à la cervelle d'or' d'Alphonse Daudet et dans 'Le Fantôme du Forum' de Jean-Pierre April." In Boivin et al., 138–52.

Birrell, Susan, and Mary G. McDonald, eds. *Reading Sport: Critical Essays on Power and Representation*. Boston: Northeastern University Press, 2000.

Black, François. *Habitants et Glorieux: Les Canadiens de 1909 à 1960*. Laval: Milles Îles, 1997.

Blake, Jason. *Canadian Hockey Literature*. Toronto: University of Toronto Press, 2010.

Bob Bissonnette.com. http://bobbissonnette.com/biographie.html.

Boileau, Roger, Fernand Landry, and Yves Trempe. "Les Canadiens français et les grands jeux internationaux (1908–1974)." In *Canadian Sport: Sociological Perspectives*, edited by Richard S. Gruneau and J.S. Albinson. Toronto: Addison Wesley, 1976. 141–69.

Boivin, Aurélien, Maurice Émond, and Michel Lord, eds. *Les Ailleurs imaginaires: Les Rapports entre le fantastique et la science-fiction*. Montreal: Nuit blanche, 1993.

Bouchard, Gérard. *Les Deux Chanoines: Contradiction et ambivalence dans la pensée de Lionel Groulx*. Montreal: Boréal, 2003.

Bouchard, Gérard, and Charles Taylor. *Building the Future: A Time for Reconciliation. Report to the Commission de Consultation sur l'Accommodement*. Government of Québec. 2008. http://www.accommodements-quebec.ca/index-en.html.

Bouchard, Guy. *Les 42,210 Univers de la science-fiction*. Montreal: Le Passeur, 1993.

–. "The Female Utopia in Canada." In Paradis, 188–96.

–. "Féminisme, utopie, philosophie." In *Ouvertures*, edited by Lise Pelletier and Guy Bouchard. Quebec: Presses de l'Université de Laval, 1988.

–. "L'Inversion des rôles masculins et féminins dans *Chroniques du Pays des Mères* d'Élisabeth Vonarburg." *Solaris* 112 (Winter 1994): 29–32.

– . "Les utopies féministes, le fantastique et la science-fiction." In Boivin et al., 53–76.

Bourgeois, Normand. "Les *Nordiques* et le nouveau Colisée: le combat de la presse sportive." In Augustin and Sorbets, 217–29.

Bowers, Maggie Ann. *Magic(al) Realism*. London: Routledge, 2004.

Bretnor, Reginald. "Science Fiction in the Age of Space." In *Science Fiction, Today and Tomorrow*, edited by Reginald Bretnor. New York: Harper and Row, 1974. 150–79.

Briley, Ron, Michael K. Schoenecke, and Deborah A. Carmichael, eds. *All-Stars and Movie Stars: Sports in Film and History*. Lexington: University Press of Kentucky, 2008.

Brodeur, Jean-Paul. "Un acteur autonome." In Lachapelle and Comeau, 286–300.

Brown, Craig, ed. *Histoire générale du Canada*. Montréal: Boréal, 1990. Translation of *The Illustrated History of Canada*. Toronto: Lester and Orpen Dennys, 1987.

Brunelle, Michel. "Rocket Knock-Out." *Moebius* 86 (2000): 21–4.

Brunt, Stephen. "Quebec Ready for Nordiques Return." *SportsNet*. 8 February 2012. www.citynews.ca/2012/02/08/brunt-on-nhl-quebec-ready-for-nordiques-return/.

Bryshun, Jamie, and Kevin Young. "Sport-Related Hazing: An Inquiry into Male and Female Involvement." In White and Young, 269–92.

Buma, Michael. *Refereeing Identity: The Cultural Work of the Canadian Hockey Novel*. Montreal and Kingston: McGill–Queen's University Press, 2012.

Burris, Susan. "She Got Game, but She Don't Got Fame." In Fuller, 85–96.

Burstyn, Varda. *The Rites of Men: Manhood, Politics, and the Culture of Sport*. Toronto: University of Toronto Press, 1999.

Canadian Press. "Hockey Riots Throughout Canadian History." *Globe and Mail*, 16 June 2011. http://www.theglobeandmail.com/news/british-columbia/hockey-riots-throughout-canadian-history/article635977.

Carrier, Roch. *Le Rocket*. Montreal: Stanké, 2000.

Castle, Gregory. *Reading the Modernist Bildungsroman*. Gainesville: University Press of Florida, 2006.

Cha, Jonathan. "'La Ville est hockey.' De la hockeyisation de la ville à la représentation architecturale: Une quête urbaine." *Journal of the Society for the Study of Architecture in Canada* 34 (2009): 3–18.

Chabot, Jean-François. *La Grande Rivalité Canadiens-Nordiques*. n.p.: Les Éditeurs Réunis, 2009.

Chamberland, Roger. "The Cultural Paradox of Rap Made in Quebec." In Durand, 124–37.

– . "Rap in Canada: Bilingual and Multicultural." Translated by Denis Belley and Madonna Hamel. In *Global Noise: Rap and Hip-Hop Outside the USA*, edited by Tony Mitchell. Middletown: Wesleyan University Press, 2001. 306–26.

Cherry, Don, and Al Strachan. *Don Cherry's Hockey Stories and Stuff*. Toronto: McClelland and Stewart, 2008.

Chito Childs, Erica. "The Prime-Time Color Line: Interracial Couples and Television." In *Fade to Black and White: Interracial Images in Popular Culture*. Lanham: Rowman and Littlefield, 2009. 33–67.

Chodos, Robert, Rae Murphy, and Eric Hamovitch. *Selling Out: Four Years of the Mulroney Government*. Toronto: James Lorimer, 1988.

Colman, Felicity J. "Cinema: Movement – Image – Recognition – Time." In *Gilles Deleuze: Key Concepts*, edited by Charles J. Stivale. Montreal and Kingston: McGill–Queen's University Press, 2005. 141–56.

Connell, R.W. *Gender and Power: Society, the Person, and Sexual Politics*. Stanford: Stanford University Press, 1987.

Corneau, Guy. *Absent Fathers, Lost Sons*. 1989. Translated by Larry Shouldice. Boston: Shambhala, 1991.

Crawford, Scott A.G.M. "Film as Art, Artifact, and Illusion: Contemporary American Sports Movies as Illustrations for Sport Sociology and Philosophy." *Aethlon: The Journal of Sport Literature* 7, no. 2 (Spring 1990): 47–55.

Csicsery-Ronay, Jr, Istvan. "Marxist Theory and Science Fiction." In *Cambridge Companion to Science Fiction*, edited by Edward James and Farah Mendlesohn. Cambridge: Cambridge University Press, 2003. 113–24.

Cunningham, Frank. "Nations and Nationalism: The Case of Canada/Quebec." In *Diversity and Community: An Interdisciplinary Reader*, edited by Philip Alperson. Malden: Blackwell, 2002. 182–208.

Dagenais, Bernard. "Est-il responsable de la mort de Pierre Laporte?" In Lachapelle and Comeau, 307–15.

D'Allemagne, André. *Le Colonialisme au Québec*. Montréal: R-B, 1966.

Daniels, Dayna B. "Gender Slurs: Motivation through Misogyny in Sports Films." In *Sexual Sports Rhetoric: Global and Universal Contexts*, edited by Linda K. Fuller. New York: Peter Lang, 2010. 217–31.

– . "You Throw Like a Girl: Sports and Misogyny on the Silver Screen." In Briley et al., 105–28.

Dejean, Paul. *The Haitians in Quebec*. Translated by Max Dorsinville. Ottawa: Tecumseh, 1980.

Demers, Jacques. Préface. In Chabot, 9–13.

Denault, Todd. *Jacques Plante: The Man Who Changed the Face of Hockey*. Toronto: McClelland and Stewart, 2009.

Dennis, Robert. "Forever Proud? The Montreal Canadiens' Transition from the Forum to the Molson Centre." In Holman, 161–79.

Désaulniers, Jean-Pierre. *De la famille Plouffe à La petite vie: les Québécois et leurs téléromans*. Quebec: Musée de la Civilisation, 1996.

DesRoches, Camil. "Nine Glorious Epochs." In Mouton, 99–109.

Dopp, Jamie. "Hockey, Zen, and the Art of Bill Gaston." Unpublished paper presented at Sports Literature Association Conference, University of Western Ontario, 24–5 June 2009.

– . "Win Orr Lose: Searching for the Good Kid in Canadian Hockey Fiction." In Holman, 81–97.

Doré, Jean-François. "Mythologie, sport et société." In Baillargeon and Boissinot, 95–113.

Dorsinville, Max. Preface. In Dejean, n.p.

Dowbiggin, Bruce. *Of Ice and Men: Steve Yzerman, Chris Chelios, Glen Sather, Dominik Hasek – The Craft of Hockey*. 2nd Ed. 1998. Toronto: Macfarlane, Walter and Ross, 1999.

Dryden, Ken. *The Game*. 1983. Rev. ed. New York: J.W. Wiley, 2005.

Dryden, Ken, and Roy MacGregor. *Home Game: Hockey and Life in Canada*. Toronto: McClelland and Stewart, 1989.

Dumont, Fernand. *Raisons communes*. 1995. Montréal: Boréal, 1997.

Dupuis, Simon. "La Science-fiction québécoise pour la jeunesse." *Solaris* 104 (1992): 70–4.

Durand, Alain-Philippe, ed. *Black, Blanc, Beur: Rap Music and Hip-Hop Culture in the Francophone World*. Lanham: Scarecrow, 2005.

Dyer, Richard. *Stars*. 1979. New ed. London: BFI, 1998.

Edensor, Tim. *National Identity, Popular Culture, and Everyday Life*. Oxford: Berg, 2002.

Elbaz, Mikhaël, Andrée Fortin, and Guy Laforest, eds. *Les Frontières de l'identité*. Ste-Foy and Paris: Presses de l'Université Laval – L'Harmattan, 1996.

Faludi, Susan. *Backlash: The Undeclared War against American Women*. New York: Crown, 1991.

Fanon, Frantz. *Black Skin, White Masks*. 1952. Translated by Charles Lam Markmann. New York: Grove, 1967.

– . *The Wretched of the Earth*. 1961. Translated by Constance Farrington. New York: Grove, 1968.

Faulkner, Tom. "A Puckish Reflection on Religion in Canada." In *From Season to Season: Sports as American Religion*, edited by Joseph L. Price. Macon: Mercer University Press, 2001. 185–211.

Flanders, Laura, ed. *The W Effect: Bush's War on Women*. New York: Feminist Press, 2004.

Fleury, Theo, with Kirstie McLellan Day. *Playing with Fire*. Chicago: Triumph, 2009.

Fortin, Pierre. "L'Économie du Québec." In Lachapelle and Comeau, 40–63.

Fosty, George, and Darril Fosty. *Black Ice: The Lost History of the Colored Hockey League of the Maritimes, 1895–1925*. Halifax: Nimbus, 2008.

Foucault, Michel. *Discipline and Punish: The Birth of the Prison*. 1977. Translated by Alan Sheridan. New York: Vintage, 1995.

Francis, Daniel. *National Dreams: Myth, Memory, and Canadian History*. Vancouver: Arsenal Pulp, 1997.

Freedman, Carl. *Critical Theory and Science Fiction*. Hanover: Wesleyan/University Press of New England, 2000.

Fuller, Linda K., ed. *Sport, Rhetoric, and Gender: Historical Perspectives and Media Representations*. New York: Palgrave Macmillan, 2006.

Gaboury, Jean-Pierre. *Le Nationalisme de Lionel Groulx: Aspects idéologiques*. 1970. Ottawa: Éditions de l'Université d'Ottawa, 1976.

Gagnon, Alain-G., and James Tully. *Multinational Democracies*. Cambridge: Cambridge University Press, 2001.

Gagnon, Lysiane. "Le 'style' social-démocrate." In Lachapelle and Comeau, 18–24.

Gainey, Bob. Introduction. In Jenish, ix–xi.

Galloway, Gloria. "No Old Boys' Club Here: Quebec's Push for Gender Parity." *TheGlobeandMail.com*, 15 October 2010. http://www.theglobeandmail.com/news/national/time-to-lead/no-old-boys-club-here-quebecs-push-for-gender-parity/article1215921.

Garneau, François X. *Histoire du Canada*. 1845–1852. 6 vols. Montreal: L'arbre, 1944–45.

Gauvreau, Michael. "From Rechristianization to Contestation: Catholic Values in Quebec Society, 1930–1970." *Church History* 69, no. 4 (2000): 803–33.

Genest, Simon. "Le Canada et l'internationalisation du hockey sur glace." In Augustin and Sorbets, 177–86.

Germain, Georges-Hébert. *Guy Lafleur: L'Ombre et la lumière*. Montreal: Art Global / Libre Expression, 1990.

Gervais, Stéphan, Christopher Kirkey, and Jarrett Rudy, eds. *Quebec Questions: Quebec Studies for the Twenty-First Century*. Toronto: Oxford University Press, 2011.

Gouanvic, Jean-Marc. "A Past, A Future: Québec Science Fiction." In Paradis, 66–75.

–. "Rational Speculations in French Canada, 1839–1974." *Science-Fiction Studies* 44 (1988): 71–81.

Gould, Jean. "La Genèse catholique d'une modernisation bureaucratique." In *Les Idées mènent le Québec: Essais sur une sensibilité historique*, edited by Stéphane Kelly. Laval: Presses de l'Université Laval, 2002. 145–74.

Greer, Allan. *The Patriots and the People: The Rebellion of 1837 in Rural Lower Canada*. Toronto: University of Toronto Press, 1993.

Grenier, Line. "Cultural Exemptionism Revisited: Québec Music Industries in the Face of Free Trade." In *Mass Media and Free Trade: NAFTA and the Cultural Industries*, edited by Emile G. McAnany and Kenton T. Wilkinson. Austin: University of Texas Press, 1996. 306–28.

Grenier, Line, and Val Morrison. "Le Terrain socio-musical populaire au Québec: 'Et dire qu'on ne comprend pas toujours les paroles ...'" *Études littéraires* 27, no. 3 (Winter 1995): 75–98.

Groulx, Lionel. *Notre maître le passé*. 1924–1944. 3 vols. Montreal: Stanké, 1977.

Gruneau, Richard S., and David Whitson. *Hockey Night in Canada: Sport, Identities, and Cultural Politics*. Toronto: Garamond, 1993.

Guay, Donald. "Problèmes de l'intégration du sport dans la société canadienne au XIXe siècle." In Augustin and Sorbets, 21–38.

Gunderson, Lisa Anne. "Memory, Modernity, and the City: An Interpretive Analysis of Montreal and Toronto's Respective Moves from Their Historic Professional Hockey Arenas." MA thesis, University of Waterloo, 2004.

Gunelius, Susan. "More Men in Executive Positions Than Women: 10:1 Ratio." *WomenInBusiness.com*, 7 November 2009. http://www.womenonbusiness.com/more-men-in-executive-positions-than-women-101-ratio.

Hadley, Jo-Anne. "Translating the Québécois Sociolect for Cinema: The Creation of a Supertext in Bon Cop Bad Cop." MA thesis, Concordia University, 2011.

Harris, Cecil. *Breaking the Ice: The Black Experience in Professional Hockey*. Toronto: Insomniac, 2003.

Harvey, Jean. "Sport and Québec Nationalism: Ethnic or Civic Identity?" In *Sport in Divided Societies*, edited by John Peter Sugden and Alan Bairner. Lansing: Meyer and Meyer Sport, 1999. 31–50.

– . "Whose Sweater Is This? The Changing Meanings of Hockey in Quebec." In Whitson and Gruneau, 29–52.

Harvey, Jean, and Alan Law. "'Resisting' the Global Media Oligopoly? The Canada Inc. Response." In *Sport and Corporate Nationalisms*, edited by Michael L. Silk, David L. Andrews, and C.L. Cole. Oxford and New York: Berg, 2005. 187–222.

Hawkins, Peter. *Chanson: The French Singer-Songwriter from Aristide Bruant to the Present Day*. Aldershot: Ashgate, 2000.

Hellekson, Karen. *The Alternate History: Refiguring Historical Time.* Kent: Kent State University Press, 2001.

Henriet, Éric. *L'Histoire revisitée: Panorama de l'uchronie sous toutes ses formes.* Amiens: Encrage, 1999.

Héroux, Claude, and Martine Pagé. *Lance et compte: Les dessous d'une grande réussite.* N.p.: Flammarion Québec, 2006.

Hoffmann, Shirl J., ed. *Sport and Religion.* Champaign: Human Kinetics, 1992.

Holman, Andrew C., ed. *Canada's Game: Hockey and Identity.* Montreal and Kingston: McGill–Queen's University Press, 2009.

Hunt, Jim. *The Men in the Nets.* Toronto: McGraw-Hill Ryerson, 1972.

Hynes, William J. "Mapping the Characteristics of Mythic Tricksters: A Heuristic Guide." In Hynes and Doty, 33–45.

Hynes, William J., and William G. Doty, eds. *Mythical Trickster Figures: Contours, Contexts, and Criticisms.* Tuscaloosa: University of Alabama Press, 1993.

Iacovino, Raffaele, and Charles-Antoine Sévigny. "Between Unity and Diversity: Examining the "Quebec Model" of Integration." In Gervais et al., 249–66.

Inglis, Christine, Anthony Birch, and Geoffrey Sherington, eds. "An Overview of Australian and Canadian Migration Patterns and Policies." In *Immigration and Refugee Policy: Australia and Canada Compared.* Vol. 1, 3–30. Toronto: University of Toronto Press, 1994.

Internet Movie Cars Database. 2012. http://www.imcdb.org/movie_479647-Bon-Cop,-Bad-Cop.html.

Janelle, Claude. "La Science-fiction au Québec: historique et perspectives d'avenir." *Solaris* 50 (March–April 1983): 6–10.

–. "Le Sport est-il littéraire?", *Solaris* 55 (Spring 1984): 13.

Janson, Gilles. "La Lente Émergeance d'une culture sportive chez les francophones montréalais, 1800–1900." In Augustin and Sorbets, 73–88.

Jenish, D'Arcy. *The Montreal Canadiens: 100 Years of Glory.* 2008. Toronto: Anchor Canada, 2009.

Jodoin, Mario, "Les Salaires au hockey: un scandale?" In Baillargeon and Boissinot, 43–60.

Jones, Christopher M. "Un interview avec Loco Locass." *Quebec Studies* 41 (2006): 27–43.

Jones, Gail. "Tricksters and Shamans in Jack London's Stories." In *Trickster Lives: Culture and Myth in American Fiction,* edited by Jeanne Campbell Reesman. Athens: University of Georgia Press, 2001. 110–20.

Jung, Karl. *Four Archetypes: Mother, Rebirth, Spirit, Trickster.* [1954]1969. Translated by R.F.C. Hull. Princeton: Princeton University Press, 1970.

Karmis, Dmitrios, and Alain-G. Gagnon. "Federalism, Federation and Collective Identities in Canada and Belgium: Different Routes, Similar Fragmentation." In Gagnon and Tully, 137–75.

Kennedy, Brian. "Confronting a Compelling Other: The Summit Series and the Nostalgic (Trans)Formation of Canadian Identity." In Holman, 44–62.

Ketterer, David. *Canadian Science Fiction and Fantasy*. Bloomington: Indiana University Press, 1992.

Kibby, Marjorie D. "Nostalgia for the Masculine: Onward to the Past in Sports Films of the Eighties." *Canadian Journal of Film Studies* 7, no. 1 (1998): 16–28.

Kidd, Bruce, and John Macfarlane. *The Death of Hockey*. Toronto: New Press, 1972.

King, C. Richard, and David J. Leonard, eds. "Screening the Social: An Introduction to Sport Cinema." In *Visual Economies of/in Motion: Sport and Film*. New York: Peter Lang, 2006. 1–11.

Kymlicka, Will. "The New Debate on Minority Rights (and Postscript)." In *Multiculturalism and Political Theory*, edited by Anthony Simon Laden and David Owen. Cambridge: Cambridge University Press, 2007.

Laberge, Suzanne. "L'Affaire Richard/Campbell: Le Hockey comme vecteur de l'affirmation francophone québécoise." In Laurin-Lamothe and Moreau, 13–29.

Lachapelle, Guy, and Robert Comeau, eds. *Robert Bourassa: Un bâtisseur tranquille*. Quebec: Presses de l'Université Laval, 2003.

Lafrance, André-A. "Je ne suis plus pratiquant, mais je n'ai jamais apostasié!" In Bauer and Barreau, 19–28.

Lamoureux, Diane. "The Paradoxes of Quebec Feminism." In Gervais et al., 307–23.

Larivière, Louise. "Diversité des règles morphologiques de féminisation dans les pays francophones industrialisés." *Études Francophones* 16 (2001): 87–108.

Lasorsa, Steve. *La Rivalité Canadien-Nordiques*. Quebec: Presses de l'Université Laval, 2011.

Laurin-Lamothe, Audrey, and Nicolas Moreau, eds. *Le Canadien de Montréal: Une légende repensée*. Quebec: Presses de l'Université Laval, 2011.

–. "Le Canadien de Montréal comme fait social," In Laurin-Lamothe and Moreau, 7–12.

Lavoie, Marc. *Désavantage numérique: Les Francophones dans la LNH*. Hull: Vents d'Ouest, 1998.

–. "The Entry Draft in the National Hockey League: Discrimination, Style of Play, and Team Location." *American Journal of Economics and Sociology* 62, no. 2 (April 2003): 383–405.

– . "Stacking, Performance Differentials, and Salary Discrimination in Professional Ice Hockey: A Survey of the Evidence." *Sociology of Sport Journal* 6 (1989): 17–35.

Lefebvre, Jean-Pierre. "Le Concept de cinéma national." In *Dialogue: Cinéma Canadien et Québécois/Canadian and Québec Cinema*, edited by Pierre Véronneau, Michael Dorland, and Seth Feldman, 83–96. Montreal: Mediatexte, 1987.

Legrand, Bill. "Those Old Montreal Maroons." In Mouton, 13–22.

Létourneau, Jocelyn. *A History for the Future: Rewriting Memory and Identity in Quebec.* Translated by Phyllis Aronoff and Howard Scott. Montreal and Kingston: McGill–Queen's University Press, 2004.

Lindros, Eric, with Randy Starkman. *Fire on Ice.* 1991. Expanded Edition. New York: HarperCollins, 1992.

Linteau, Paul-André, René Durocher, Jean-Claude Robert, and François Ricard. *Histoire du Québec contemporain.* Vol. 2: *Le Québec depuis 1930.* Montréal: Boréal, 1989.

Lisée, Jean-François. *The Trickster: Robert Bourassa and Quebecers, 1990–1992.* Translated and abridged by Robert Chodos, Simon Horn, and Wanda Taylor. Toronto: James Lorimer, 1994. Translation of *Le Tricheur* and *Le Naufragé.* Montreal: Boréal, 1994. 2 vols.

Longley, Neil. "Measuring Employer-Based Discrimination Versus Consumer-Based Discrimination: The Case of French Canadians in the National Hockey League." *American Journal of Economics and Sociology* 62, no. 2 (April 2003): 365–81.

Lucas, C.P. *Lord Durham's Report on the Affairs of British North America.* Vol. II: *Text of the Report.* Oxford: Clarendon, 1912.

Luckhurst, Roger. *Science Fiction.* Cambridge: Polity, 2005.

Ludwig, Jack. *The Great Hockey Thaw, or The Russians are Here!* New York: Doubleday, 1974. Alt. pub. *Hockey Night in Moscow.* Richmond Hill: Pocket-Penguin, 1972.

Macdougall, Heather. "Facing off: French and English in *Bon Cop, Bad Cop.*" *Reconstruction* 11, no. 1 (2011): n.p. http://reconstruction.eserver.org/111/Macdougall.shtml.

Macfarlane, John. (see Kidd, Bruce)

MacGregor, Roy. (see Dryden, Ken)

Maguire, Joseph. "Blade Runners: Canadian Migrants and European Ice Hockey." In *Sport and Migration: Borders, Boundaries, and Crossings*, edited by Joseph Maguire and Mark Falcous. New York: Routledge, 2011. 141–56.

Markosun. "NHL Average Attendance Since 1989–90," *Markosun's Blog*, 26 December 2011, http://markosun.wordpress.com/2011/12/26/nhl-average-attendance-since-1989-90.

McCallum, Jack. "Green Cars, Black Cats, and Lady Luck." In Hoffmann, 203–11.

McClean, Shilo T. "So Here's the Deal: A Case Study Considering the Influence of Franchise Filmmaking and Its Relationship to Digital Visual Effects." In *Digital Storytelling: The Narrative Power of Visual Effects in Film.* Cambridge: MIT Press, 2007. 171–84.

McDonell, Chris, ed. *For the Love of Hockey: Hockey Stars' Personal Stories.* 2001. Toronto: Firefly, 2004.

McFarlane, Brian. *The Habs.* Toronto: Stoddart, 1996.

McKenna, Brian, and Susan Purcell. *Drapeau.* Toronto: Clarke, Irwin, 1980.

McSorley, Marty. Foreword. In Ross Bernstein, *The Code: The Unwritten Rules of Fighting and Retaliation in the NHL.* Chicago: Triumph, 2006. ix–xi.

Mead, David G., and Pawel Frelik, eds. *Playing the Universe: Games and Gaming in Science Fiction.* Lublin: UMCS, 2007.

Melançon, Benoît. "La Langue du hockey à travers les âges." *L'Oreille tendue,* 4 April 2011. http://oreilletendue.com/2011/04/04/la-langue-du-hockey-a-travers-les-ages-comme/.

–. "Hockey spectral." *L'Oreille tendue,* 24 January 2011. http://oreilletendue.com/2011/01/24/hockey-spectral.

–. "Notre père le Rocket qui êtes au cieux': Les Religions de Maurice Richard." In Bauer and Barreau, 111–38.

–. *The Rocket: A Cultural History of Maurice Richard.* Translated Fred A. Reed. Vancouver: Greystone, 2009. Translation of *Les Yeux de Maurice Richard. Une histoire culturelle.* Montréal: Fides, 2006.

–. "Le Roman de la puck." *L'Oreille tendue,* 10 March 2011. http://oreilletendue.com/2011/03/10/le-roman-de-la-puck.

Messier, Audrey. "André Fortin: Un mythe en devenir?" MA thesis, University of Sherbrooke, 2010.

Messner, Michael A. *Power at Play: Sports and the Problem of Masculinity.* Boston: Beacon, 1992.

Mills, Sean. *The Empire Within: Postcolonial Thought in 1960s Quebec.* Montreal and Kingston: McGill–Queen's University Press, 2010.

Minister of Industry. *Canadian Demographics at a Glance.* 2008. http://www.statcan.gc.ca/pub/91-003-x/91-003-x2007001-eng.pdf.

Morin, Edgar. "Salut les copains." *Le Monde,* 6 July 1963, 1, 11.

Morin, Marie-Claude. "Les femmes sont rares dans l'antichambre du pouvoir au Québec." *Les Affaires.com,* 16 September 2010, http://www.lesaffaires.com/recherche?mot=les+femmes+sont+rares+dans+l%27antichambre&location=article.

Mouton, Claude, ed. *The Montreal Canadiens: A Hockey Dynasty.* Toronto: Van Nostrand Reinhold, 1980.

Moylan, Tom. *Demand the Impossible: Science Fiction and the Utopian Imagination.* London: Methuen, 1986.

Nadel, Ira B. *Various Positions: A Life of Leonard Cohen.* 1996. Austin: University of Texas Press, 2007.

Nathan, Daniel A. "'I'm Against It:' The Marx Brothers' *Horse Feathers* as Cultural Critique; or, Why Bit-Time College Football Gives Me a Haddock." In Briley et al., 40–51.

Nora, Pierre. "Between Memory and History: Les Lieux de Mémoire." Translated by Marc Roudebush. *Representations* 26 (1989): 7–24.

– , ed. *Les Lieux de mémoire.* 3 vols. Paris: Gallimard, 1984–1992. Translated as *Rethinking France: Les Lieux de Mémoire.* Chicago: University of Chicago Press, 1999–2009.

Office Québécois de la Langue Française. *Au Féminin: Guide de Féminisation des Titres de Fonction et des Textes.* Québec: Publications du Québec, 1991.

Paradis, Andrea, ed. *Out of this World: Canadian Science Fiction and Fantasy Literature.* Ottawa: Quarry /National Library of Canada, 1995.

Parpart, Lee. "The Nation and the Nude: Colonial Masculinity and the Spectacle of the Male Body in Recent Canadian Cinema(s)." In *Masculinity: Bodies, Movies, Culture,* edited by Peter Lehman. New York and London: Routledge, 2001. 167–92.

Patoine, Tony. "'On est Canayen ou ben on l'est pas:' Hockey, nationalisme et identités au Québec et au Canada." In Baillargeon and Boissinot, 9–26.

Pellerin, Jean-Marie. *Maurice Richard: L'Idole d'un peuple.* 1976. Édition augmentée. Montréal: Trustar, 1998.

Pelletier, Gérard. *La Crise d'octobre.* Montréal: Le Jour, 1971.

Peterman, Michael. "Hockey Dreams." *Canadian Literature* 202 (2009): 141–50.

Pinard, Maurice. "The Quebec Independence Movement: From Its Emergence to the 1995 Referendum." In *Political Sociology: Canadian Perspectives,* edited by Douglas Baer. Oxford: Oxford University Press, 2002. 238–68.

Pitter, Robert. "Racialization and Hockey in Canada: From Personal Troubles to a Canadian Challenge." In Whitson and Gruneau, 123–39.

Poliquin, Daniel. *Le Roman colonial.* Montreal: Boréal, 2000.

Pomerance, Murray, and Frances Gateward, eds. Introduction. In *Where the Boys Are: Cinemas of Masculinity and Youth.* Detroit: Wayne State University Press, 2005. 1–18.

Poulter, Gillian. *Becoming Native in a Foreign Land: Sport, Visual Culture, and Identity in Montreal, 1840–85.* Vancouver: UBC Press, 2009.

Prévost-Thomas, Cécile. "Céline, Isabelle, Lynda Pierre et … les autres?" In *À la rencontre d'un Québec qui bouge,* edited by Robert Laliberté. Paris: CTHS, 2009. 167–86.

Pronger, Brian. *The Arena of Masculinity: Sports, Homosexuality, and the Meaning of Sex*. New York: St Martin's, 1990.

Provencher, Jean. *La Grande Peur d'octobre '70*. Montréal: L'Aurore, 1974.

Raboy, Marc. "Public Television, the National Question, and the Preservation of the Canadian State." In *Television in Transition: Papers from the First International Television Studies Conference*, 1985, edited by Philip Drummond, 64–86. London: BFI, 1986.

Ransom, Amy J. "Constructions of the Future: Science-Fictional Visions of Montréal's Olympic Stadium." *Contemporary French Civilization* 34.2 (Spring/Summer 2010): 23–47.

– . "Deterritorialization and the Crisis of Recognition in Turn of the Millennium Québec Film." *American Review of Canadian Studies* 43, no. 2 (June 2013): 176–89. Special Issue on Québec Cinema, edited by Denis Bachand, Vincent Desroches, André Loiselle, and Miléna Santoro.

– . "La Gamme du fantastique: L'Éclatement des genres et l'écriture migrante haïtiano-québécoise," dans Amy J. Ransom et Sophie Beaulé (dirs.), *@nalyses: revue de critique et de théorie littéraire* 8.2 (Spring-Summer 2013): 146–74. Special Issue on *Nouvelles perspectives sur le polar et les genres de l'imaginaire et le polar du Canada d'expression française*. https://uottawa.scholarsportal.info/ojs/index.php/revue-analyses/index.

– . "*He Shoots! He Scores!*: Language and Gender Politics in the Québec Television Series *Lance et compte*." In *Ice Hockey in Quebec – The Same, but Different?*, edited by Jason Blake and Andrew C. Holman. Forthcoming.

– . "History Making and Canon Fodder: The Battle of SFQ." *Foundation* 112 (2011): 7–26.

– . "Hockey of the Future: Canada's Game in Québec's Science Fiction." *Aethlon: The Journal of Sport Literature* 27 (Spring–Summer 2010): 65–87.

---. "Hockeyers cybernétiques et disparus: le sport et l'identité dans la science-fiction québécoise," unpublished paper, Conseil International des Études Francophones Conference, Montréal, 27 June–4 July 2010.

– . "Language Choice and Code Switching in Current Popular Music from Québec." *Glottopol* 17 (January 2011). Special Issue on *Variétés de la chanson francophone*. http://glottopol.univ-rouen.fr/telecharger/numero_17/gpl17_10ransom.pdf.

– . "*Lieux de mémoire* or *lieux du dollar*?: Montreal's Forum, the Canadiens, and Popular Culture." *Quebec Studies* 51 (Spring–Summer 2011): 21–39.

– . "Parabolas of SFQ: Canadian SF in French and the Making of a 'National' Sub-Genre." In *Parabolas of Science Fiction*, edited by Brian Attebery and Veronica Hollinger. Westport: Greenwood, 2012. 89–105, 265–7.

–. "Québec History X." *American Review of Canadian Studies* 43, no. 1 (2013): 12–29.
–. *Science Fiction from Québec: A Postcolonial Study*. Jefferson: McFarland, 2009.
–. "L'Uchronie québécoise: Histoire et politique dans un sous-genre de la science-fiction." *Études francophones* 25, nos. 1–2 (Spring–Fall 2010). Special issue on Quebec Literature.
–. "(Un)common Ground: National Sovereignty and Individual Identity in Contemporary SF from Québec." *Science Fiction Studies* 82 (November 2000): 439–60.
–. "Un utopiste québécois: Le cas de Jacques Brossard." *Temporalités* 12, no. 2 (January 2011). Special issue "Utopies/Uchronies," edited by Michel Lallement and Jean-Marc Ramos. http://temporalites.revues.org/1295.
–. "Warping Time: Alternate History, Historical Fantasy, and the Postmodern *uchronie québécoise*." *Extrapolation* 51, no. 2 (2010): 258–80.
Reid, Malcolm. *The Shouting Sign Painters: A Literary and Political Account of Quebec Revolutionary Nationalism*. New York: MR, 1972.
Richard, Simon. *La Série du siècle: Septembre 1972*. Montreal: Hurtubise, 2002.
Robidoux, Michael A. "Imagining a Canadian Identity through Sport: A Historical Interpretation of Lacrosse and Hockey." *Journal of American Folklore* 115 (Spring 2002): 209–25.
–. *Men at Play: A Working Understanding of Professional Hockey*. Montreal and Kingston: McGill–Queen's University Press, 2001.
Robidoux, Michael A., and Pierre Trudel. "Hockey in Canada and the Body-checking Debate in Minor Hockey." In Whitson and Gruneau, 101–22.
Roy, Michel. *Le Guerrier*. Montreal: Libre Expression, 2008.
Sabo, Donald F. "The Politics of Homophobia in Sport." In *Sex, Violence, and Power in Sports: Rethinking Masculinity*, edited by Michael A. Messner and Donald F. Sabo. Freedom: Crossing, 1994. 101–12.
Saint-Éloi, Rodney. "Des Haïtiens, le hockey et quelques éléments de philosophie de la culture." In Baillargeon and Boissinot, 245–54.
Sanaker, John Kristian. *La Rencontre des langues dans le cinéma francophone: Québec, Afrique subsaharienne, France, Maghreb*. Quebec et Paris: Press de l'Université Laval – L'Harmattan, 2010.
Santoro, Miléna. *Mothers of Invention: Feminist Authors and Experimental Fiction in France and Quebec*. Montreal and Kingston: McGill–Queen's University Press, 2002.
Saudohar, P.D. "The Hockey Lockout." *Monthly Labor Review*, December 2005, 23–29.

Saul, John Ralston. *Reflections of a Siamese Twin: Canada at the End of the Twentieth Century*. Toronto: Viking/Penguin Canada, 1997.

Saunders, Michael William. *Imps of the Perverse: Gay Monsters in Film*. Westport: Praeger, 1998.

Savard, Serge. Preface. In Richard, 13–15.

Savoie, Donald J. *Thatcher, Reagan, Mulroney: In Search of a New Bureaucracy*. Pittsburgh: University of Pittsburgh Press, 1994.

Scanlan, Lawrence. *Grace under Fire: The State of Our Sweet and Savage Game*. Toronto: Penguin Canada, 2002.

Senn, Bryan. "The Sport of Violence: *Death Race 2000* and *Rollerball*." In *Science Fiction in America: Essays on SF Cinema*, edited by David J. Hogan. Jefferson: McFarland, 2006. 207–16.

Serruys, Nicholas. "Xénototalité: l'utopie, l'uchronie et l'anticipation canadiennes-françaises et québécoises dans l'optique de l'allégorie nationale." *Voix plurielles* 5, no. 2 (2008): 28–44.

Silliman, Barbara A. "Batter Up!: The Mythology and Psychology of Sports and Games in *Star Trek: Deep Space Nine*." In *The Influence of* Star Trek *on Television, Film, and Culture*, edited by Lincoln Geraghty. Jefferson: McFarland, 2008. 100–14.

Simard, Jean-Claude. "Hockey et politique, même combat!" In Baillargeon and Boissinot, 27–41.

Sinden, Harry, and Dick Grace. *The Picture History of the Boston Bruins: From Shore to Orr and the Years Between*. Indianapolis: Bobbs-Merril, 1976.

Sirois, Bob. *Discrimination in the NHL: Quebec Hockey Players Sidelined*. Montreal: Baraka, 2010. Translation of *Le Québec mis en échec*. Montreal: L'Homme, 2009.

Skinazi, Karen E.H. "The Mystery of a Canadian Father of Hockey Stories: Leslie McFarlane's Break Away from the Hardy Boys." In Holman, 98–124.

Skinner, David. "Television in Canada: Continuity or Change?" In *Television and Public Policy: Change and Continuity in an Era of Global Liberalization*, edited by David Ward, 3–26. New York: Lawrence Erlbaum / Taylor and Francis, 2008.

Somay, Bülent. "Towards an Open-Ended Utopia." *Science-Fiction Studies* 11 (1984): 25–38.

Stalker, Richard. "Bruins Fans Flood Twitter with Racist Remarks: Racial Slurs Put NHL in Bad Light." *Web Pro News*. 26 April 2012. http://www.webpronews.com/bruins-fans-flood-twitter-with-racist-remarks-2012-04.

Stangl, Jane M. "White *Sauvage-ry*: Revisiting the Collegians and Coeds of Old *Siwash* College." In Fuller, 71–84.

Stein, Gil. *Power Plays: An Inside Look at the Big Business of the National Hockey League*. Secaucus: Carol, 1997.

Stevens, Julie. "Women's Hockey in Canada: After the 'Gold Rush.'" In Whitson and Gruneau, 85–99.

Summerfield, Giovanna, and Lisa Downward. *New Perspectives on the European* Bildungsroman. London and New York: Continuum, 2010.

Suvin, Darko. "The SF Novel as Epic Narration." 1982. *Positions and Presuppositions in SF*. Kent: Kent State University Press, 1988. 74–85.

Taylor, Charles. "The Politics of Recognition." In *Multiculturalism: Examining the Politics of Recognition*, edited by Amy Gutman. Princeton: Princeton University Press, 1994. 25–73.

Theberge, Nancy. *Higher Goals: Women's Ice Hockey and the Politics of Gender*. Albany: SUNY Press, 2000.

–. "Playing with the Boys: Manon Rheaume, Women's Hockey, and the Struggle for Legitimacy." *Canadian Women's Studies* 15, no. 4 (1995): 37–41.

Tremblay, Manon. *Quebec Women and Legislative Representation*. Translated by Käthe Roth. Vancouver: UBC Press, 2010.

Tremblay, Marie-Claude. *Loco Locass: La Parole en gage*. Montréal: Triptyque, 2011.

Tremblay, Victor-Laurent. "Masculinité et hockey dans le roman québécois." *French Review* 78, no. 6 (May 2005): 1104–16.

Trudel, Marcel. *The Beginnings of New France: 1524–1663*. Translated by Patricia Claxton. Toronto: McClelland and Stewart, 1973.

Trujillo, Nick. "Hegemonic Masculinity on the Mound: Media Representations of Nolan Ryan and American Sports Culture." In Birrell and McDonald, 14–39.

Vallières, Pierre. *White Niggers of America*. Translated by Joan Pinkham, 1971. Translation of *Nègres blancs d'Amérique*. Montréal: Parti pris, 1969.

van Compernolle, Rémi A. "What Do Women Want?: Linguistic Equality and the Feminization of Job Titles in Contemporary France." *Gender and Language* 3, no. 1 (2009): 33–52.

van der Vossen, Philip. "The All-Black Hockey Team." *Gunixin Sports*, 2 February 2011. http://sports.gunaxin.com/the-all-black-hockey-team/75145.

Vautier, Marie. *New World Myth: Postmodernism and Postcolonialism in Canadian Fiction*. Montreal and Kingston: McGill–Queen's University Press, 1998.

Warwick, Jack. *L'Appel du Nord dans la littérature canadienne-française*. Montréal: Hurtubise/HMH, 1972.

Waugh, Thomas. "Boys and The Beast." In *The Romance of Transgression in Canada: Queering Sexualities, Nations, Cinemas*. Montreal and Kingston: McGill–Queen's University Press, 2006. 180–211.

Werneburg, M. "Origins of 'Canuck.'" *EMUU.net*. 2001. http://emuu.net/origins-of-%27Canuck%27.

Westfahl, Gary. *Hugo Gernsback and the Century of Science Fiction*. Jefferson: McFarland, 2007.

White, Philip, and Kevin Young, eds. *Sport and Gender in Canada*. Oxford: Oxford University Press, 1999.

Whitson, David. "Sport in the Social Construction of Masculinity." In *Sport, Men, and the Gender Order*, edited by Michael A. Messner and Donald F. Sabo. Champaign: Human Kinetics, 1990. 19–30.

Whitson, David, and Richard Gruneau, eds. *Artificial Ice: Hockey, Culture, and Commerce*. Peterborough: Broadview, 2006.

Willes, Ed. *The Rebel League: The Short and Unruly Life of the World Hockey Association*. Toronto: McClelland and Stewart, 2004.

Wilson, Brian. "Selective Memory in a Global Culture: Reconsidering Links between Youth, Hockey, and Canadian Identity." In Whitson and Gruneau, 53–70.

Wind, Herbert Warren. "Les Canadiens sont là." In Mouton, 23–91.

Wright, Robert. *Virtual Sovereignty: Nationalism, Culture, and the Canadian Question*. Toronto: Canadian Scholars' Press, 2004.

Womack, Mari. "Why Athletes Need Ritual: A Study of Magic among Professional Athletes." In Hoffman, 191–202.

Yelle, François. "Les Études en communications médiatique au Québec et l'approche Cultural Studies." *Commposite* 1 (2000): 1–21. http://www.commposite.org/index.php/revue/ article/viewArticle/40.

Index

www.ingramcontent.com/pod-product-compliance
Lightning Source LLC
LaVergne TN
LVHW090806070826
844660LV00022B/1097
9781442616196